W9-BRE-198

OCT 2 1 2005

DK COLLECTOR'S GUIDES

ARTS & CRAFTS

Textile by William Morris, p.70; previous page: table lamp by Dirk van Erp, p.180

DK COLLECTOR'S GUIDES

ARTS & CRAFTS

JUDITH MILLER

with Jill Bace

Photography by Graham Rae
with Byron Slater, John McKenzie, and Adam Gault

LONDON, NEW YORK,
MELBOURNE, MUNICH, DELHI

A joint production from **DK** and
THE PRICE GUIDE COMPANY

DORLING KINDERSLEY LIMITED
Senior Editor Paula Regan
Senior Art Editor Mandy Earey
Managing Editor Julie Oughton
Managing Art Editor Heather McCarry
Art Director Peter Luff
Publishing Director Jackie Douglas
Production Sarah Dodd
DTP Designer Adam Walker
Picture Research Sarah Duncan
US Editor Christine Heilman

Produced for Dorling Kindersley by
Sands Publishing Solutions
Project Editors Sylvia & David Tombesi-Walton
Project Art Editor Simon Murrell

THE PRICE GUIDE COMPANY LIMITED
Publishing Manager Julie Brooke
Managing Editor Cathy Marriott
Editorial Assistants Jessica Bishop, Dan Dunlavey,
Karen Morden
Digital Image Coordinator Ellen Sinclair
Consultants Keith Baker,
John Mackie (Lyon & Turnbull)
Contributors Keith Baker, John Wainwright

While every care has been taken in the
compilation of this guide, neither the authors
nor the publishers accept any liability for any
financial or other loss incurred by reliance
placed on the information contained in
DK Collector's Guides: Arts & Crafts.

First American Edition, 2005

Published in the United States by
DK Publishing, Inc., 375 Hudson Street,
New York, New York 10014

05 06 07 08 09 10 9 8 7 6 5 4 3 2 1

Copyright © Judith Miller and Dorling
Kindersley Limited 2004

The Price Guide Company (UK) Ltd.
info@thepriceguidecompany.com

All rights reserved under International and
Pan-American Copyright Conventions. No part of
this publication may be reproduced, stored in a
retrieval system, or transmitted in any form or by any
means, electronic, mechanical, photocopying,
recording or otherwise, without the prior written
permission of the copyright owner. Published in
Great Britain by Dorling Kindersley Limited.

A Cataloging-in-Publication record for this book is
available from the Library of Congress.

ISBN 0-7566-0963-1

Color reproduction by Colourscan, Singapore
Printed and bound in China
by L. Rex Printing Co. Ltd.

Discover more at
www.dk.com

Contents

Rocking chair by Plail Brothers, p.56

Furniture 20

Textiles 68

Ceramics 78

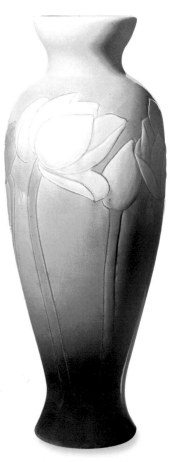

Vase by Rookwood, p.100

Lamp by Tiffany Studios, p.206

Bracelet by Edward E. Oakes, p.151

Glass and Lamps 202

Jewelry 130

Books and Graphics 216

Silver and Metalware 156

Silver clock by Liberty & Co., p.164

Appendices and Index 226

How to use this book

DK Collector's Guides: Arts & Crafts is divided into seven chapters: furniture; textiles; ceramics; jewelry; silver and metalware; glass and lamps; and books and graphics. Each section opens with an introductory overview that discusses the historical background to the medium and its place in Arts and Crafts. This is followed by profiles of the most important Arts and Crafts designers and factories from Great Britain, continental Europe, and the United States, as well as examples of their work. Highlighted sidebars provide an at-a-glance list of the key features for each designer or factory, and A Closer Look pieces are expertly selected and carefully annotated to show what makes them icons of Arts and Crafts design. Every item is briefly and concisely described, given an up-to-date price, and, where possible, dated.

Key Features
Lists the particular characteristics, influences, motifs, and marks for each designer and factory.

A Closer Look
Selects, annotates, and highlights the features that make the piece stand out as an icon of Arts and Crafts style.

FURNITURE

KEY FEATURES

Hand-hammered repoussé copper panels are common, usually with stylized floral designs.

Inlays of metal or marquetry are often elaborate, intended to showcase the skill of the craftsmen employed at the Raleigh Cabinet Works.

Multiple shaped spindles and slats are often included as decorative elements.

Carving and pierced hearts, a favorite motif of Arts and Crafts cabinet makers, were sometimes used as extra decoration.

Remarkable stained-glass panels featuring colorful floral forms are occasionally included.

Shapland & Petter

Based in Barnstaple, England, the commercial firm of Shapland & Petter became a leading maker of furniture in the Arts and Crafts style, producing a distinctive range that was celebrated for fine design and high-quality craftsmanship.

In 1854, Henry Shapland (1823–1909) established a cabinet-making business in north Devon, and accountant Henry Petter joined him to create a highly successful commercial enterprise. Although devastated by a fire in 1888, their Raleigh Cabinet Works was rebuilt to include state-of-the-art production facilities.

Shapland & Petter combined modern machine technology with traditional craftsmanship. Mechanized processes were employed to produce well-made furniture in quality materials. Items were then embellished with a variety of handcraft techniques—woodcarving, marquetry, metal inlay, mounted ceramic and enamel cabochons, and the application of decorative copperwork. Shapland & Petter furniture also includes restrained pieces using heart-shaped

piercing, geometric shapes with angled arches, and a medieval style heavily ornamented with hand-hammered repoussé copper panels.

The company paid great attention to training its staff. Carvers, for example, perfected their craft by attending classes at the Barnstaple School of Art and completing seven-year apprenticeships.

Many pieces were made from hundreds of standard designs promoted in local and London showrooms and through catalogs. Creating its own unique style by copying the designs of other Arts and Crafts luminaries, such as C. R. Ashbee and Hugh Baillie Scott, the company also produced furniture for retailers across Great Britain, including Morris & Co. The company is still in business under the name Leaderflush Shapland.

Above: Mahogany and stained-glass firescreen with stylized buds in colored glass against a textured ground, flanked by embossed copper panels. *c. 1900. 39 in (99 cm) high* **$1,200–1,800** DN

MARQUETRY AND LEADED GLASS

Unlike many of its peers, Shapland & Petter was conspicuous in its extravagant use of surface decoration. Floral marquetry panels, often using three or more different woods, acted as attractive embellishments that set Shapland & Petter furniture apart. The stylized stained-glass designs included on some of the company's furniture are equally distinctive. It is unclear whether these leaded-glass panels were made at the Raleigh workshop or in nearby glassworks.

Mahogany display cabinet with marquetry decoration. The door has a decorative metal panel and is flanked by open shelving and cupboards with elaborate wood and mother-of-pearl inlay. *c. 1900. 54 in (137 cm) wide* **$5,000–8,000** V2

Lady's walnut desk with a stained-glass panel of stylized plant forms, a flat leather writing surface, a frieze drawer with ring-pulls, and open supports united by shaped slats. *c. 1905. 42 in (107 cm) wide* **$3,000–4,000** PUR

28

SHAPLAND & PETTER

Mahogany bookcase topped by a copper panel embossed "Reading Maketh a Full Man," with three leaded-glass doors, open shelving, cupboards, and a drawer. *c. 1900. 83 in (211 cm) high* **$5,000–7,000** LAT

Oak umbrella stand with a copper panel embossed with stylized foliage and a slatted lower gallery with a pierced heart motif, on square supports. *c. 1905. 43 in (109 cm) high* **$1,200–1,800** PUR

Oak stick stand with a shaped copper panel embossed with stylized flowers and tendrils. The slatted front and sides feature a further copper panel with raised bosses. *c. 1905. 41½ in (106 cm) high* **$2,000–2,500** PUR

Oak wardrobe with two paneled doors featuring carved foliate detail at the top, with shaped copper strap hinges and pulls and a fitted interior. *c. 1905. 82½ in (209 cm) high* **$5,000–7,000** PUR

A CLOSER LOOK

Mahogany high-backed side chair by Shapland & Petter in the Glasgow style, with a cherub's head with tousled forelock carved in pewter on a heart-shaped base applied to the wide central slat. The rear seat rail is joined to a stretcher below by three shaped spindles. The upholstered seat is a replacement. Shapland & Petter designs were created in house, although none were ever registered. *c. 1905. 42 in (107 cm) high* **$1,500–2,000** PUR

This pewter cherub's head is a good example of the applied metalwork of Shapland & Petter's work. They employed skilled craftsmen to produce these details in their factory.

High back is reminiscent of the work of Charles Rennie Mackintosh and Frank Lloyd Wright.

Oak stick stand with a shaped copper panel embossed with stylized flowers and tendrils. The slatted front and sides feature a further copper panel with raised bosses. *c. 1905. 41¼ in (106 cm) high*

$2,000–2,500	PUR

Designer Information
Gives a fascinating insight into the career and history of an Arts and Crafts designer or factory. Also highlights the particular characteristics of their work, and offers advice on what to look for when collecting.

The Caption
Describes the piece in detail, including the materials used, the date it was made, and its length, height, or width.

The Price Guide
All prices are shown in ranges to give you a ballpark figure. If the piece is in a museum or has not been seen on the market for some time and no price is available, the letters NPA will be used.

The Source Code
With the exception of museum pieces, most items in the book were specially photographed at an auction house, dealer, antique market, or private collection. Each source is credited here. See pp.230–31 for full listings.

Foreword

Trying to quantify the appeal of an antique can be a difficult business. You might love an object for its beauty, its function, or the way it speaks to you of a bygone era. Pieces by the best Arts and Crafts designers will fulfill all of these criteria, making them especially rewarding to collect. My own interest in this area was sparked when a remarkable stained-glass window in the Chapel of St. Salvatore, at St. Andrews in Fife, Scotland, caught my eye. Designed by Henry Holiday, it is a wonderfully naturalistic riot of color, and I was inspired enough to delve deeper into its historical context.

William Morris, the de facto father of Arts and Crafts, summed up his philosophy succinctly when he said: "If you want a golden rule that will fit everything, this is it: have nothing in your houses that you do not know to be useful or believe to be beautiful." Utility and beauty are at the heart of the Arts and Crafts ideal, and these twin concepts can be traced back to the intellectual and emotional roots of the movement—John Ruskin's cerebral Christian socialist manifesto was a powerful influence on William Morris, and this was coupled with a sentimental longing for a preindustrial golden age of unhurried and scrupulous labor.

The delight of the craftsman at work is explicitly evident in little details— from the amusing mice of Robert Thompson to the painstaking decoration on the pages of the Kelmscott Chaucer. George Ohr, "the Mad Potter of Biloxi," was adamant that each of his "clay babies" should be unique: his mantra was "No two alike." The working communities established by visionaries such as Charles Robert Ashbee and Elbert Hubbard are a testament to the commitment of those who made Arts and Crafts the focus not just of their working lives but also of their family and social lives.

The very best and most famous Arts and Crafts artifacts are now museum pieces, or else only available to the fabulously wealthy. The good news for the rest of us is that beautiful and practical objects by many well-known and lesser-known designers are still very affordable. With a trained eye, who knows what you might unearth?

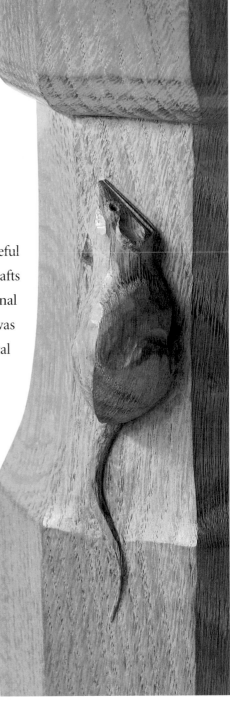

Detail of an oak table by Robert "Mouseman" Thompson, p.27

Judith Miller.

Green-glazed pottery table lamp by Fulper.
It is of mushroom shape with a flared base
and a domed shade inset with leaded
sections of yellow and green glass. *c. 1910*
17¼ in (44 cm) high **$30,000–40,000 GDG**

What is Arts and Crafts?

The Arts and Crafts movement that emerged in England in the late 19th century
completely redefined the decorative arts. Inspired by John Ruskin and William
Morris, British artists and social reformers lamented the diminished role of the
artist-craftsman and the increasing dependence on the machine to meet the
demands of a burgeoning middle class. Morris condemned mass production
and blamed it for a decline in values that he felt had been brought about by the
proliferation of inferior-quality decorative household wares.

The Arts and Crafts movement aimed to strengthen the balance between art and
craftsmanship. Morris believed in the importance of the individual craftsman and in
a vision of beauty and harmony that looked back to the medieval guild system for
inspiration. The movement sought to revive traditional craft techniques
and restore the dignity and prestige of the artisan, which had
been sacrificed in the name of Victorian progress and
industrialization. It was not just a style but a way of living
founded upon Utopian ideals. Morris and his followers were
convinced that bringing artistic integrity to everyday household
objects played a vital role in improving the quality of life. To this

Enameled silver clock designed by
Archibald Knox for Liberty & Co., with a
spandrel showing a tree motif against
colored enamels, above a circular enameled
dial. *c. 1905. 4¼ in (11 cm) high*
$20,000–30,000 GDG

Bentwood nest of four tables designed by
Josef Hoffmann for J. & J. Kohn, in beech
with mahogany staining. The largest table
has lattice sides. *c. 1905. Tallest: 29¾ in
(75.5 cm) high* **$3,000–5,000 (the set) QU**

end, the movement emphasized humble, local materials, the importance of honesty to function, and the veneration of handcraftsmanship.

The principles championed by William Morris were embraced across Europe, where the Arts and Crafts movement was interpreted by artist-craftsmen in a host of different ways, from Paris to Vienna. Fresh ideas for new forms of expression mingled and were redefined, making their way back to Great Britain enriched and revitalized, and crossing the Atlantic to the United States, where Morris's visionary ideals were warmly received and adapted to create a uniquely American incarnation of the Arts and Crafts style.

English oak elbow chair featuring a tall paneled back with scrolling finials and a panel of turned spindles, curved armrests, and a solid seat. It rests on turned supports united by stretchers. *c. 1900 51¼ in (130.5 cm) high* **$1,000–1,500 FRE**

Gustav Stickley fixed-back oak armchair the sides of which have five vertical slats below broad, plain armrests. It is raised on square supports and has replacement leather upholstery. *c. 1900. 42½ in (108 cm) high* **$2,000–3,000 DRA**

Origins and influences

William Morris's writings, lectures, and lifestyle exercised a profound influence on a new generation of architects, craftsmen, and decorators on both sides of the Atlantic. Morris based much of his philosophy on the medieval ideal celebrating the central role of the craftsman and the establishment of workers' guilds. He and his followers—including A. H. Mackmurdo, Walter Crane, and Philip Webb—aimed to bring renewed vitality to native English traditions and stem the decline in quality resulting from marginalizing the craftsman in favor of industrialization.

To this end, a number of Arts and Crafts guilds were established in the 1880s to try to elevate crafts to the status of fine art. Among these were Ruskin's short-lived St. George's Guild, A. H. Mackmurdo's Century Guild—where a team of craftsmen designed houses and furnishings in a collaborative spirit—and the Art Workers' Guild, which aimed to bring artists and architects, designers and craftsmen together in the name of decorative unity.

The message moved from London to urban centers, including Birmingham and Glasgow, via publications such as *The Studio* and colleges dedicated to promoting the Arts and Crafts philosophy in the decorative arts. Along with the socialist and aesthetic principles of William Morris and John Ruskin, the

Dove and rose detail of handwoven silk wall hanging on a wool base, designed by William Morris. Produced for a short period only due to high production costs. *c. 1905*
48 in (122 cm) wide **$3,000–5,000 PC**

Large stoneware bird by the Martin Brothers. The bird, in shades of green, ocher, and brown, has a hooked beak and quizzical eyes and rests with folded wings on a circular base. Signed and dated. *1894*
17 in (43 cm) high **$70,000–100,000 WW**

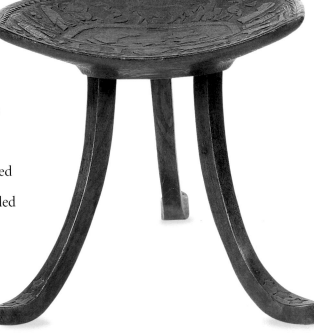

Large Peacock pottery tile by William de Morgan. It is decorated in Persian colors with confronting peacocks with extending tails amid blue flowers and olive-colored foliage. *c. 1890. 9 in (23 cm) square* **$2,000–3,000 PC**

Oak Thebes stool by Liberty & Co. (one of a pair), supported on three curved legs. The concave seat is carved with Egyptian and astrological symbols. *c. 1890. 13½ in (34 cm) high* **$3,000–5,000 (the pair) PUR**

success of the Arts and Crafts movement was framed by a number of influential designers trained as architects, including A. H. Mackmurdo, C. F. A. Voysey, Charles Rennie Mackintosh, and C. R. Ashbee.

In keeping with the medieval ideal, Arts and Crafts designs were often based on simple, organic shapes and a vocabulary of decorative motifs such as flowers, birds, and foliage rendered in stylized patterns. The broad range of design influences included Persian colors and style, as used by William de Morgan; Egyptian motifs, evident in Liberty's Thebes stool; as well as medieval romances, late romantic poetry, and Pre-Raphaelite painting.

Development of the style

From the writings and lectures of William Morris, the Arts and Crafts style evolved into an international movement. Not only did Morris base his principles on the rules and methods of the medieval craft system, he also supported the idea that the artist should be intimately involved with his craft; a painter should grind his own pigments and a jeweler should hand-hammer his own designs.

This philosophy crossed the English Channel and made itself known in European workshops from Brussels to Darmstadt and also across the Atlantic. In France, artists such as Léon Jallot seized on the Arts and Crafts penchant for handcraftsmanship and natural motifs, while in Austria and Germany, designers including Josef Hoffmann and Richard Riemerschmid evolved a style that focused on the geometric outlines featured in the designs of Ernest Gimson and C. R. Mackintosh.

In the United States came entrepreneurs such as Elbert Hubbard and the Stickley family, who developed a new style of furniture and metalware made affordable to

Rare Rookwood vase painted by William P. McDonald in natural colors with a panoramic view of a seagull in relief against a dawn seascape. *1899. 11¾ in (30 cm) high* **$70,000–100,000 DRA**

Gustav Stickley oak sideboard with a raised back, a plain work surface, and four short drawers flanked by cupboards. It is applied with copper handles and hinges, and raised on square supports. *c. 1900 70 in (178 cm) wide* **$20,000–30,000 G5**

Entrance to the Roycroft Inn menu cover
by Dard Hunter, showing a stylized image
of the hostelry with geometric plants in
the foreground. *1920. 5¼ in (13.5 cm) wide*
$500–700 DRA

the middle class through carefully controlled mass production. The Arts and Crafts style found a voice in the simple shapes and minimal decoration of the furniture created by Gustav Stickley and the Gothic and medieval designs produced by Charles Rohlfs. Inspired by a trip to England, in 1896 Elbert Hubbard established the Roycroft community in East Aurora, New York, which was based on the English guilds and produced handcrafted books, furniture, and leather goods. Both American individual potters and ceramics companies such as George Ohr, Artus Van Briggle, and Rookwood also strove to live up to Ernest Batchelder's motto, "No two tiles are the same." Most American Arts and Crafts makers shared William Morris's ideal of the craftsman while remaining open to the possibilities offered by the machine.

Gustav Stickley early oak lunch table with
a plain plank top raised on square supports
united by stretchers with exposed tenons
and joints. *c. 1900. 40 in (101.5 cm) wide*
$3,000–4,000 DRA

Rookwood Iris Glaze plaque painted by Sturgis Laurence and called *A Bit of New England Coast*. A rare item, it shows a rocky coastline and waves under a cloudy blue sky. *1903 12¼ in (31 cm) wide* **$30,000–50,000 DRA**

Rare Artichoke tile by William Morris, painted in blues and grays on a fragile body. Few have survived. *c. 1880. 6 in (15 cm) wide* **$1,200–1,800 PC**

Pair of cast-iron firedogs by Gustav Stickley, with ball finials, scrolling legs, and rings linked by a chain *c. 1910. 21¾ in (55 cm) wide* **$15,000–20,000 GDG**

An integrated style

The Arts and Crafts ideology was based upon the belief that beautiful and artistic furnishings should be created in local materials with an eye on function, to achieve a harmonizing, unified interior. Furniture had clear, simple lines and the inherent beauty of the wood was emphasized. Gone was the gloominess brought about by Victorian clutter—the oppressive accumulation of furniture and bric-a-brac was replaced by a lighter, cheerful, and more reasoned program that rethought the use of space.

William Morris pioneered this new interior decorative style, and Morris & Co. produced influential and distinctive textiles, wallpapers, and tiles with stylized repeated patterns inspired by nature. As Morris himself said, "Do not be afraid of large patterns—if properly designed, they are more restful to the eye than small ones." The art of textile making, embroidery, and wallpaper design rose to such prominence at the end of the 19th century that a host of gifted individuals such as C. F. A. Voysey and M. H. Baillie Scott not only designed textiles, but also wrote on the subject.

As well as the fixtures and structural decoration of a room, carpets, wallpapers, furniture, ceramics, metalware, and glass lamps were created as part of a cohesive design scheme that often depended upon recurring decorative motifs for unity. In the hands of a new breed of architect-designers led by M. H. Baillie Scott, the Arts and Crafts interior was a warm and welcoming evocation of

M. H. Baillie Scott design for the music room of a house in Crowborough, Sussex. Baillie Scott developed the idea of the integrated interior, aiming for simplicity and flexibility in his design. *1902.* **NPA MEPL**

the simple life, and balanced the practical with the domestic, with the fireplace the designated focus of a long room boasting a low-beamed ceiling, leaded windows, and an abundance of finely crafted wood that included paneling and built-in, multipurpose furniture. Others Arts and Crafts designers had their own interpretation of the integrated style: Voysey, for example, favored bright interiors with light, whitewashed walls and little ornament, while C. R. Mackintosh developed stunning decorative schemes that used delicate, elongated geometric lines to punctuate everything from cutlery to carpets. The Greene Brothers' design of the Gamble House in California displayed an inspired use of clean lines, natural wood, and art glass to create a warm, integrated interior with abundant natural light.

Charles Limbert table lamp with a hammered-copper base supporting a flaring pierced shade with Dutch scenes in silhouette against hammered amber glass. *c. 1910* 24½ in (62 cm) high **$12,000–18,000 DRA**

W.M.F. silver-plated shaped photograph frame the pierced top of which has two girls' heads in profile, on a truncated-pyramid base. *c. 1905. 6¾ in (17 cm) high*
$800–1,200 STY

A diverse movement

William Morris and John Ruskin, the pioneers of what was to become the Arts and Crafts movement, blamed mass production for the decline in the quality of life. How could one really live a worthy life, they reasoned, surrounded by the shabby furniture, cheap glass- and metalware, and general clutter typical of the Victorian home? Their followers—architects, designers, and craftsmen aiming to create a better, more authentic world—looked to nature for inspiration, from the inherent beauty of the wood and the construction of a piece of furniture, to the shape of a silver candlestick based on the trunk of a tree, to the sumptuous colors and decorative motifs based on birds, flowers, and foliage that embellished a glass lampshade, a brooch, or a textile wall hanging.

The disillusionment with industrialization was felt not only in England, but also in Europe and the United States. In France, the Arts and Crafts movement encouraged the development of the Art Nouveau style, which took the dependence on the natural world to imaginative, inspired heights. In Austria, Germany, and Belgium, Josef Hoffmann, Joseph Maria Olbrich, and Henry van de Velde interpreted nature with an abstract, geometric twist influenced by Charles Rennie Mackintosh. In the United States,

Thonet beech elbow chair with curved arms and a short backrest on three circular supports linked by curved bands. The wickerwork seat has been replaced. *c. 1900. 32 in (81.5 cm) high*
$1,800–2,200 QU

workshops for furniture, metalware, glass, and ceramics grew up around the country prompted by the success of Gustav Stickley and the Roycrofters, or inspired by the dedication to handcraftsmanship and truth to materials championed by George Ohr.

American, German, and Austrian Arts and Crafts practitioners differed from their British counterparts in their willingness to accept the creative possibilities offered by the machine, although commercial companies in Great Britain such as Murrle Bennett and Liberty & Co. exploited the fashionable taste for the Arts and Crafts style.

By the onset of World War I, the Arts and Crafts movement had moved beyond its socialist aims, and the world looked ahead to Modernism. Nevertheless, Arts and Crafts always was—and still remains—a philosophy, style, and lifestyle for those who appreciate simplicity, quality materials, and handcraftsmanship.

Silver knife and fork from the Flat Model set designed by Josef Hoffmann for the Wiener Werkstätte. Hallmarks include a woman's head, a greyhound, and the maker's mark "WW." *1903. Knife: 7¼ in (18.5 cm) long* **$20,000–30,000 WKA**

Pewter wine jug designed by Joseph Maria Olbrich for Eduard Hueck. It resembles a stylized peacock, with tail-feather motifs around the lower base. *c. 1900 13½ in (34 cm) high* **$2,000–3,000 VZ**

Thonet beech coat stand designed by Josef Hoffmann. It is of tapering square form, with a rounded top applied with hooks for hats, and a central space for canes and umbrellas. *c. 1900 82½ in (209.5 cm) high* **$5,000–7,000 WKA**

Furniture

From elaborate sideboards and cabinets embellished with carving, painting, or inlaid work, to simple chairs and tables in solid oak, craftsmen from Great Britain to Austria and across the Atlantic shared the vision of William Morris by creating both "the necessary workaday furniture... simple to the last degree" and "the other kind... the blossoms of the art of furniture."

In late 19th-century Britain, the writings and lectures of Arts and Crafts pioneer William Morris touched the imagination of a new breed of architects and designers who moved furniture design in a revolutionary direction.

Looking to provide an alternative to the gloomy Victorian interior that typically boasted a range of mismatched styles, Arts and Crafts designers reconsidered the use of space and developed the concept of the room interior as part of a cohesive, integrated whole. Buildings were decorated from the inside out, with interiors and furniture—both built-in pieces, such as bookcases, and freestanding ones—conceived with an eye on the overall design.

Most designers looked back to the traditional ideal that furniture should be well crafted from solid, honest materials and—above all—functional. This idea was interpreted across Europe and the United States in a variety of ways. British designers—C. F. A. Voysey, C. R. Ashbee, and Charles Rennie Mackintosh—shared with the French Art Nouveau movement a dependence on nature for decorative themes for their restrained furniture. On the other hand, their continental counterparts, such as Carlo Bugatti and Louis Majorelle, favored exuberant, flamboyant confections created in luxurious materials that saw decoration take precedence over function.

At the same time, German and Austrian designers defined the style in a straightforward, abstract manner, while in the United States the purity of the British Arts and Crafts movement was reflected in the taste for clean-lined, undecorated furniture.

Detail of a Gustav Stickley oak sideboard (see p.12) with a plain work surface and four drawers flanked by cupboards. It is applied with copper handles and hinges. c. 1900
70 in (178 cm) wide **$20,000–30,000 G5**

HONESTY AND FUNCTION

The Arts and Crafts furniture that sprang from the vision of William Morris and The Firm, the enterprise he ran along the lines of a medieval workshop, was sturdy, well proportioned, and functional, made from local woods such as oak, elm, and ash, and boasting minimal decoration.

Many craftsmen—including Ernest Gimson, Philip Webb, and M. H. Baillie Scott—fell under the spell of Morris's philosophy. They combined traditional and new ideas and forged a variety of individual paths for furniture design in the Arts and Crafts style. Simple, homey, and useful pieces in local materials were made alongside more elaborate and monumental "blossoms." The latter were rendered in rich timbers such as walnut and ebony and often featured inlays made of ivory, brass, or precious woods, decorative cutout patterns, painted panels, or metal handles and strap hinges.

The influence of William Morris was far-reaching and had a lasting impact on the development of Arts and Crafts furniture. His ideas were taken up both in continental Europe and across the Atlantic, where they were echoed in the works of leading American designers, from Charles Limbert to Charles Rohlfs. Signature designs, such as the humble Sussex Chair and various incarnations of the popular Morris Chair, were created in the prestigious workshop of Gustav Stickley.

As in the US, European designers who were inspired by the Arts and Crafts movement—among them Henry van de Velde at the Deutscher Werkbund and Josef Hoffmann and Koloman Moser at the Wiener Werkstätte—put their own spin on the style. Their clean-lined utilitarian furniture—designed for handcraft as well as for mass production—owed much to the simple geometric forms created by Charles Rennie Mackintosh in Glasgow. These pieces would ultimately open the door to the modern age.

PERSONAL INTERPRETATIONS

In Great Britain, designers such as C. F. A. Voysey and the innovative Glasgow Four led by C. R. Mackintosh adopted Morris's ideology while

Shapland & Petter mahogany bowfront cabinet with a rounded top. The center has a glazed door flanked by open shelving and cupboard doors inlaid with boxwood stringing, mother-of-pearl, and abalone. On straight legs with block feet. *c. 1905* *75¼ in (191 cm) high* **$1,800–2,200 DN**

William Morris (on the right), the founder of the English Arts and Crafts movement and of leading furniture manufacturer Morris & Co., with painter and illustrator Edward Burne-Jones, circa 1890.

KEY POINTS

The majority of Arts and Crafts furniture is austere, relatively free of surface embellishment, and strongly architectural in form. Craftsmen made a virtue of the varied joints and abutments they used and made them the decorative focus. Where surface decoration was used, it took the form of marquetry inlays, cutouts, piercing, and chamfering, adornments that showcased both the wood and the talents of the craftsman.

Morris & Co. ebonized-walnut armchair designed by Philip Webb. It has a reclining back and turned spindle sides, and rests on curved back legs and square front supports united by turned stretchers. The padded arm supports and separate cushions are upholstered with Morris's Bird pattern woven fabric. *c. 1865. 36¼ in (92 cm) high* **$12,000–18,000 PUR**

Liberty & Co. oak three-tier bookshelf with extended planklike sides with shaped tops and pierced decoration. The top rail is pierced with a bird motif, while the three front panels are carved in relief with scrolling flowers and foliage. *c. 1905* *35 in (89 cm) high* **$800–1,200 PUR**

developing their own individual interpretations of the Arts and Crafts style. This personal reading also took place in the United States, with Elbert Hubbard and the Roycrofters, Gustav Stickley, and Frank Lloyd Wright.

Mackintosh created bold, imaginative tables, dining chairs, and cabinets in simple but elegant shapes, but concerned himself less with function than with beauty, and always kept an eye on the decoration of the interior space. On the other hand, Voysey's plain and elegant furniture was distinctive for its dependence on shape for expression and the spare use of decorative ornaments. Across the Atlantic, the talented designer Harvey Ellis pushed the boundaries of the English Arts and Crafts style by bringing a sophisticated European dimension to Stickley's Mission oak designs. He was partial to ornamental inlays in stylized floral motifs made from sumptuous materials—exotic woods, copper, and pewter—and elongated proportions in the manner of Mackintosh.

The guilds that had been created to further the social reforms and ideals of Morris and Ruskin—including A. H. Mackmurdo's Century Guild, C. R. Ashbee's Guild of Handicraft, and the Art Workers' Guild, led by William Lethaby—were modeled after the medieval guild system. They celebrated the role of the individual designer-craftsman and aimed to create modest, well-made, functional furniture in honest materials with imagination and originality. Ernest Gimson and the Barnsley Brothers

in the Cotswolds brought the spirit of William Morris and the rural tradition to their solidly constructed furniture, which highlighted, as decoration, rustic joinery features such as mortise-and-tenon joints, wooden pins, and dovetails.

THE PRICE OF ARTISTRY

Inevitably, the machine answered the siren call for less expensive furniture, which in Germany, Austria, and the United States was considered as an important adjunct in the effort to create functional quality pieces. While holding fast to the Arts and Crafts principles advocating a return to the medieval ideals of handcraftsmanship and design based on an honesty of purpose and truth to materials, the movement in Great Britain could not sustain itself with furniture that had become, by necessity, increasingly costly to produce. Ultimately, it was left to commercial retailers such as Liberty & Co. and Heal & Son to provide the middle classes with decorative machine-made furniture in the simple Arts and Crafts style.

L. & J. G. Stickley oak magazine stand with slatted sides, four shelves, and an arched apron and top rails. It is raised on square-section supports. With the original finish and a handcrafted decal mark. *c. 1900 42¼ in (107.5 cm) high* **$3,000–4,000 DRA**

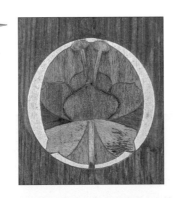

Gustav Stickley oak drop-front desk designed by Harvey Ellis, with a flat extending top and plain planklike sides and undershelf. The hinged desk flap has three panels with inlaid colored fruitwoods and pewter stylized floral motifs (*see detail above*). *c. 1910 30¼ in (77 cm) wide* **$40,000–60,000 GDG**

Limbert oak lamp table with a plain octagonal top on flared planklike supports with pierced inverted heart motifs and united by a cruciform stretcher. With the original finish and a branded maker's mark. *c. 1910 28½ in (72.5 cm) high* **$800–1,200 DRA**

Ebonized wood was typically used for early Morris furniture, although later designs favored timbers traditionally associated with country furniture, such as oak, ash, and occasionally mahogany.

Traditional country designs, which are usually handcrafted and boast sturdy, solid construction, heavily influenced Morris furniture.

Rush seating is common for dining chairs, while armchairs are typically upholstered with Morris fabrics inspired by medieval designs.

Joints and hinges used in construction play an important role as decorative details on Morris furniture.

Copies of Morris furniture abound, and authentic pieces are marked with the "Morris & Co." stamp.

Morris & Co.

Encouraging the use of traditional skills in the quest to produce quality handcrafted decorative objects, William Morris is credited—along with John Ruskin—as the founding father of the Arts and Crafts movement.

Deeply opposed to mechanical production, William Morris (1834–96) campaigned for the revival of traditional techniques. Teaming up with a circle of talented artist friends, including the architect Philip Webb (1831–1915), his London-based design firm Morris, Marshall, Faulkner & Co. (est. 1861) looked to natural materials and handicraft traditions to produce highly original ceramics, textiles, wallpaper, carpets, and furniture. Decorative fabrics, often featuring narrative themes drawn from nature or medieval romantic legends, were sometimes used on furniture.

Morris assumed sole control of the company in 1875, producing solid, heavy, conventional furniture, frequently in mahogany with satinwood inlay decoration. The Sussex Chair was one of the company's many successful items. Webb's original 1880s design was based on a traditional country chair: an ash frame with a hand-woven rush seat and decoration confined to turned vertical spindles at the back. It was produced in a variety of forms, such as a single chair, an armchair, a corner chair, a round-seat piano stool, and a settee. Another enduring design was the Morris Chair, a large, adjustable armchair typically upholstered by Morris with medieval-inspired fabrics.

In the 1890s, following the appointment of American craftsman George Jack (1855–1932) as chief designer, Morris embraced a more elaborate taste influenced by the newly popular Queen Anne style. Alongside simple country-style bedroom furniture and chairs, large mahogany buffets and dressers were embellished with sumptuous marquetry, glazed doors, and pierced carvings.

Morris & Co. finally closed its doors in 1940, after 65 years of production.

Above: Upholstered reclining chair with back legs and arms curving in parallel and united by slightly turned spindles. *c. 1890 40 in (101.5 cm) high* **$2,000–3,000 G5**

PHILIP WEBB DESIGNS

From 1861, architect Philip Webb, who had designed the Red House in Bexleyheath, Kent, for William Morris, worked exclusively for the Morris firm as a designer. His distinctive furniture is massive and solid, with the joinery exposed for decorative effect. Webb favored plain oak, which was usually stained green or black, but occasionally decorated on the surface by painting, gesso work, or lacquered leather. His early enthusiasm for Gothic design eventually gave way to a variety of influences, including the Queen Anne and Japanese styles. He set an example for aspiring Arts and Crafts designers by emphasizing the importance of high-quality manufacturing techniques.

Large mahogany dining table designed by Philip Webb. The oval top has an incised edge above a central turned support surrounded by six ring-turned legs united by stretchers. *1860s 70¼ in (176 cm) long* **$50,000–70,000 L&T**

This detail of the mahogany dining table shows the central plain circular support with typical radiating ring-turned spokes uniting the six outer supports, which are further united by horizontal rods.

Mahogany settee designed by George Jack, with upholstered back, seat, and armrests, open rod sides, and turned supports terminating in casters. *c. 1900*

37 in (94 cm) high

$8,000–12,000   **PUR**

Dark-colored walnut sideboard designed by Philip Webb. The superstructure has a plain solid top, with arched panels at the front and sides supported by turned columns. The base has a rectangular top and three frieze drawers with cupboards below, including original brass drop pulls. *c. 1890*

61½ in (156 cm) wide

$20,000–30,000   **DN**

A CLOSER LOOK

Mahogany draft screen enclosing panels of flowering foliage worked in colored silks, possibly from a design by J. H. Dearle. The frame has a shaped top surmounted by finials and a pierced wavy frieze. *c. 1890. 73¾ in (187 cm) high* **$20,000–30,000 L&T**

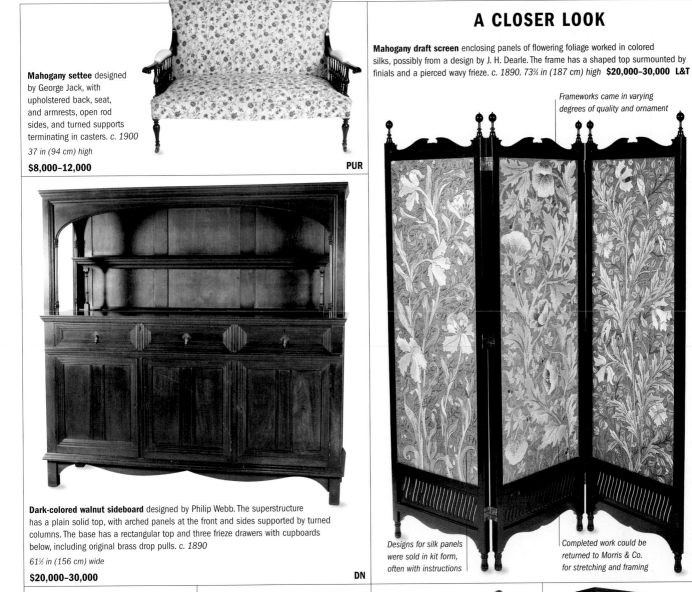

Frameworks came in varying degrees of quality and ornament

Designs for silk panels were sold in kit form, often with instructions

Completed work could be returned to Morris & Co. for stretching and framing

Suffolk chair (one of a pair) in ebonized elm, the back with spindles and horizontal rails. The chair has open armrests above a rush seat on turned legs linked by stretchers. *c. 1870*

$1,000–1,500 (the pair)   **L&T**

Sussex ash armchair with three shaped horizontal bands in the back, curved armrests, a rush seat, and supports united by stretchers. Damaged. *c. 1890*

33½ in (85 cm) high

$400–600   **WW**

Mahogany firescreen inlaid with boxed ebony stringing and enclosing an embroidered panel of silks. Stamped on the underside "Morris & Co., 449 Oxford St." and numbered. *c. 1890*

41¼ in (105 cm) high

$1,000–1,500   **DN**

Mahogany bookcase in the manner of Morris & Co., with a molded and projecting cornice above an arcaded open shelf with fixed shelves below and stile supports. *c. 1900*

86½ in (220 cm) high

$3,000–5,000   **L&T**

Oak, mahogany, and walnut were the favored timbers for commercially produced furniture by Liberty & Co.

Clean, symmetrical shapes of simple construction are highlighted with a minimum of decoration.

Decorative details commonly feature pierced or cut-out square, rectangle, heart, and trefoil patterns; painted- or stained-glass panels; and elaborate hinges in hand-beaten copper or brass.

Furniture is mostly marked "Liberty & Co." within rectangular ivorine plaques.

Liberty & Co.

From its founding in 1875, the London emporium of Liberty & Co. served as a vanguard for progressive, innovative design while responding to the demand for fashionable but affordable furniture in the Arts and Crafts style.

In 1883, Arthur Lasenby Liberty (1843–1917), founder of the London store that bears his name, set up a furnishing and decorating studio directed by Leonard F. Wyburd. Wyburd's mandate was to meet the growing demand for fashionable interiors by developing a style that merged commercial needs with Arts and Crafts design.

Wyburd's furniture for Liberty borrowed freely from Arts and Crafts designers, but the company commissioned designs from them as well. The Liberty inventory included furniture by C. F. A. Voysey (*see p.26*), George Walton (*see p.33*), and a line of 81 pieces by M. H. Baillie Scott.

By 1887 Liberty's cabinet-making workshop was turning out a range of simple chairs— stools, carvers, and side chairs—and country-style oak furniture embellished with inlaid decoration, leaded-glass panels, strap hinges and metal handles, and occasionally inset tiles by William de Morgan (*see pp.86–87*). A number of manufacturers were subcontracted to produce the more complex pieces.

Liberty played on both the visual and the ideological appeal of Arts and Crafts design, liberally sprinkling quotations by John Ruskin throughout its illustrated catalog. Although the movement's fundamental—and expensive— notion of the artist-craftsman was brushed aside, it was a path that proved to be hugely popular, and by 1900 Liberty & Co. was celebrated worldwide as a leader in the production of Arts and Crafts furniture.

Liberty's success in selling cheaper versions of art furniture ultimately contributed to the commercial demise of the guilds and hastened the end of the movement in the 1900s.

Above: Mahogany table with molded hexagonal top, on tapering square supports with pad feet, united by broad pierced panels. *c. 1900. 28¾ in (73 cm) high* **$800–1,200 L&T**

Large oak bureau-bookcase with a projecting cornice above open shelves and a leaded-glass door. The lower section has a sloping fall above a single drawer, cupboard, and open area. *c. 1890 58¾ in (149 cm) wide* **$3,000–5,000 L&T**

THE LIBERTY STYLE

Liberty responded to the demand for fashionable but affordable furniture by creating a range of high-backed chairs with cut-out patterns and simply constructed cabinets boasting painted- or stained-glass panels, metal handles, and elaborate hinges. Country-style oak chairs, stools, tables, and cupboards by Leonard F. Wyburd are among the most widely recognized items of Liberty furniture. Although the company's catalogs offered an eclectic array of furniture styles, it is the range of Quaint furniture that most closely mirrored the Arts and Crafts designs and decorative motifs.

Mahogany Thebes stool with solid D-shaped and dished seat supported on three spreading square-section legs terminating with pointed pad feet. This design is based on an archaic Egyptian original. *c. 1880. 14½ in (36.5 cm) high* **$800–1,200 L&T**

Oak day bed of open boxlike construction, with plain plank armrests, open sides with vertical struts, a hinged reclining back, and footrest extending at the front. *c. 1900*

31 in (79 cm) high

$700–1,000   **TDG**

Anglo-Moorish walnut plant stand with ebonized brackets and *musharabeyah* (turned-bobbin) panels. *c. 1890*

33 in (84 cm) high

$1,800–2,200   **PUR**

Mahogany Thebes-style tapering plant stand with thin rods uniting the supports; probably retailed by Liberty & Co. *c. 1880*

41¾ in (106 cm) high

$600–900   **WW**

Oak stick stand with back pierced with heart motifs; on square supports with capped feet united by stretchers. *c. 1905*

32½ in (83 cm) high

$500–700   **PUR**

Oak étagère by L. F. Wyburd, with two galleried undertiers. Turned and blocked supports enclose latticed grilled sides. *c. 1895*

30¾ in (78 cm) high

$700–1,000   **L&T**

Mahogany chair retailed by Liberty & Co. with curved solid top-rail carved with interwoven scrollwork above a tapering spindle-back. Complete with original paper label. *c. 1900*

39¾ in (101 cm) high

$800–1,200   **WW**

Oak bookcase with removable long shelves above a cupboard flanked by further shelves. The top is pierced with heart motifs. *c. 1900*

70 in (178 cm) high

$20,000–30,000   **PUR**

Oak buffet probably retailed through Liberty & Co., with a glazed cupboard as well as shelves, alcoves, cupboards, and drawers. *c. 1890*

69¼ in (176 cm) high

$700–1,000   **DN**

KEY FEATURES

Voysey's furniture is typically rendered in pale-colored oak that was prized for its visual beauty.

Decoration is spare, with cut-out vertical panels, pierced heart patterns, and low-relief carvings among the favored techniques.

Tapering legs or supports frequently terminate in a wide square cap—a feature also found in furniture by A. H. Mackmurdo.

Elaborate metal strap hinges and brass or leather panels often decorate otherwise simple cabinets.

Chairs feature rush or leather seats with vertical, tapering uprights and heart-shaped cutouts.

C. F. A. Voysey

Many of the characteristics of the Arts and Crafts style can be attributed to English architect and designer C. F. A. Voysey, who embraced a highly individual approach in his designs for furniture, textiles, and metalwork.

A disciple of William Morris (*see p.22–23*) and A. H. Mackmurdo, Charles Francis Annesley Voysey (1857–1941) was one of Great Britain's most innovative designers of furniture in the Arts and Crafts style.

A maverick with a distaste for all things foreign, Voysey embarked on his career as a furniture designer in 1890. His imaginative items were characterized by an elegant simplicity that reflected his philosophy that furniture should be honest and suited to the everyday needs of the people who used it.

Voysey's light, graceful furniture celebrates the inherent beauty and visual quality of the wood and boasts an engaging rustic quality that mirrors the style of his architecture. Pieces were typically rendered in pale oak—which was often left untreated and free of stain or polish—with a minimum of decoration.

Voysey frequently embellished his finely crafted cabinets with elaborate metal strap hinges, carvings in low relief, or panels of brass and leather, and highlighted his rush-seated high-backed chairs with a favorite pierced heart motif. However, it is his emphasis on structure and proportion that lends his highly original designs freshness and vitality.

Above: Oak dining chair featuring a broad back splat pierced with a heart motif, with tapering armrests, a drop-in leather seat, and tapering supports. *c. 1900. 39½ in (100 cm) high* **$10,000–15,000 BRI**

Oak table made by F. C. Nielsen, London, originally unpolished and unstained. The present dark varnish is a later addition. *c. 1905*
29½ in (75 cm) wide

NPA   **V&A**

Oak hall chair with five broad back splats, paddle-shaped armrests, tapering supports, and vertically extending back posts; the leather seat is a replacement. *c. 1895*
55 in (140 cm) high

$12,000–18,000   **DRA**

Unvarnished oak writing desk featuring an upper door with elaborate copper hinges and a panel pierced to show a rural family group strolling through a pastoral landscape. *c. 1905*
66 in (167.5 cm) high

NPA   **V&A**

Robert "Mouseman" Thompson

Yorkshire craftsman Robert Thompson devoted his career to the revival of traditional solid English-oak furniture, which he made, using traditional tools and methods of manufacture, in his rural workshop.

Starting out as an apprentice in his father's joinery in the village of Kilburn, Yorkshire, Thompson (1876–1955) soon developed a love of English oak and became interested in traditional techniques. By 1895, Thompson had taken over the family business and was producing solid handcrafted oak furnishings inspired by the medieval carvings he had seen at nearby Ripon and York cathedrals, as well as by traditional 17th-century designs.

In 1919, Thompson received his first major commission for a carving from Ampleforth Boys' School. He went on to work for several schools and churches, including York Minster. His firm expanded rapidly, and by the 1930s, Thompson employed 30 men.

The famous carved mouse that adorns every piece by Robert Thompson was registered as a trademark in the 1930s, but was used by the firm from the start. The company is still in existence today.

Above: A carved oak mouse was the signature of Robert Thompson, who once considered himself "as poor as a church mouse."

KEY FEATURES

English oak was Thompson's material of choice, though he occasionally incorporated wrought iron and cowhide in his designs.

Wooden surfaces are uneven and rippled, an effect created by the use of an adze.

The handcrafted pieces are inspired by traditional English country furniture.

The carved-mouse signature can be found on every piece of furniture made by Robert Thompson.

Oak refectory table on two octagonal supports linked by a flat stretcher. One of the supports has a signature mouse running up toward the tabletop. *c. 1910*

NPA   **DP**

Oak nest of three small tables with rectangular tops, all slightly adzed, on chamfered supports united by stretchers. Each is carved with a signature mouse. *c. 1950*

Largest: 15 in (38 cm) wide

$1,000–1,500   **DN**

Oak desk chair with a curved back and solid shaped arm supports, a pierced lattice back splat and side panels, and a leather seat. It is raised on octagonal baluster supports united by plain cross stretchers. *c. 1910*

31½ in (80 cm) high

NPA   **DP**

KEY FEATURES

Hand-hammered repoussé copper panels are common, usually with stylized floral designs.

Inlays of metal or marquetry are often elaborate, intended to showcase the skill of the craftsmen employed at the Raleigh Cabinet Works.

Multiple shaped spindles and slats are often included as decorative elements.

Carving and pierced hearts, a favorite motif of Arts and Crafts cabinet makers, were sometimes used as extra decoration.

Remarkable stained-glass panels featuring colorful floral forms are occasionally included.

Shapland & Petter

Based in Barnstaple, England, the commercial firm of Shapland & Petter became a leading maker of furniture in the Arts and Crafts style, producing a distinctive range that was celebrated for fine design and high-quality craftsmanship.

In 1854, Henry Shapland (1823–1909) established a cabinet-making business in north Devon, and accountant Henry Petter joined him to create a highly successful commercial enterprise. Although devastated by a fire in 1888, their Raleigh Cabinet Works was rebuilt to include state-of-the-art production facilities.

Shapland & Petter combined modern machine technology with traditional craftsmanship. Mechanized processes were employed to produce well-made furniture in quality materials. Items were then embellished with a variety of handcraft techniques—woodcarving, marquetry, metal inlay, mounted ceramic and enamel cabochons, and the application of decorative copperwork. Shapland & Petter furniture also includes restrained pieces using heart-shaped piercing, geometric shapes with angled arches, and a medieval style heavily ornamented with hand-hammered repoussé copper panels.

The company paid great attention to training its staff. Carvers, for example, perfected their craft by attending classes at the Barnstaple School of Art and completing seven-year apprenticeships.

Many pieces were made from hundreds of standard designs promoted in local and London showrooms and through catalogs. Creating its own unique style by copying the designs of other Arts and Crafts luminaries, such as C. R. Ashbee and Hugh Baillie Scott, the company also produced furniture for retailers across Great Britain, including Morris & Co. The company is still in business under the name Leaderflush Shapland.

Above: Mahogany and stained-glass firescreen with stylized buds in colored glass against a textured ground, flanked by embossed copper panels. *c.* 1900. 39 in (99 cm) high **$1,200–1,800 DN**

MARQUETRY AND LEADED GLASS

Unlike many of its peers, Shapland & Petter was conspicuous in its extravagant use of surface decoration. Floral marquetry panels, often using three or more different woods, acted as attractive embellishments that set Shapland & Petter furniture apart. The stylized stained-glass designs included on some of the company's furniture are equally distinctive. It is unclear whether these leaded-glass panels were made at the Raleigh workshop or in nearby glassworks.

Mahogany display cabinet with marquetry decoration. The door has a decorative metal panel and is flanked by open shelving and cupboards with elaborate wood and mother-of-pearl inlay. *c.* 1900. 54 in (137 cm) wide **$5,000–8,000 VZ**

Lady's walnut desk with a stained-glass panel of stylized plant forms, a flat leather writing surface, a frieze drawer with ring-pulls, and open supports united by shaped slats. *c.* 1905 42 in (107 cm) wide **$3,000–4,000 PUR**

Mahogany bookcase topped by a copper panel embossed "Reading Maketh a Full Man"; with three leaded-glass doors, open shelving, cupboards, and a drawer. *c. 1900*
83 in (211 cm) high
$5,000–7,000   **L&T**

Oak umbrella stand with a copper panel embossed with stylized foliage and a slatted lower gallery with a pierced heart motif; on square supports. *c. 1905*
43 in (109 cm) high
$1,200–1,800   **PUR**

A CLOSER LOOK

Mahogany high-backed side chair by Shapland & Petter in the Glasgow style, with a cherub's head with tousled forelock carved in pewter on a heart-shaped base applied to the wide central slat. The rear seat rail is joined to a stretcher below by three shaped spindles. The upholstered seat is a replacement. Shapland & Petter designs were created in house, although none were ever registered. *c. 1905. 42 in (107 cm) high* **$1,500–2,000 PUR**

This pewter cherub's head is a good example of the applied metalwork of Shapland & Petter's work. They employed skilled craftsmen to produce these details in their factory.

Oak stick stand with a shaped copper panel embossed with stylized flowers and tendrils. The slatted front and sides feature a further copper panel with raised bosses. *c. 1905*
41¾ in (106 cm) high
$2,000–2,500   **PUR**

Oak wardrobe with two paneled doors featuring carved foliate detail at the top, with shaped copper strap hinges and pulls and a fitted interior. *c. 1905*
82¼ in (209 cm) high
$5,000–7,000   **PUR**

High back is reminiscent of the work of Charles Rennie Mackintosh and Frank Lloyd Wright.

Oak and beech were favored timbers, frequently painted white or in pale, pastel colors, although rich, dark shades of gray, brown, and olive are not uncommon.

Decoration is sparse, featuring motifs in clean, geometric shapes, such as squares and rectangles, with inset panels of leaded glass, embroidery, or metalwork also used.

Simple, rectilinear forms are hallmarks of Mackintosh furniture: tables feature long, slender supports; cupboards and cabinets boast wide projecting cornices; and chairs have high, attenuated backs.

Charles Rennie Mackintosh

One of the most talented designers of his generation, the prize-winning architect Charles Rennie Mackintosh challenged the traditional Arts and Crafts style with bold rectilinear shapes and slender attenuated proportions.

Born and educated in Glasgow, Charles Rennie Mackintosh (1868–1928) took his promising career as an architect in a new direction when he ventured into furniture, textiles, and interior design. Along with fellow artists J. H. MacNair and sisters Margaret and Frances Macdonald, he helped forge an innovative new design movement as an alternative to the Arts and Crafts ideology favored in most parts of Great Britain. "The Glasgow Four" pooled their talents to create a universal style for decorative designs that included not only furniture, but also metalwork, textiles, and posters.

Fundamental principles at the heart of the Arts and Crafts movement that mattered little to Mackintosh were the preoccupation with the details of fine craftsmanship and the desire to exploit the natural beauty of wood for decorative effect. His sophisticated and highly original furniture designs part company with the more robust Arts and Crafts furniture. Cupboards are topped with broad projecting cornices, tables feature long and narrow supports, and chairs boast tall, attenuated backs.

Although at odds with prevailing British tastes, Mackintosh's pioneering style was widely celebrated in continental Europe, leaving an enduring impression on contemporary designers in Germany and Austria. The Secessionists went on to develop furniture that relied heavily on hallmarks of the Mackintosh style.

Above: Stained-oak side chair (one of a pair), designed for the Argyle Street Tearooms, with a simple slatted back and a drop-in seat. *1897 39¼ in (99.5 cm) high* **$10,000–15,000 (the pair) L&T**

ARCHITECT AND DESIGNER

Although Mackintosh provided designs for the Glasgow furniture makers Guthrie & Wells, it was his pioneering plans for buildings and interiors that were central to his success as an architect and designer. Having created integrated furniture and interior programs for commissions ranging from private houses to a new building for the Glasgow School of Art in 1897, he collaborated with decorator George Walton (*see p.33*) on a chain of tearooms in Glasgow for Miss Kate Cranston. His signature rectilinear high-backed chairs and his unified decorative themes sealed his reputation as a designer of considerable talent.

MACKINTOSH WATERCOLOR DESIGN (1902) FOR "HOUSE OF ART LOVER" COMPETITION

Ebonized-sycamore chair designed for Miss Cranston's "Hous'hill." The geometric trellis back resembles a stylized tree. *1904. 28¼ in (72 cm) high* **$100,000–150,000 L&T**

Ebonized-oak chair for the interior at 78 Derngate, Northampton, with trellislike back and drop-in rush seat, raised on square supports united by a stretcher. *1916*

$20,000–30,000   **BRI**

Green lacquered-beechwood armchair from the Argyle Street Tearooms, resembling a Windsor chair. It has a curved top rail, spindle back, and solid seat on four spreading legs and a stretcher. *1906*

29½ in (75 cm) high

$12,000–18,000   **VZ**

Stained oak tub armchair designed for the blue bedroom at "Hous'hill," with a tall curved back with mother-of-pearl squares, armrests, and upholstered back and seat. *1905*

51 in (129.5 cm) high

$90,000–120,000   **BRI**

Dark-stained oak Domino table and chairs. The table has a solid circular top and under-shelves and the tub chairs have curved top rails and splats extending to base rails. *c. 1905*

Table: 30 in (76.5 cm) high

$50,000–70,000   **V&A**

Beech bijouterie table cabinet designed by Mackintosh's brother-in-law James Herbert MacNair for the 1902 Turin Exhibition. *c. 1900*

30¼ in (77 cm) high

$10,000–15,000   **L&T**

Tall dark-stained oak chair from the luncheon room at the Argyle Street Tearooms. It has an oval top pierced with a bird motif and a drop-in rush seat. *c. 1895*

53¾ in (136.5 cm) high

$100,000–150,000   **BRI**

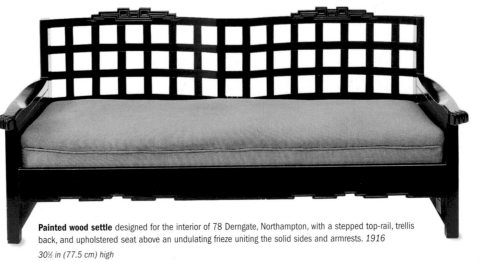

Painted wood settle designed for the interior of 78 Derngate, Northampton, with a stepped top-rail, trellis back, and upholstered seat above an undulating frieze uniting the solid sides and armrests. *1916*

30½ in (77.5 cm) high

$30,000–50,000   **V&A**

KEY FEATURES

Oak and mahogany are the favored timbers for E. A. Taylor furniture.

Sideboards and display cabinets boast elegant, restrained lines.

Decorative details include panels of marquetry in precious woods or colorful stained glass with flower motifs, pierced heart patterns, and metal inlays of copper or pewter.

Mackintosh's influence can be seen in rush-seat chairs with elongated, tapering backs.

Handles and strap hinges are usually hand-hammered in copper or pewter.

E. A. Taylor

The versatile Scottish designer E. A. Taylor was celebrated for subdued, graceful, and highly finished Arts and Crafts furniture that owed much to the innovative, elegant style of Charles Rennie Mackintosh and his fellow craftsmen in the Glasgow Four.

Trained as a shipyard draftsman, Scottish furniture and stained-glass designer Ernest Archibald Taylor (1874–1951) studied at the Glasgow School of Art (*see p.175*), where he fell under the spell of the Glasgow Four. He joined the highly respected Glasgow cabinet-making manufacturer of Wylie & Lochhead Ltd. (*see p.35*), designing the drawing room shown by the firm at the prestigious Glasgow International Exhibition of 1901. Taylor also won a medal when he exhibited alongside other Glasgow School artisans, including Charles Rennie

Mackintosh (*see pp.30–31*), at the 1902 Esposizione Internazionale in Turin.

Taylor's use of marquetry panels, sometimes with metal inlays, was characteristic. He often depicted medieval themes or stylized designs that showed Mackintosh's influence.

After a stint designing stained glass for Manchester's George Wragge Ltd., Taylor and his wife—textile and jewelry designer Jessie M. King—founded the Shealing Atelier of Fine Art in Paris in 1911. However, the outbreak of World War I drove them back to Scotland.

Above: Oak chair (one of a pair) with the top-rail pierced with a heart motif, a slatted back, and a rush seat on square supports. *c. 1900.* **$300–500 (the pair) L&T**

Mahogany display cabinet with marquetry top and a mirrored back flanked by open shelving. The glazed area below has silver-plated embossed fenestration flanked by stylized marquetry blossoms. The supports are united by an undershelf. *c. 1905*
69 in (175 cm) high

$12,000–18,000   PUR

Oak sideboard designed for Wylie & Lochhead, with a marquetry panel depicting a knight in a landscape, a pewter-inlaid river in the foreground, and a castle in flames in the distance. Below are drawers, shelves, and cupboards. *c. 1900*
67 in (170 cm) wide

$12,000–18,000   PUR

George Walton

Along with Charles Rennie Mackintosh, George Walton was the most important Scottish interpreter of the Arts and Crafts style, creating highly original and elegant furniture, as well as textiles, metalwork, and glass.

The Scottish architect and interior designer George Walton (1867–1933) studied at the Glasgow School of Art (*see p.175*) before establishing his own design and decorating business—George Walton & Co. Ecclesiastical & House Decorators—on Wellington Street, Glasgow, in 1888.

A prestigious commission given to him by Miss Cranston for the interior design of the Buchanan Street Tearooms in 1896 allowed Walton to work in collaboration with Charles Rennie Mackintosh (*see p.30–31*). It also sealed his reputation as one of the most important Scottish Arts and Crafts furniture designers. Based on a traditional Scottish design, Walton's rush-seated chairs for the Buchanan Street Tearooms boasted a narrow, solid back with arms sweeping in a wide curve and pierced heart-shaped decoration.

Walton's furniture was more flamboyant and lavish than the designs being produced by his English Arts and Crafts counterparts, such as A. H. Mackmurdo or Ernest Gimson.

Moving to London in 1897, Walton took on a number of high-profile projects, including designing the furniture, fixtures, and storefronts for branches of the Kodak camera company in Great Britain and across Europe.

Above: Oak bracket clock of architectural form, carved with the initials "GWB" on top. The dial is flanked by classical columns. With Camerer Cuss movement. *c. 1900* 23¼ in (59 cm) high **$3,000–5,000 PUR**

Mahogany Holland cabinet featuring extended top and twin glazed doors. The cabinet is raised on square supports united by a double-H stretcher. *c. 1900*
48 in (122 cm) high
$3,000–5,000   **TDG**

Satin-birch cabinet with two small drawers flanked by mirrored doors above short and long drawers with cut-out handles and silvered backplates. *c. 1900*
45 in (114 cm) wide
$7,000–10,000   **L&T**

Mahogany dining chair (one of six) with three openwork and tapering splats in the back surmounted by floral marquetry roundels in colored woods and flanked by upholstered panels. *c. 1900*
37¾ in (96 cm) high
$2,500–3,000 (the set)   **PUR**

KEY FEATURES

Oak was the favored timber for most furniture designed by Sir Robert Lorimer.

Traditional 17th- and 18th-century styles influenced Lorimer's refectory tables, benches and high-back settles, cupboards, and display cabinets.

Exposed peg joints and adzed surface finishes are typical decorative details.

Sir Robert Lorimer

An important influence in Scottish furnishing and decorating, Sir Robert Lorimer embraced the ideals of the Arts and Crafts movement by adapting traditional designs and techniques to create furniture that looked to the past for inspiration.

Robert Stodart Lorimer (1864–1929) was born in Edinburgh and educated at the city's Academy and University. In 1893, following the completion of his apprenticeship with Sir Robert Rowand Anderson and a four-year stint in London, he established his own architectural practice.

After developing an interest in Scottish vernacular architecture and being influenced by the work of R. N. Shaw, Lorimer joined the Arts and Crafts movement and was instrumental in promoting the Scottish Vernacular Revival. He devoted a significant portion of his career to the restoration and alteration of a large number of country houses, castles, and national monuments, including the War Memorial at Edinburgh Castle.

Although considered the east coast's answer to Charles Rennie Mackintosh (*see pp.30–31*), Lorimer had a very different philosophy. He favored designs that were faithful to traditional 17th- and 18th-century styles over the innovative and unconventional, and his furniture—featuring details such as exposed peg joints and adzed surface finishing—was created to combine effortlessly with antiques and older furnishings.

Above: Scott Morton oak stool from a Lorimer design, with chamfered trestle ends and a curved stretcher. It bears the original retail label. *c. 1920. 17¼ in (44 cm) wide* **$800–1,200 L&T**

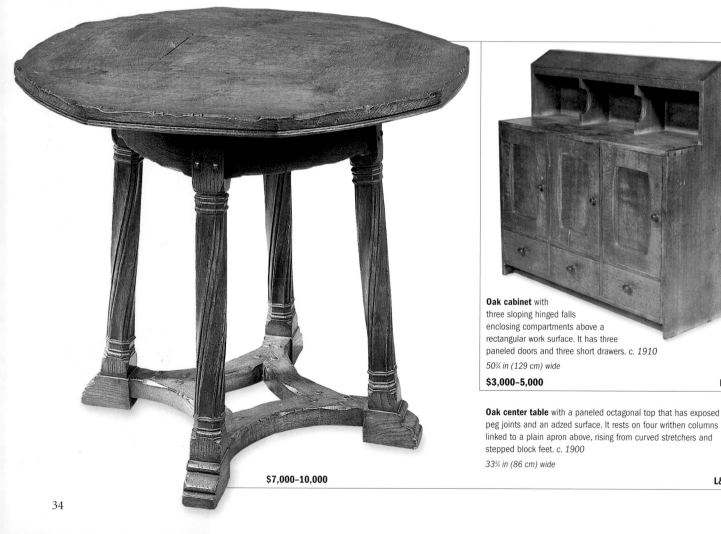

Oak cabinet with three sloping hinged falls enclosing compartments above a rectangular work surface. It has three paneled doors and three short drawers. *c. 1910*
50¾ in (129 cm) wide

$3,000–5,000 **L&T**

Oak center table with a paneled octagonal top that has exposed peg joints and an adzed surface. It rests on four writhen columns linked to a plain apron above, rising from curved stretchers and stepped block feet. *c. 1900*
33¾ in (86 cm) wide

$7,000–10,000

L&T

Wylie & Lochhead

Brothers-in-law Robert Wylie and William Lochhead set up a department store in Glasgow together. They employed local furniture-makers such as E. A. Taylor and John Ednie and developed a solid, architectural style.

Robert Wylie and William Lochhead went into business together running a Glasgow department store. They stocked home furnishings made by local and foreign manufacturers, as well as by craftsmen employed at their own workshops. Each partner brought different skills to the business: Wylie was a feather and hair merchant, and Lochhead a cabinetmaker and funeral director. The company still operates as a funeral parlor today.

They prospered on the back of Glasgow's shipping industry—the luxury boats built on the Clyde had to be appointed with good-quality furnishings. Other commissions include the case for the organ at Wallneuk North church in Paisley.

Wylie & Lochhead employed many luminaries of the Glasgow scene, including E. A. Taylor (*see p.32*), and John Ednie, who had been heavily influenced by Charles Rennie Mackintosh (*see pp.30–31*). Their furniture is firmly within the tradition of the Glasgow School of Art (*see p.175*), albeit a less rigorous interpretation of Mackintosh's vision. The briar rose motif is a common feature, as are solid, architectural forms and surface decorations picked out in contrasting woods or stained glass.

Above: Stained-beech tub armchair with a double curved top rail with marquetry roundels, an upholstered seat, and a stretcher uniting the supports. *c. 1900.* **$500–700 L&T**

KEY FEATURES

Oak was the timber of choice for Wylie & Lochhead. Elm, beech, and walnut were also used.

Carved or inlaid stylized briar roses, with long stems and geometric leaves and petals, feature frequently.

Brass fittings include elongated hinges and molded ring handles.

Lines are generally clean and straight, and always simple, with projecting surfaces and edges.

Stylized hearts are often pierced into top rails and supports.

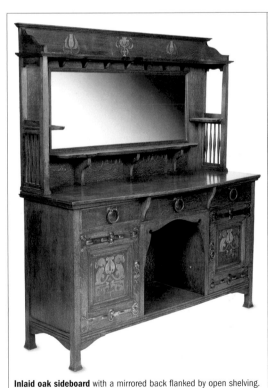

Inlaid oak sideboard with a mirrored back flanked by open shelving. The curved work surface sits above three short drawers, a pair of floral-inlaid doors, and an open area, all on splayed square feet. Complete with maker's label. *c. 1900*
74 in (188 cm) high
$1,800–2,200 L&T

Stained beech-and-elm tub chair possibly by Wylie & Lochhead, with three pierced back slats inlaid with boxwood lines, an upholstered paneled seat, and feet linked by stretchers. *c. 1900*

$400–600 L&T

Oak bookcase with an overhanging top and leaded glazed doors with floral motifs, flanked by copper panels embossed with stylized flowers. Below is a frieze drawer and two doors with metal pulls. The bookcase rests on block supports. *c. 1900*
72 in (183 cm) high
$8,000–12,000 PUR

35

The color and grain of the local timber used for the furniture were highlighted through the absence of varnishes or paint.

Joints were exposed rather than hidden to draw attention to the handcrafted nature of the furniture.

Designs can be almost stark in their simplicity, with smooth, flat surfaces to show off the wood.

Cotswold School

Architect and designer E. W. Gimson moved from London to the Cotswolds with Sidney and Ernest Barnsley in 1893. Later they were joined by Peter Waals and Gordon Russell. The furniture they created became known as "Cotswold School."

Ernest William Gimson (1863–1919) and Sidney and Ernest Barnsley established a workshop in Pinbury Park, an idyllic rural setting that fostered the artist-craftsman ideal. Sidney Barnsley constructed his entire output with his own hands, while a team of highly skilled craftsmen executed Gimson's clean-lined designs. They exploited the natural color and grain of local woods, such as ash, elm, oak, and fruitwoods.

Typically, the dovetails and wooden pins used to join the timbers were left visible in the finished product. Decoration was kept to a minimum, restricted to chamfering and gouging the wood, although inlays

of ivory, pearl, brass, and even silver were sometimes used on the more elaborate creations.

Later, due to the success of the business, they moved to larger premises in Shapperton, where they were joined by designers Peter Waals and Gordon Russell. With the latter's acceptance of machinery, a bridge was built between Barnsley and Gimson's rarefied, handcrafted furniture and the need for functional and affordable pieces designed for the mass market. The Shapperton premises closed on Gimson's death in 1919.

Above: Gordon Russell Cuban light-oak dressing table with a frieze drawer and two pairs of drawers with walnut pulls and an ebony inlay. The square supports are united by stretchers. *c. 1930*
50 in (127 cm) wide **NPA DP**

Oak hallstand featuring two central drawers with solid pulls flanked by two open compartments for umbrellas and canes. The supports are united by stretchers. *c. 1930*
41¾ in (106 cm) wide
$1,000–1,500

WW

Peter Waals walnut fireside armchair to a Gimson design, with a lattice back, tapering armrests, and an upholstered drop-in seat. On square supports united by stretchers. *c. 1930*
38 in (96.5 cm) high
NPA **DP**

Sidney Barnsley oak monk's bench with storage under the seat. The table hinges back to a vertical position, forming a support for the bench. *c. 1925*
60 in (152.5 cm) wide
NPA **DP**

E. W. Godwin

One of the leading figures of the Aesthetic movement, E. W. Godwin produced light, elegant furniture with a Japanese sensibility that is celebrated for its superior construction and high-quality materials.

Architect Edward William Godwin (1833–86) was the most important furniture designer of the Aesthetic movement. The ideals of quality materials and superb construction central to the Arts and Crafts philosophy were realized in his sumptuous furniture, which embraced the Japanese principles of design in its careful balance of vertical and horizontal components.

Elegance, lightness, and refined proportions are the hallmarks of Godwin's distinctive items, with ebonized wood his material of choice. Decoration is minimal, with molding and carving dispensed with in favor of inset panels of embossed Japanese paper, or occasionally painted or stenciled symmetrical designs featuring stylized geometric patterns. Some examples incorporate panels painted by artist friends such as James McNeill Whistler and Edward Burne-Jones.

Since they were widely copied, Godwin patented the designs for his furniture, which was produced by London cabinet-makers William Watt, John Gregory Crace, and the firm Collinson & Lock. Godwin never marked his furniture, and attribution is largely based on the style found in the few sketches that have survived.

Above: Oak-framed gong attributed to E. W. Godwin, resembling the "tori" gates of the Shinto shrine, with a round beaten-brass gong suspended in the center. *c. 1880. 30 in (76 cm) high* **$8,000–12,000 PUR**

KEY FEATURES

Ebonized wood was the favored material for Godwin furniture.

Cabinets, chairs, and tables are light, elegant, and well proportioned and strongly influenced by Japanese design.

Decoration is minimal, with inset panels of embossed Japanese paper most common, although painted or stenciled designs in stylized geometric patterns also feature.

Mahogany sideboard by E. W. Godwin and made by William Watt. It has an open lattice top and a mirrored back, two frieze drawers flanked by cupboards with open shelving below, and Japanese lacquer panels set into embossed leather paper. Raised on slender supports. *c. 1880*
50 in (127 cm) wide
$120,000–180,000   **PUR**

Old English or Jacobean-style oak office chair in the manner of E. W. Godwin. It has a curved lattice back, turned finials on the uprights, curved tapering armrests, and an oval rush seat. It swivels on four curved supports. *c. 1880*
40 in (102 cm) high
$7,000–10,000   **PUR**

British Furniture

As the Arts and Crafts style grew in popularity, many British designers and furniture manufacturers emulated the style of leading designers such as William Morris, C. F. A. Voysey, Charles Rennie Mackintosh, and the Cotswold School. Much of the furniture was mass-produced by retailers such as Heals, which resulted in varying quality of the finished pieces. Designers such as C. R. Ashbee continued to produce handcrafted, sturdy furniture, often in oak, pine, and mahogany. Decoration was often minimal—usually only a heart-shaped or stylized motif. Shapland & Petter was an exception to this rule, often embellishing furniture with fine inlays.

Walnut armchair designed by E. Punnet, with a heart-shaped motif, upholstered back, and armrests on vertical slats. *c. 1905*
32¼ in (82 cm) high

$3,000–5,000 PUR

Mahogany music cabinet showing Anglo-Japanese influence. The glazed doors are partially colored with green glass foliage; an apron below unites the front supports. *c. 1895*
49¼ in (125 cm) wide

$5,000–7,000 PUR

Coalbrookedale cast-iron garden bench designed by Christopher Dresser. The top rail has a band of florets, while the back features a repeat pattern of geometric plant forms. With openwork armrests; supported on simple feet. *c. 1875*
76 in (193 cm) wide

$12,000–18,000 PUR

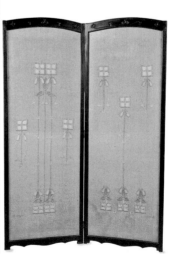

Glasgow-style two-fold mahogany screen the edges of which are carved in bas-relief with buds. The linen panels are embroidered with stylized plant forms in silk and wool. *c. 1900*
71¼ in (181 cm) high

$4,000–6,000 L&T

Gothic Revival tiled oak hallstand by Christopher Dresser, with stylized floral cutouts above the central mirror, which is flanked at each top corner by butterfly fretwork. *c. 1880*
96½ in (245 cm) high

$5,000–7,000 PUR

Scottish stained-pine and pokerwork-decorated hall settle with a molded top rail and a tongue-and-groove back decorated with stylized flowering roses. It has open-sided arms and is raised on square supports further embellished with rose and checker decoration. *c. 1900*
73¾ in (187 cm) wide

$1,800–2,200 L&T

A CLOSER LOOK

Large mahogany wardrobe designed by Barry Parker and Sir Raymond Unwin, for Goodall, Lamb & Heighway Ltd. of Manchester. It has two large central doors, flanked by glazed cupboards, above a series of drawers. The item was once the property of the famous ceramicist Clarice Cliff, and stood in her home, Chetwynd, in Staffordshire. *c. 1900*
86½ in (220 cm) wide **$4,000–6,000 L&T**

Copper backplates and shaped handles

Panel doors decorated with pierced club motifs

Sturdy and simple solid-wood design

Guild of Handicraft pine music cabinet designed by C. R. Ashbee. The twin doors have elaborate wraparound hinges and lock plates; on Moorish-inspired bracket feet. *c. 1900*
49 in (124.5 cm) high
$20,000–30,000 **DRA**

Walnut side chair attributed to Heals, with curved top rail, a shaped and heart-pierced splat, tapering uprights, and a rush seat raised on tapering supports. *c. 1890*
41¾ in (106 cm) high
$600–900 **DN**

Heals oak child's chair with a simple slatted back and a rush seat raised on square supports united by stretchers. It is of pleasing golden tone. *c. 1920*
35½ in (90 cm) high
$180–220 **WW**

Harry Lebus oak bookcase with an extended top, a drop-down writing slope, a frieze drawer, and open bookshelves. The solid sides are pierced with stylized heart motifs. *c. 1900*
65 in (165 cm) high
$3,000–5,000 **PUR**

Harry Lebus mahogany hallstand featuring an arched top with carved floral detail and a central mirror above a panel of tube-lined floral tiles. It has a central drawer and compartments for walking sticks. *c. 1905*
82¾ in (210 cm) high
$3,000–4,000 **PUR**

KEY FEATURES

Heavy, quartered oak covered with rich, fumed finishes is one of the hallmarks of Stickley furniture.

Circular pins, mortise-and-tenon joints, dovetails, chamfered boards, and long arched corbels are emphasized by decorative design.

Floral motifs inlaid in nickel, pewter, and copper or stained and exotic woods are favored decorative details, as are hand-hammered handles and hinges.

Furniture is mostly upholstered in green or brown leather.

Pieces are usually signed beneath the slogan "Als Ik Kan" (Flemish for "As I can") set within a carpenter's compass.

Stickley

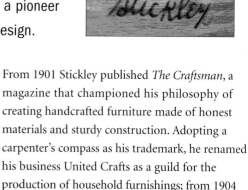

The eldest of five furniture-maker brothers, Gustav Stickley was the leading light of the American Arts and Crafts movement. His workshop made furniture with a pioneer spirit that set a new standard in American design.

Born in Wisconsin, Gustav Stickley (1858–1942) learned his craft as a furniture-maker in the chair factory of his uncle Jacob Schlager. In 1898, Stickley traveled to Europe, where he became captivated by the ideals of John Ruskin and the work of England's Arts and Crafts designers.

Back in the United States, in 1898 he founded the Gustav Stickley Co. in Eastwood, New York, producing a line of household furniture that looked to the designs of William Morris (*see pp.22–23*) for inspiration. Stickley shunned the elaborate curves and fussy ornament typical of Victorian taste in favor of simple, geometric lines and heavy, solid forms— exemplified by the Craftsman range made in American white oak that he introduced in 1900.

From 1901 Stickley published *The Craftsman*, a magazine that championed his philosophy of creating handcrafted furniture made of honest materials and sturdy construction. Adopting a carpenter's compass as his trademark, he renamed his business United Crafts as a guild for the production of household furnishings; from 1904 it became known as The Craftsman Workshops.

HARMONY OF FUNCTION AND MATERIAL

Stickley's mission was to create "furniture that shows plainly what it is and in which the design and construction harmonize with the wood." Furniture was made by hand from thick sections of heavy, quarter-sawn oak. Construction

Above: Gustav Stickley's branded shopmark features a carpenter's compass. Variations in black or red include "Stickley" or "Gustav Stickley" in script, a surrounding rectangle, and the Flemish words "Als Ik Kan" ("As I can").

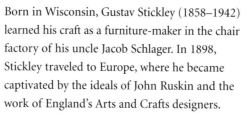

HARVEY ELLIS INLAID DESIGNS

The talented architect Harvey Ellis joined Gustav Stickley's Craftsman Workshops in 1903 to provide new designs for furniture items and interiors. He would also bring to the enterprise a taste for a lighter style of furniture embellished with small inlaid motifs. Although the pair worked together for a mere seven months owing to Ellis's untimely death, Stickley embraced his partner's light, subtle approach in his later furniture designs. The Ellis influence can be seen in subtle patterns featuring decorative flowers or Jugendstil-type designs that have been inlaid with metals such as copper, pewter, and nickel, and with exotic or local timbers that have been stained.

Rare Gustav Stickley armchair in dark-stained oak, with stylized plant-form inlay by Harvey Ellis on the slats of the back splat, and a leather-covered drop-in seat pad. *1903–10. 44 in (112 cm) high* **$30,000–50,000 GDG**

Detail of a rare Gustav Stickley writing desk designed by Harvey Ellis. It is made of various woods, copper, and pewter. *1903 29½ in (75 cm) wide* **$50,000–70,000 DRA**

THE STICKLEY FAMILY

After an unhappy childhood with their struggling German immigrant parents on a small farm in Wisconsin, the five ambitious Stickley brothers all broadened their horizons by joining the furniture industry. Each boasted a unique and formidable talent—Gustav's eye for design, Albert's marketing skills, Charles's production talents, Leopold's management ability, and John's sales techniques—and together they might have built a thriving and prosperous furniture empire that could have survived long after Arts and Crafts furniture fell from favor. Instead, their fractured relationships led the Stickley brothers to establish solo and joint furniture companies that—although successful—would eventually rival one another in a highly competitive market. While flourishing during the heyday of the Arts and Crafts movement, each Stickley-endorsed company eventually foundered as fashions changed and moved on.

INFLUENCES

Gustav Stickley was profoundly influenced by the philosophy behind the Arts and Crafts movement as promoted by founding fathers John Ruskin, the English writer and social reformer, and William Morris, who wrote of the importance of high standards of craftsmanship and the pivotal role played by the individual craftsman.

INTERIOR STYLE

Gustav Stickley held to Ruskin's ideal that design begins with interior spaces, and his vision extended to creating simple furniture that was suited to both "the place it had to occupy and the work it had to do."

THE CRAFTSMAN

In addition to promoting his Mission oak furniture, textiles, lamps, and carpets for the home, Stickley spread the principles of the Arts and Crafts movement through his influential magazine, *The Craftsman*.

---

features—arched corbels, mortise-and-tenon joints, and chamfered boards, for example—were incorporated into the design of pieces that were covered with "fumed" finishes, which relied on a chemical reaction with the wood rather than stain for their rich, dark color.

Many forms, such as stools, trestle tables, and high-backed settles, looked back to colonial furniture of the 17th century. More innovative designs that combined the ideals of craftsmanship with mechanized techniques included cabinets, beds, bookcases, desks, dining and writing tables, and horizontal and vertical slat-back chairs, such as the adjustable upholstered reclining chair inspired by a Morris original. Spindle-sided and spindle-backed chairs produced by Stickley from 1905 reveal the influence of furniture designed by Frank Lloyd Wright (1867–1956) for Darwin House near Buffalo, New York.

A brief collaboration with architect and designer Harvey Ellis starting in 1903 brought the influence of Charles Rennie Mackintosh (*see pp.30–31*) to the US and saw the Stickley workshops adopt a lighter, elegant, and more sophisticated style, using smaller pieces of oak covered with a pale-brown patina.

Although Stickley's furniture became more widely available across the US, competition and changing tastes ultimately forced Gustav Stickley to close his factory in 1916.

Gustav Stickley's Morris chair No. 332, a Mission-style interpretation of an armchair originally designed by Philip Webb for William Morris. *c. 1910. 41 in (104 cm) high* **$10,000–15,000 G5**

Gustav Stickley

The fame of Gustav Stickley, the most successful of the five brothers, rested on his unwavering vision as a designer and manufacturer of American Arts and Crafts furniture. As well as believing passionately in the philosophy behind the movement founded by Ruskin and Morris, Gustav Stickley also helped publicize the fundamental principles of reform throughout the United States with his highly original furniture and through his monthly magazine *The Craftsman*. Stubborn, independent, and creative, Stickley proved throughout his career that he was willing to sacrifice financial security to realize his beliefs and find a way to express them freely.

The legs are tenoned flush, rather than protruding through the top. The stretcher tenons lower down protrude through the legs.

An X-frame stretcher (two corseted stretchers secured with a crossed lap joint) lends strength to the legs supporting the seat.

Clip-cornered low seat or tabouret, marked "No. 52" and made in oak with conforming square-post legs. The latter are flush through-tenoned to the top and united by corseted, X-frame, through-tenoned stretchers. *c. 1900*

22 in (56 cm) high

$3,000–4,000

DRA

Oak piano bench with the seat and an underlying stretcher through-tenoned flush with the sides. The sides have handles and bases cut out in serpentine profile. *1902–12*

36 in (91.5 cm) wide

$6,000–9,000

DRA

Oak magazine stand with top and bottom shelves through-tenoned into sides with demilune cutouts and arched bases, the latter echoed in an arched toeboard. *1905–16*

40 in (101.5 cm) high

$3,000–4,000　　　　DRA

Oak magazine stand with an overhanging corbeled top, flared and canted sides with cutouts at the base and Tree of Life decoration, and graduated shelves. *1902–15*

43 in (109.25 cm) high

$1,000–1,500　　　　DRA

Rare blanket chest in rich brown-stained white oak with paneled hinged top and sides, and arrowhead and arched wrought-iron straps and hinges. Set on square-post feet. *1902–03*

34¾ in (88.25 cm) wide

$30,000–40,000　　　　DRA

ORIGINAL FINISH

Many furniture designers working in the Arts and Crafts style produced pieces that were not only constructed with an eye to high standards of craftsmanship, but also boasted a time-worn surface appearance. Craftsmen such as Gustav Stickley—who strongly believed in the Arts and Crafts ideal—used a variety of methods to age chairs, cabinets, chests, and tables. Stickley's furniture boasted a rich, dark patina that was created not with stain, but by applying chemicals that reacted with the wood. A well-worn finish—whether achieved by natural aging or by artificial means—that maintains the original integrity of a piece and that has not been compromised by overpolishing or excessive restoration remains the most desirable for collectors.

Rare oak china cabinet by Harvey Ellis. It has an overhanging top, glass-paneled door and sides, four internal shelves, a multiple-plank back, and an arched apron. *1903–04*

60 in (152.5 cm) high

$8,000–12,000 G5

Rare side chair No. 2600 with a horizontal back splat, an inverted-V top rail, blind-tenoned stretchers uniting slightly flared square legs, and a woven rush seat. *c. 1900*

33½ in (85 cm) high

$5,000–7,000 DRA

Ladderback armchair No. 349 with a tacked-on brown-leather seat, three horizontal back splats, flat arms, and blind-tenoned stretchers uniting the square legs. *c. 1900*

38 in (96.5 cm) high

$1,200–1,800 DRA

Slim oak lamp table with a circular top and square-section legs. The latter are united by gently arched X-frame stretchers, topped at the center with an oak acorn finial. *1902–12*

24 in (61 cm) wide

$3,000–4,000 DRA

Oak rocker No. 323 with vertical side splats and flat open arms supported at the front by short corbels. The back and seat cushions have been reupholstered. *1902–12*

40 in (101.5 cm) high

$3,000–5,000 DRA

A CLOSER LOOK

Oak bureau-bookcase designed by Harvey Ellis. It comprises a drop-front desk above two drawers, with open shelf space above and below. It is flanked by two bookcases with leaded glass-paneled doors. Its substantial desirability and value largely reside in the fact that it was designed by Harvey Ellis who, due to his untimely death, worked for Stickley for just nine months. However, the item is further enhanced by its exceptional provenance, namely: it descended through the family of a Chief Judge of the US District Court in New Jersey. *1903. 56 in (142.25 cm) wide*

$100,000–150,000 DRA

Bookcase doors with their original glass panels

Original finish increases desirability

The bureau-bookcase is fitted with long strap hinges and, as here, door pulls made of handwrought and hammered iron.

The interior of the Harvey Ellis-designed bureau is finished in a pale hardwood. Its architecturally compartmented design displays a pleasing lightness of touch characteristic of Ellis's work.

L. & J. G. Stickley

In 1904, after working with Gustav for a while, Leopold Stickley (1869–1957) moved out on his own, setting up the Onondaga Shops. Later that year, he joined his brother John George (1871–1921), who had been working with another brother, Albert, to establish L. & J. G. Stickley in Fayetteville, New York. Though they looked to Gustav for inspiration, Leopold and John George rejected handcrafted methods in favor of mechanical production techniques. In 1906 the company was renamed Handcraft, and from 1912 it was known as The Work of L. & J. G. Stickley. The company is still trading.

Low seat or tabouret made from pale oak, with square-section legs united by an X-frame stretcher, and mortise-and-tenoned through an octagonal top. *1906–22*

17 in (43 cm) high

$1,200–1,800   **DRA**

Circular-top tea table made from oak. It has four square-section legs united by an X-frame stretcher, with the latter lending additional support to a lower shelf. *1906–22*

24 in (61 cm) wide

$1,800–2,200   **DRA**

Pale-oak sideboard with a plate-rail splashback, above three central drawers, two flanking cupboards, and a bottom linen drawer, all with hammered-copper metalware. *1906–22*

66 in (167.5 cm) wide

$5,000–7,000   **DRA**

Even-arm oak settle with broad vertical slats to the back and sides, square-section corner posts, and a drop-in seat cushion still finished in its original brown leather. *1906–22*

71 in (180.25 cm) wide

$3,000–4,000   **DRA**

Drop-front oak desk with an overhanging bookshelf, three drawers flanked by two cupboards, square-section corner posts, and internal cupboards, drawers, and letter racks. *1906–22*

45 in (114.25 cm) wide

$4,000–6,000   **G5**

Rare oak book table with an overhanging top, square-section corner posts, and two internally divided undershelves, each with vertical slats on two sides. *1906–22*

29 in (73.5 cm) high

$5,000–7,000   **DRA**

Stickley Bros.

In 1891, John George Stickley and his brother Albert (1862–1928) adopted the Stickley Bros. company name, which paid tribute to the name that Albert and brother Charles had employed when they worked for Gustav in New York. John George eventually left the firm to work with brother Leopold, who shared his talent as a clever businessman. The company carried on with Albert at the helm under the family name, although his style was decidedly different from that practiced by his brothers. Looking to the designs of England and Scotland for inspiration, Albert added more decorative detail to his furniture, and he marked his pieces with the "Quaint" logo by which he defined his style. The company closed around 1940.

The gold decal, paper-label, and, as here, metal-tag shopmarks on Stickley Bros. furniture carry the name "Quaint" and the factory location in Grand Rapids.

The mortise-and-tenon joint securing the stretchers to the corner posts is called a "through tenon," because it protrudes through the corner post.

Plank-top side table made from quarter-sawn oak. The top is supported on a frieze mortise-and-tenoned into square-section corner posts. The latter are united near the base by two through-tenoned stretchers that are, in turn, united by an undershelf secured with blind mortise-and-tenon joints. Three vertical slats running between the stretchers and the frieze at either end are similarly jointed. *1900–15*

30 in (76.25 cm) wide

CALD

$6,000–9,000

Unsigned oak Morris chair attributed to Stickley Bros., with through-tenoned stretchers and corner post, corbel-supported arms, and leather-upholstered cushion and back pad. *1900–15*

37 in (94 cm) high

$1,800–2,200 **DRA**

Pedestal mahogany dining table with a round top, and four additional leaves (not shown). It has a large, square-section column with four splayed feet with carved brackets. *c. 1915*

48 in (122 cm) wide

$6,000–9,000 **G5**

Oak tea table with a circular, overhanging plank top, on flared square-section legs united by through-tenoned X-frame stretchers. *1900–15*

42 in (106.5 cm) wide

$1,800–2,200 **DRA**

Mahogany magazine stand with square-section corner posts chamfered on top, four shelves, and slatted sides; the lower shelf also has an apron. *1900–15*

34 in (86.5 cm) high

$800–1,200 **DRA**

KEY FEATURES

Furniture was typically made of oak, from pale hues to the favored rich, dark finishes, sometimes with staining in contrasting shades. Mahogany was occasionally used.

The simple, rectilinear lines of cabinets, chairs, and tables echo the furniture styles produced by the Secessionist designers in Germany and Austria, including Josef Hoffmann.

Decorative details, especially in the early period, feature cut-out patterns of heart, rectangle, and square shapes that show the influence of designs created by Charles Rennie Mackintosh and the Glasgow School.

Stylized designs that were inlaid with metal or fruitwood feature on some pieces.

Furniture was usually branded with a large rectangular mark.

Limbert

The strong, rectilinear style promoted by Charles Rennie Mackintosh, the Glasgow School, and the Secessionist designers is echoed in the well-crafted Arts and Crafts furniture created by the Michigan-based Limbert Furniture Co.

Established in 1894 by Charles P. Limbert (1854–1944) near Grand Rapids, Michigan, the Limbert Furniture Co. produced a broad range of elegant, well-proportioned furniture in the Arts and Crafts style. Limbert's furniture favored rectilinear shapes and—while not as finely crafted as examples produced by Gustav Stickley (*see pp.40–45*)—it nonetheless used high-quality materials and took advantage of the creative possibilities offered by the machine.

From the beginning, Limbert's designs looked to Europe for inspiration. Lamp tables, desks, and "Morris" chairs in geometric forms were decorated with patterns of cut-out squares or hearts that were clearly influenced by the Glasgow School of designers in Scotland (*see p.175*) and by Charles Rennie Mackintosh (*see pp.30–31*), whose work was widely publicized and prominently displayed at exhibitions showcasing the new style. Echoes of the simple, rectilinear designs championed by the Secessionist

movement in Austria and Germany also resonate in Limbert's work, along with Japanese style and the Arts and Crafts tradition of the Dutch settlers who worked at the Michigan factory.

Early examples of Limbert's furniture show a taste for darker finishes similar to Stickley's fumed oak, with most pieces in medium- to rich dark-brown shades and sometimes inlaid in metal and fruitwood, with stylized decorative motifs.

Up until World War I, the Limbert factory produced its most celebrated range: solid, well-balanced tables, chairs, and cabinets in geometric shapes that were frequently rendered in sumptuous, tiger-grained oak. The last phase of production after the war witnessed a shift to spindly forms and a watered-down version of the furniture that had characterized the successful early period. The factory operated until 1944.

Above: Branded maker's mark applied to Limbert furniture from 1906. It depicts a craftsman at work, with the words: "Limberts Arts Crafts Furniture Trade Mark Made in Grand Rapids and Holland."

Single-drawer library table in autumn-leaf brown oak, with serpentine ends on the corbeled top, an undershelf, and cutouts on the flared sides. *c. 1880.* 48 in (122 cm) long **$5,000–7,000 DRA**

RECTILINEAR DESIGN

Charles Limbert's furniture designs boldly reflect European influences, in particular the furniture produced by the innovative Scottish pioneer Charles Rennie Mackintosh and the Glasgow School, and the work of avant-garde Secessionist designers from Germany and Austria, including Josef Hoffmann and Koloman Moser. In Limbert's furniture, the confluence of these two strands of Arts and Crafts style can be seen in a marked dependence on strong rectilinear forms, complemented by highly stylized decorative details featuring cut-out geometric shapes—squares, rectangles, hearts, and triangles.

Limbert's use of geometric cutouts was inspired by similar decorative motifs that featured on the European furniture of Mackintosh, Baillie Scott, and Voysey.

Rare single-door bookcase in oak, with a leaded glass-panel door, keyed-through tenons, and wrought-iron hardware. *1900–05*

55 in (140 cm) high

$5,000–7,000 DRA

Four-shelf magazine stand in oak. Its flared sides feature scalloped tops and pairs of demilune cutouts near the base. *1905–10*

37 in (94 cm) high

$1,800–2,200 G5

Two-door vice cabinet in oak, with a below-cupboard trough, circular cutouts on the sides, and copper metalware. *1906–10*

32½ in (82.5 cm) high

$2,000–3,000 DRA

Single-drawer oak desk with a spline-jointed top, long corbels, and square-post legs. The latter are united by two through-tenoned stretchers supporting an undershelf. *1906–15*

42 in (106.5 cm) wide

$2,000–3,000 G5

Oversized oak armchair with an angled back, corbel-supported flat-paddle arms, a scooped apron, and leather-upholstered back pad and sprung seat. *c. 1910*

33 in (84 cm) high

$5,000–7,000 DRA

Five-shelf magazine stand made from ammonia-fumed oak. Its flared sides have spade-shaped cutouts and the bottom shelf is finished with an apron. *1906–10*

40 in (101.5 cm) high

$4,000–6,000 DRA

Three-drawer oak server with a flush top and backsplash, an arched apron, stile legs united by three stretchers, and copper drawer-pulls. *1906–10*

39½ in (100.5 cm) wide

$1,500–2,000 DRA

Even-arm oak settle made with vertical slats to the back and sides, square corner post with faceted tops, and a seat pad still upholstered in its original brown leather. *1906–10*

74 in (188 cm) wide

$4,000–6,000 DRA

Rectilinear forms are solidly constructed with prominent pins, pegs, and mortise-and-tenon joints.

Pieces are mostly made of oak, frequently with a warm, nut-brown patina, although ash and mahogany were also used.

Decoration is minimal, with hand-wrought iron or copper metalware.

Distinctive tapered legs, canted sides, and rounded bun feet are among the hallmarks.

Furniture is marked with an orb-and-cross symbol or with an incised "Roycroft."

Roycrofters

Founded in 1895 by Elbert Green Hubbard, the Roycroft community of craftsmen (known as Roycrofters) in East Aurora, New York, followed the principles established in England by William Morris.

Roycroft—which resembled an idealistic guildlike community more than a factory—developed a unique interpretation of the Arts and Crafts movement in the United States. The company focused its earliest efforts on book printing, its founder Elbert Hubbard (1856–1915) having been greatly influenced by William Morris's (*see pp.72–73*) Kelmscott Press in England.

Roycroft initially produced leatherwork, lighting, wrought metalwork, and simple Mission furniture—oak benches, tables, and chairs—designed to meet the needs of the burgeoning brotherhood. From 1896, the woodwork shop expanded to produce souvenirs for visitors to the community. By about 1910 such objects had become the cornerstone of the company's stock, and they were sold through mail-order catalogs.

The relatively small Roycroft wood shop produced some of the finest furniture of the time. Rectilinear forms with strong proportions were solidly constructed in oak with pins, pegs, and mortise-and-tenon joints, and they boast a warm, nut-brown patina. Decoration tends to be limited to hand-hammered iron or copper metalware. After Roycroft designer Dard Hunter (1883–1966) visited Vienna in 1908, the company began to incorporate motifs inspired by the Wiener Werkstätte (*see pp.198–99*) into its designs. Roycroft furniture was marked with either the orb-and-cross symbol (a cross with two horizontal bars and an "R" within a circle) or an incised "Roycroft."

When Hubbard, who was often called "the American William Morris," and his wife met an untimely death aboard the ill-fated *Lusitania* in 1915, the Roycroft workshops and their commercial aspirations were taken over by their son Elbert Jr., who went on to establish Roycroft departments in several hundred stores across the United States. The company closed in 1938.

Above: *Little Journeys* **oak bookstand** with two keyed tenons and a trefoil cutout at either end. These stands were supplied free with Elbert Hubbard's 14-volume *Little Journeys* series. *c. 1915* 24½ in (62.5 cm) wide **$700–1,000 G5**

ROYCROFTERS BRANDING AND CARVING

Although Roycroft furniture keeps decorative detail to a minimum, examples occasionally feature carved leaves and stylized flowers (*see right*). Gothic-style carved letters mark the pieces: both the Roycroft name and the orb-and-double-barred-cross symbol. This Gothic influence is also reflected in the choice of wood and austere designs of much of the Mission-style furniture produced at Elbert Hubbard's Roycroft Arts and Crafts community.

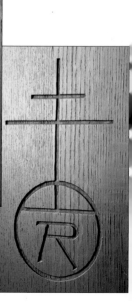

Roycroft's main mark (right) was a carved cross and orb enclosing an "R." It was adapted from a 14th-century monastic mark used on hand-copied manuscripts. Some oak pieces were also carved with a decorative oak leaf (above).

Large pyramidal bookcase made from dark-stained oak. Its graduated shelves are flanked by flared sides scalloped at the base and secured with pegged-through tenons. *1900–10* 20 in (51 cm) wide at base **$15,000–20,000 GDG**

A CLOSER LOOK

Circular-top lamp table made from solid oak. Its bolection-molded apron, square tapering legs, X-stretchers, and Mackmurdo-style feet are combined in a solid and distinctly masculine construction typical of Roycroft furniture. *1902–10. 30 in (76.25 cm) wide*
$4,000–6,000 DRA

Top is of solid rather than veneered oak

Feet are in the style of English architect and designer A. H. Mackmurdo

Oak open-arm chair with a single back slat, flat paddle arms with curved supports, square-section legs joined by two pairs of stretchers, and a tacked-over leather seat. *1902–10*
40¾ in (103.5 cm) high
$2,000–3,000   **DRA**

Prototype oak child's chair with a vertically slatted back, square-section tapering legs joined by three stretchers, and Mackmurdo-style feet. *1905–10*
29 in (73.5 cm) high
$2,000–3,000   **G5**

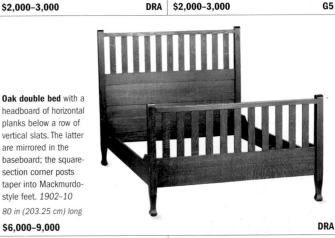

Oak double bed with a headboard of horizontal planks below a row of vertical slats. The latter are mirrored in the baseboard; the square-section corner posts taper into Mackmurdo-style feet. *1902–10*
80 in (203.25 cm) long
$6,000–9,000   **DRA**

Rectangular oak *Journey* stand on shoe feet with two pegged-tenoned undershelves. It was originally designed to hold Hubbard's *Little Journeys. c. 1910*
26¼ in (66.5 cm) high
$1,500–2,000   **G5**

Four-drawer oak dresser with an integrated swivel mirror, an overhanging top, square corner posts terminating in Mackmurdo-style feet, and brass drawer pulls. *1902–10*
61½ in (156 cm) high
$10,000–15,000   **DRA**

Architectural mahogany bookcase with a cornice top and a glass-paned door above a single-drawer cupboard. It also has adjustable shelves and copper metalware. *1902–10*
67 in (170 cm) high
$15,000–20,000   **DRA**

KEY FEATURES

Gothic, Moorish, and Scandinavian traditions, among others, all influenced Rohlfs's furniture.

Oak was the favored timber for elongated, solidly constructed tables, desks, chairs, and storage chests boasting a rich, dark patina. Mahogany is occasionally used.

Elaborately hand-carved cut-out designs featuring Gothic ornament and lettering, fretwork, brass embellishments such as nailheads, and Art Nouveau whiplash and tendril motifs are recurring decorative hallmarks.

Charles Rohlfs

The imaginative and successful American designer Charles Rohlfs created a distinctive brand of highly original furniture in the Arts and Crafts style that was widely celebrated on both sides of the Atlantic.

Charles Rohlfs (1853–1936) was the New York–born son of a cabinetmaker who received his training at the Cooper Union college. In around 1889, he turned his talents to furniture-making and design, specializing in elaborately pierced and carved oak furniture in the Gothic manner. Early success led to the establishment, two years later, of a small workshop in Buffalo, New York.

Here Rohlfs created custom-built solid-oak pieces that looked to the English Arts and Crafts style for inspiration—with exposed joinery and stylized abstract ornament that anticipated the Art Nouveau style. His furniture won widespread acclaim when exhibited at Marshall Field & Co. in Chicago in 1899. By 1909, Rohlfs was still working in his workshop, although he employed eight artisans to execute his designs.

Rohlfs's unusual designs for chairs, chests, small tables, and desks combine a variety of influences—including Gothic,

Moorish, and Scandinavian traditions—yet they remain decidedly unique. Of solid construction in oak—or more rarely, mahogany—and covered with a rich, dark patina, his one-of-a-kind pieces typically tend to be elongated and enriched by elaborately hand-carved fretwork, decorative Gothic lettering, and sinuous Art Nouveau-inspired motifs. Rohlfs himself described his style as having "the spirit of today blended with the poetry of the medieval ages."

Rohlfs's high standard of craftsmanship and careful attention to detail won him a host of international admirers, especially after he showed his furniture at the 1902 International Exhibition of Modern Decorative Art in Turin, and he received many prestigious commissions from around the globe, including Buckingham Palace. He retired in the mid-1920s.

Above: Rohlfs's carved maker's mark (often burned in, instead) with the shopmark "R" set within the rectangular outline of a wood saw. Sometimes the marks are highlighted in white or, as here, red.

Rare mahogany corner unit with four shelves, the lower with a serpentine carved apron, and square-section corner posts with square-block finials.
1905. 57½ in (146 cm) high **$4,000–6,000 DRA**

CONSTRUCTION AND BRANDING

A hallmark of the individual furniture made by Charles Rohlfs was his enthusiasm for the pure, traditional "honesty of construction" methods that were being promoted by pioneering designers of the English Arts and Crafts movement, including the multitalented William Morris (*see pp.22–23*). Metalwork strap hinges form a crucial part of the decoration, along with time-honored craftsman techniques—mortise-and-tenon joints, faceting, chamfering, and dovetailing. The maker's mark of an "R" and the date are usually branded—or burned with a hot iron—on to the surface of the wood.

Unlike other Arts and Crafts furniture-makers, Rohlfs sometimes used screws instead of dowels or tenons, disguising them with wooden buttons (the latter is missing on this corner-unit joint).

Charles Rohlfs's shopmark (an "R" within a saw) is accompanied by the date of manufacture (1905, on the right). Both the mark and the date are branded into the wood.

Rare hanging drawer-shelf made from ebonized oak. The rectangular shelf sits above a curved and pegged drawer front with a square wooden drawer pull. *1900*

15 in (38 cm) wide

$1,800–2,200 **DRA**

Rare oak lamp table with an octagonal top and two lower shelves mortised through cut-out plank legs and fastened with long, keyed-through tenons. *c. 1905*

29 in (73.5 cm) high

$6,000–9,000 **DRA**

Oak octagonal-top library table with fretworked, conforming sides, two of which form a door, with stamped metal hinges and latch, that opens to two interior shelves. *1900–05*

Top: 32 in (81.25 cm) wide

$4,000–6,000 **DRA**

Rare long case clock made from oak with stepped sides, four side posts, a cross of rectangular cutouts in the door, and a circular dial with copper-painted numerals. *1900–10*

85½ in (217 cm) high

$60,000–90,000 **DRA**

A CLOSER LOOK

Characteristic, linear Arts and Crafts elements

Typically functional but decorative brackets

Curvaceous Art Nouveau-style carving

Rare Arts and Crafts settee made of dark-stained oak with Art Nouveau–style carving. It is constructed from slim, plank-form top and floor rails united by slender, square-section corner and center posts, supporting a plain wooden seat. The unit is strengthened by elaborately carved and pierced corner brackets, with the seat being additionally supported at the front by a carved bracket-leg. *1900. 45 in (114.25 cm) wide* **NPA PC**

Charles Rohlfs was able to blend harmoniously the flowing forms of Art Nouveau with the more linear qualities of Arts and Crafts.

Ebonized-oak desk with drawers on one side and a cabinet on the other, and a high-back, swivel chair with carved decoration, a fleur-de-lys finial, and a brass-tacked leather seat. *1902*

Desk: 60 in (152.5 cm) wide; Chair: 59 in (150 cm) high

$20,000–30,000 **DRA**

KEY FEATURES

Simple, unornamented Lifetime pieces are rendered in oak and typically include bookcases, drop-front desks, china cabinets, settles, armchairs, and rocking chairs.

Popular Stickley styles—such as the bow-arm Morris chair and a trestle library table—inspired several Lifetime designs.

Drawer pulls and handles tend to be of lightweight, hand-hammered copper or brass.

Exposed tenons on the fronts of bookcases, china cabinets, and rocking chairs are a distinctive Lifetime decorative feature, as is faux-mullion latticework.

Lifetime furniture is marked with a decal or a paper label, or the words "Lifetime Furniture" branded into the wood within a rectangle, sometimes centered above "Grand Rapids Bookcase & Chair Co. Hastings, Mich."

Lifetime

At the turn of the 20th century, Michigan-based A. A. Barber introduced a line of Mission oak Lifetime furniture that he called Cloister Furniture in an effort to identify it with a high level of medieval craftsmanship.

In 1911, the enterprising salesman A. A. Barber merged two companies producing furniture in the Arts and Crafts style—the Grand Rapids Bookcase Co. and the Barber Brothers Chair Co.—to form a new enterprise called the Grand Rapids Bookcase and Chair Co. The firm's Cloister line of Lifetime furniture tended to be simple and unadorned and was often inspired by the styles popularized by designers such as the Stickleys (*see pp.40–45*). A number of distinctive design features remain unique to Lifetime, however, among them exposed tenons on the fronts of pieces rather than the sides, and the use of faux-mullion latticework in place of individual panes of glass on cabinet doors as a cost-cutting measure.

Much of the construction of Lifetime furniture was carried out by machine, while metalware details were often of hand-hammered copper. Although the quality was extremely high—boasting well-finished pieces made of fine timbers—the majority of even the best designs lack the grace and proportion necessary to elevate the functional furniture to the realm of the artistic. Nonetheless, Lifetime was one of the most successful commercial companies to produce quality furniture in the Arts and Crafts style. It is not known when the factory closed down.

Above: Rocking chair in oak with three vertical back splats, open arms, and a leather sprung-seat cushion. Numbered "624." *c. 1910* *33¾ in (85.5 cm) high* **$500–700 DRA**

Single-door oak bookcase on stile feet with a single drawer above a faux-mullion door, three interior shelves, and remnants of the paper label. *c. 1910* *32 in (81 cm) wide*
$3,000–4,000 DRA

Two-door oak bookcase on stile feet with three drawers above single-pane faux-mullion doors and with copper drawer pulls and handles. The exposed tenons on the front rather than the sides are typically Lifetime. *c. 1910* *54 in (137 cm) high*
$5,000–7,000 G5

The Shop of the Crafters

Following a visit to the 1904 Louisiana Purchase Exposition held in St. Louis, showing Arts and Crafts furniture, glassware, and metalware by pioneering US designers, retailer Oscar Onken founded the Shop of the Crafters in Cincinnati, Ohio.

Teaming up with the acclaimed Budapest designer Paul Horti (1865–1907), Oscar Onken (1858–1948) expanded his manufacturing company to include Arts and Crafts furniture with a distinctive European flavor. A shrewd businessman, Onken promoted his new venture through advertisements in a wide range of magazines. Horti's most important contribution was furniture that incorporated inlaid marquetry panels of colorful imported Austrian woods.

Unlike many of the companies that jumped on the Arts and Crafts bandwagon after it had been popularized by pioneers such as Gustav Stickley (*see pp.40–45*), the Shop of the Crafters resisted the temptation simply to replicate craftsman design.

Onken also developed furniture finishes in "Weathered, Fumed, Flemish, Austrian, or Early English shades." By 1920, the Shop of the Crafters stopped producing Arts and Crafts furniture, although the Oscar Onken Co. did not close until 1931.

Above: Fumed oak cabinet in the style of C. F. A. Voysey, with marquetry decoration, pierced heart motifs, and wrought-iron handles. *c. 1905.* 44½ *in (113 cm) high* **$6,000–9,000 CALD**

KEY FEATURES

Decorative embellishments on Shop of the Crafters furniture include inlaid marquetry patterns, Limbert-style cutouts, and Art Nouveau–inspired stained- and leaded-glass panels.

Oak was the favored timber, although occasionally mahogany was used.

Metalware typically features strap hinges, beveled square brass knobs, and brass nails. The latter were heavily relied on to stud leather tops.

Arts and Crafts furniture bears a gold paper label with black lettering reading "Shop of the Crafters" above a simple drawing of a lantern, below which are found the words "At Cincinnati Oscar Onken Co. Sole Owners."

Large oak library table with a bronze-handled partner's drawer. Its spade-footed, slatted legs are united by two stretchers supporting an undershelf. *c. 1910*
54 in (137 cm) wide
$2,000–3,000　　　　　**DRA**

Stained and waxed oak cabinet with a single drawer over an open shelf above a two-door cupboard. The drawer and doors have Austrian fruitwood marquetry panels. *1905–10*
51 in (129.5 cm) high
$3,000–5,000　　　**DRA**

Large oak display cabinet on stile feet, with five interior shelves behind two three-over-five-pane mullion doors, above a two-door cupboard. Its earthy, dull waxed finish and its large metal strap hinges are characteristic of Shop of the Crafters designs. *1905–10*
65 in (165 cm) high
$10,000–15,000　　　**G5**

American Furniture

Furniture made during this period in the United States is often known as Mission furniture. The term is said to derive from the functionalist beliefs of the designers, who declared that furniture has a mission—to be used. Creating clean-lined, straightforward, solid furniture primarily in oak, makers such as Frank Furness, the Barber Brothers, Greene & Greene, Joseph McHugh, and George Mann Niedecken emphasized simplicity of design, with the quality of the materials and the elements of construction—exposed pegs and tenons, for example—as the only decoration. Stylized inlays in metal, wood, and shell were occasionally used as embellishments, but American Mission furniture is mostly simple and unadorned.

Pair of twin beds by the Brooks Manufacturing Co. Their mortise-and-tenoned frame is made of stained and waxed oak, and has spindled head- and footboards. *c. 1910*

81 in (205.75 cm) long

$3,000–4,000 (the pair) **DRA**

Double-door blanket chest by Greene & Greene, made in oak and yellow pine with unusual mortised corners secured with square dowel pegs. *c. 1910*

65 in (165 cm) long

$20,000–30,000 **DRA**

Mission furniture oak footstool with a drop-in cushion re-covered in brown leather. It was made by the Barber Brothers Chair Co., which became Lifetime around 1911. *c. 1905*

16½ in (42 cm) wide

$300–500 **DRA**

Slatted oak umbrella stand of cylindrical form secured with leather lacing, and on ball feet. It was made by the Lakeside Craft Shops of Sheboygan, Wisconsin. *c. 1905*

25 in (63.5 cm) high

$300–400 **DRA**

Oak smoking stand made by the Lakeside Craft Shops. The lower door has butt-jointed and double-braced oak slats; the upper door has a leaded, slag-glass panel. *c. 1905*

33 in (83.75 cm) high

$800–1,200 **DRA**

Single-door pine bookcase made by the Honeoye Falls Furniture Co., New York. It has a clip-corner gallery top and, behind the glazed door, three interior shelves. *Early 20th century*

55 in (139.75 cm) high

$800–1,200 **DRA**

Pagoda-shaped magazine stand made by the Byrdcliffe Arts and Crafts Colony in cherry wood, with white lilies painted in wood stain on its flared sides. *1902–10*

30 in (76.25 cm) high

$12,000–18,000   **DRA**

Large oak church pew with plank seat and back, by Frank Furness. The rear supports for each side have chamfered edges and are topped with roundel standards. The molded armrests have turned supports and applied geometric designs. *Early 1880s*

65 in (165 cm) long

$3,000–5,000   **FRE**

Harden Furniture Co.

The genesis of the Harden Furniture Co. can be traced to 1880, when Charles Harden and his son Frank began to make kitchen chairs as a sideline at their sawmill in Camden, New York. The sideline soon became the company's full-time business, and the firm began to specialize in the production of fine-quality Mission furniture, including rocking chairs, footstools, and tables in mahogany, maple, birch, and oak. Early Harden furniture can be identified by a red paper label reading "From the Harden Line, Factory No. 2 Camden, New York." Designs from the turn of the 20th century emulated those of Gustav Stickley and other Mission furniture-makers, with whom Harden was competing.

Harden Furniture Co. oak footstool with open mortise-and-tenon construction, curved seat rails, and short vertical slats. It is missing its original seat cushion. *Early 20th century*

18½ in (47 cm) wide

$1,200–1,800   **DRA**

Harden Furniture Co. rocker with scrolled arms and slatted back and sides. The original sprung seat is yet to be restored. *Early 20th century*

37¾ in (96 cm) high

$400–600   **DRA**

Mission furniture oak director's table by Joseph P. McHugh & Co. It has a rectangular top and apron, five legs, and shoe feet. *Late 1890s*

108 in (274.50 cm) long

$3,000–5,000　　　　　　　　　　　　**DRA**

Oak vice cabinet made possibly by Joseph P. McHugh & Co., with an iron-studded panel door enclosed by flared sides with serpentine-profile tops. *Late 1890s*

38 in (96.5 cm) high

$500–800　　　　　　　　　　　　**DRA**

Rare square side-table designed by Frank Lloyd Wright and made by George Mann Niedecken. Its top and cross-pedestal base are made from waxed, unstained oak. *c. 1910*

30½ in (77.5 cm) high

$7,000–10,000　　　　　　　　　　**DRA**

Open-arm oak rocker made by the J. M. Young Furniture Co. It has four vertical back slats, paddle arms, and a new brown leather-upholstered seat cushion. *1904–20*

33½ in (85 cm) high

$400–600　　　　　　　　　　　　**DRA**

Oak armchair by the J. M. Young Furniture Co., with four vertical back slats and a seat cushion reupholstered in vinyl. Its leg stretchers form a square. *1904–20*

39¼ in (99.5 cm) high

$600–900　　　　　　　　　　　　**DRA**

Plail Brothers Chair Co. rocker constructed from oak. The top rail of its slat-barrel back, which encloses a reupholstered sprung seat, is steeply curved by steam-bending. *1906–10*

31¼ in (79.5 cm) high

$6,000–9,000　　　　　　　　　　　**G5**

Bureau-style dressing table with a large swivel mirror, by the Luce Furniture Co. Made from solid mahogany and mahogany-veneered softwood, it is embellished with pierced hearts and floral-motif fruitwood inlay. *c. 1905*

70 in (178 cm) high

$1,200–1,800 DRA

Large oak settle by the Phoenix Chair Co., with vertical slats to the back and sides, square-section corner posts, and a drop-in seat cushion reupholstered in brown leather with matching cushions. *c. 1910*

65 in (165 cm) wide

$3,000–5,000 DRA

Unsigned mahogany armchair with the original cane seat and back panel, and open paddle arms with diagonal supports. *c. 1910*

35 in (89 cm) high

$400–600 DRA

Unsigned mahogany rocker made to match the armchair shown left. (Unattributable pieces command lower prices.) *c. 1910*

32½ in (82.5 cm) high

$500–700 DRA

Onondaga Shops

Leopold and John George Stickley (*see p.44*) chose the name Onondaga Shops when they set up business together in Fayetteville, New York, in 1904. The name was only in use for two years before the brothers rebranded themselves as Handcraft, and Onondaga furniture is now collected in its own right. During the Onondaga period, L. and J. G. Stickley produced furniture that was based on the designs of their pioneering but less business-savvy brother, Gustav. Realizing that, by scaling down and simplifying his designs, they could cut prices and thus increase the volume of their sales, they did just that.

Onondaga Shops library table No. 518 with the top resting on slatted sides and an undershelf stretcher. *c. 1905*

40 in (101.5 cm) wide

$1,000–1,500 DRA

Onondaga Shops Morris chair No. 790 with open paddle arms, a drop-in seat, and a reclining slatted back with a leather support strap. *c. 1905*

38 in (96.5 cm) high

$1,000–1,500 DRA

C. R. Mackintosh's elegant, linear style was a great influence on Hoffmann's furniture.

Utilitarian Austrian Biedermeier furniture produced earlier in the 19th century provided another source of inspiration for Hoffmann's stark, functional furniture designs.

Tables, chairs, and cupboards are rendered in limed oak, beechwood, mahogany, and other ebonized woods.

Furniture pieces are frequently decorated with geometric patterns featuring open-centered rectangles and squares, circles, and spheres.

Josef Hoffmann

A cofounder of the Wiener Werkstätte, Josef Hoffmann was a pioneer of functional Arts and Crafts design, embracing a philosophy based on the unity of architecture, furniture, and interior decoration.

A major force behind the founding of the forward-looking Wiener Werkstätte—which was patterned after Charles Robert Ashbee's Guild of Handicraft (*see pp.160–61*) in Great Britain—the Moravian-born Josef Hoffmann (1870–1956) pioneered the creation of useful, functional, yet aesthetically pleasing furniture.

Although Hoffmann's earliest designs reflected the fluid lines characteristic of French Art Nouveau, by 1900 his furniture bore the unmistakable influence of the Scottish Arts and Crafts luminary Charles Rennie Mackintosh (*see pp.30–31*), whose work was widely celebrated in Vienna. Favoring timbers including beechwood, mahogany, limed oak, and other ebonized woods, Hoffmann continued to push the boundaries, moving beyond a purely aesthetic canon to endorse a philosophy that endowed functional furniture with both elegance and restraint.

His early belief in the fundamental Arts and Crafts principle that brought architecture, furniture, and interior decoration into a cohesive whole led him to design both the interior and the exterior of many of his building projects. Hoffmann adopted a style that was stark, functional, and directly opposed to the flamboyant, curvilinear fashion embraced by his French contemporaries.

Among Hoffmann's many highly acclaimed designs were those he created for Vienna's Purkersdorf Sanatorium and the Palais Stoclet in Brussels. He was also ranked as one of the premier designers for the prestigious company established by Michael Thonet, whose international renown was largely based upon the invention of the bentwood technique.

Above: Stained-beechwood armchair made by J. & J. Kohn of Vienna. It has a slatted back and sides, a curved back rest, and ball brackets under the seat. *c. 1910. 31½ in (80 cm) high* **$1,200–1,800 VZ**

FUNCTIONAL DESIGN

An essential component of the furniture created by Josef Hoffmann and his fellow designers at the Wiener Werkstätte was the continuous attention paid to the importance of function. In contrast to their French and Belgian counterparts—who placed greater emphasis on decoration, organic shapes, and sumptuous materials—furniture designers and craftsmen in Germany and Austria followed the lead of many British and American Arts and Crafts designers including Voysey, Mackintosh, and Gustav Stickley, who believed that form should be subordinate to function.

Stained-beechwood side chair made by J. & J. Kohn of Vienna. It has bentwood back posts and top rail, a stuffed seat and a shield-shaped back rest covered in leather, and spherical brackets under the seat rails. *1890s. 38¾ in (98.5 cm) high* **$1,000–1,500 SDR**

Dark-stained beechwood table made by Thonet for Cabaret Fledermaus. Its circular top and base are united by turned posts, alternative pairs of which are united top and bottom with ball brackets. *c. 1905. 40 in (101.5 cm) high* **$1,800–2,200 QU**

Walnut-veneered sideboard with figured inlay and brass metalware, by the school of Josef Hoffmann. Its top cupboards are on spindle supports in front of a mirrored splashback and over a marble-topped base. *c. 1900*

70 in (178 cm) high

$10,000–15,000   DOR

Veneered cherrywood casket of cubelike form with black-stained vertical bands on the corners and sides. It is raised on black-stained square block feet and has a hinged cover with a stuffed seat cushion. *c. 1910*

8¾ in (22.5 cm) wide

$1,000–1,500   BMN

Cupboard (one of a pair) made by the Wiener Werkstätte. Its softwood carcass and doors are lacquered in black, and the doors have geometric-pattern panels with green and white glazing. *c. 1910*

39½ in (100 cm) high

$12,000–18,000 (the pair)   QU

Viennese nutwood armchair probably by Josef Hoffmann. It has a slatted back with a curved top rail sweeping into flat paddle arms, above a D-shaped seat and stretchered, square-section legs. *c. 1905*

34 in (86.5 cm) high

$3,000–4,000   DOR

Cabaret Fledermaus chair in stained beechwood, with turned legs, ebony ball brackets under the top rail and seat rails, and an upholstered seat. *c. 1905*

29½ in (75 cm) high

$2,000–3,000   DOR

Koloman Moser

A founder of both the Vienna Secession and—with Josef Hoffmann—the Wiener Werkstätte, the Austrian designer Koloman Moser (1868–1918) had conceived a broad range of designs for jewelry, metalwork, glass, and textiles before adding furniture to his repertoire in the 1890s. His highly refined furniture in severe, rectilinear shapes was widely celebrated for its rich, colorful ornamentation that was so different from the austere, unadorned, and functional furniture being produced in Vienna. Moser gave his attention to decoration rather than form, using veneers made from luxurious timbers including rosewood and maple and stylized ornamental inlays featuring opulent materials such as exotic woods and mother-of-pearl.

Koloman Moser Fauteuil No. 413 made by J. & J. Kohn of Vienna, in dark mahogany-stained beech with brass rivets and feet. The seat and buttoned back are upholstered in brown leather. *1901*

39 in (99 cm) high

$7,000–10,000   DOR

Koloman Moser painted softwood cupboard with twin glazed doors above two drawers and a double-door cupboard; in white with brass metalware. *c. 1900*

84 in (213.5 cm) high

$30,000–40,000   DOR

KEY FEATURES

Clear-cut forms, rather than ornamentation, define the furniture pieces by Olbrich.

Rectilinear, functional furniture combines monumentality with delicacy, formal structures with organic detailing.

The geometric lines of Olbrich's work reveal the influence of C. R. Mackintosh.

Oak, beechwood, nutwood, and maple are his most typically used materials.

Bold and simple chairs are common, often varnished and with a leather seat, occasionally with some detailing.

Joseph Maria Olbrich

In the spirit of the Arts and Crafts movement, the prolific Austrian architect and designer Joseph Maria Olbrich created distinctive furniture that relied on the integrity of form rather than ornament for definition.

A founding member of the Vienna Secessionists, the architect and designer of metalwork, textiles, and graphics Joseph Maria Olbrich (1867–1908) ventured into furniture-making with relatively few—although highly original—designs. Travels in Rome and Africa were followed by a stint working with Josef Hoffmann (*see pp.58–59*) in the workshop of Otto Wagner.

Along with Koloman Moser (*see p.59*) and others, Olbrich and Hoffmann broke from the main arts organization of 19th-century Vienna, the conservative Kunstlerhaus, in 1897 to form the Vienna Secession. This group embraced the ideas of William Morris and aimed to elevate the applied

arts to the status of fine art. In its 1900 exhibition, it featured the work of C. R. Ashbee (*see p.160*), the Guild of Handicraft (*see p.136 and pp.160–61*), the Glasgow Four (*see p.30*), and other leading British Arts and Crafts designers.

In 1899, Olbrich established an artists' colony in Darmstadt, Germany, where he designed and produced wooden furniture. Pieces were restrained in design and featured clean, geometric forms with little decorative ornamentation and occasionally embellished with leather.

Above: Beechwood-and-mahogany armchair made by Thonet of Vienna, with steam-curved arms and sides and green leather upholstery. *c. 1900. 30 in (76 cm) high* **$1,200–1,800 DOR**

Black-varnished maple armchair by Josef Niedermoser of Vienna. It has serpentine arms, slatted sides, and stretchered legs with brass terminals; yellow-leather upholstery. *1898–99*
32 in (81 cm) high

$1,800–2,200   **QU**

Viennese chair (one of four) in the style of Joseph Maria Olbrich, in stained beechwood in lighter and darker shades of brown and with a rectilinear open fretwork back and a seat pad covered in new black leather. *c. 1900*
39 in (99 cm) high

$2,000–3,000 (the set)   **DOR**

Stained-nutwood armchair with diagonal and arched supports on the arms and legs. The vertical back slats are augmented with a pair of brass-tacked brown leather pads matching the seat cover. *c. 1900*
37 in (94 cm) high

$3,000–4,000   **DOR**

Henry van de Velde

Belgian architect Henry van de Velde believed that natural lines perfectly complemented the solid wood he used. His furniture followed the curved, organic lines of nature and eschewed the use of decorative ornament.

Henry van de Velde (1863–1957) won acclaim with Bloemenwerf, the house he built for himself near Brussels in 1894, for which he created the furniture, silver, cutlery, and decorative fixtures.

Influenced by the ideals of William Morris (*see pp.22–23*), van de Velde championed the importance of the artist over the machine in the Arts and Crafts tradition. He based his designs for furniture on the theory that art should always follow the organic forms found in nature, and he considered the function of furniture to be of overriding importance. The sweeping, energetic lines of his early pieces eventually gave way to more restrained designs. The influence of English

Arts and Crafts designers such as C. F. A. Voysey (*see p.26*) can be detected in the sculptural lines of van de Velde's chairs, tables, and cabinets that were rendered in light-colored woods and boasted little, if any, decoration.

Van de Velde established and directed the Grand Ducal School of Arts and Crafts from 1906 and continued to design furniture, ceramics, and jewelry until his retirement in the 1940s.

Above: Oak bedside table (one of a pair), with raised and fielded oval panel doors, arched stretchers, and pairs of stylized hoof feet. *1897–98*
32 in (81 cm) high **$1,800–2,200 (the pair) QU**

Lady's mahogany writing desk made by H. Scheidemantel, with a kidney-shaped top, two cupboards, and an open shelf. *c. 1905*
48½ in (123 cm) wide
$20,000–30,000   **QU**

Oak head- and footboards of curvilinear form with bowed and arched profiles and shield-shaped panels; on brass casters. *1897–98*
80 in (203 cm) wide
$10,000–15,000   **QU**

Mahogany corner cupboard from a bedroom suite, with an overhanging top, a scooped base, and bowed sides and door, the latter with an arched center panel and a brass escutcheon. *1903*
30 in (76 cm) high
$5,000–7,000   **QU**

Green-and-red stained umbrella stand attributed to Henry van de Velde. Its open, drum-shaped brass-and-wood center is raised on and supported by three angular braces. *1904*
30 in (76 cm) high
$2,000–3,000   **QU**

KEY FEATURES

Simple, straightforward construction is typical of Riemerschmid's furniture designs.

Modest materials such as oak, yew, or pine tend to be most used.

Clean, straight lines typically enhanced by soft, subtle curves are hallmarks of his furniture.

The construction of the furniture is often highlighted as part of the overall design.

Decorative ornament favored by Riemerschmid includes carving, brasswork, and inlays of metal or precious materials such as mother-of-pearl.

Richard Riemerschmid

Munich's esteemed place in the pantheon of internationally acclaimed Arts and Crafts furniture owes a great debt to the versatile and prolific German architect and designer Richard Riemerschmid.

One of the founders of the Munich Werkstätten für Kunst im Handwerk (the United Workshops for Art and Handicraft), which encouraged designers and manufacturers to work for the benefit of the common man, Richard Riemerschmid (1868–1957) initially trained as a painter in Munich. He then turned his hand to decorative objects for the home, including metalwork, ceramics, glass, textiles, and, by 1895, furniture, where his elegant, abstract designs were inspired by historical sources, the Arts and Crafts movement, and contemporary Art Nouveau.

By 1905, Riemerschmid was allied with the Deutscher Werkbund and had ventured into creating designs for machine-made furniture—Maschinenmobel—for the Dresden atelier of his brother-in-law, cabinet-maker Karl Schmidt. Schmidt's workshop heralded the Arts and Crafts principles, although both he and Riemerschmid accepted the practical benefits of using machinery to create useful, well-made furniture.

Above: Dark-stained beech elbow chair with a rhombus seat, curved arms, and heart, moon, and demilune cutouts on the back slat. *1900. 33½ in (85.5 cm) high* **$2,500–3,000 VZ**

Six-drawer gentleman's stained-pine commode by the Dresdner Werkstätten. The top has a three-sided splashback, and the drawers have nickel-plated pulls. *c. 1905*
51½ in (130.5 cm) high
$5,000–7,000   **QU**

Stained-oak cupboard with a pair of glazed-panel doors above an overhanging shelf, and two drawers and two doors with recessed center panels below. Its strap hinges and drawer pulls are nickel-plated. *c. 1905*
80¼ in (204 cm) high
$2,500–3,000   **BMN**

Stained-oak armchair designed for the German Art Exhibition in Dresden, in 1899. It has an undulating top rail and arms (the latter with scrolled ends), square-section tapering legs, and diagonal side supports. *1899*
38½ in (98 cm) high
$8,000–12,000   **VZ**

Léon Jallot

Turning his back on the highly popular, flamboyant designs typical of the French Art Nouveau style, furniture designer Léon Jallot forged his reputation on clean-lined, solidly constructed pieces inspired by the Arts and Crafts style.

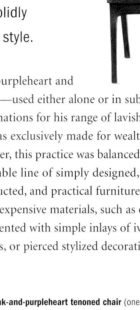

KEY FEATURES

Well-proportioned, simple shapes and clean lines are typical of the furniture designed by Jallot.

Colorful, luxurious woods such as purpleheart and walnut embellish his more expensive pieces of furniture.

Frequently rendered in oak, Jallot chairs, tables, and cabinets often feature inlays of ivory or metals, or pierced decorative patterns.

Having left the employment of the influential dealer Samuel Bing in 1903, Léon Jallot (1874–1967) established his own atelier. Here, he confirmed his place as one of the most creative members of an emerging generation of furniture designers who rejected the early, nature-inspired Art Nouveau style. Jallot looked in new directions for inspiration—including the British Arts and Crafts movement—and he eventually found his niche with a decorative style that favored a precise and restrained sense of proportion coupled with pure shapes and simple, clean lines.

Jallot remained true to his French roots as a furniture designer by favoring rare, highly colored, and luxurious timbers—among them purpleheart and walnut—used either alone or in subtle combinations for his range of lavish furniture that was exclusively made for wealthy clients. However, this practice was balanced by a more affordable line of simply designed, soundly constructed, and practical furniture rendered in less expensive materials, such as oak, and ornamented with simple inlays of ivory, rare timbers, or pierced stylized decoration.

Above: Oak-and-purpleheart tenoned chair (one of six), with pierced, stylized leaf decoration on the serpentine-topped back rest, and a brown-leather seat pad. *c. 1910.* 36 in (91.5 cm) high **$10,000–15,000 (the set) CALD**

Oak-and-purpleheart tenoned server with a serpentine-topped back rail pierced with a stylized floral motif. It also has a pair of frieze drawers above arched aprons and two open shelves, and four gently flared corner posts. *c. 1910* 48¼ in (122.5 cm) wide
$10,000–15,000   **CALD**

Walnut side chair (one of six) with a leather-covered back panel rising from a leather seat pad, and flanked by carved stylized floral decoration. Its square-section tapering legs are united by a high double-H stretcher. *c. 1910*
17 in (43 cm) wide

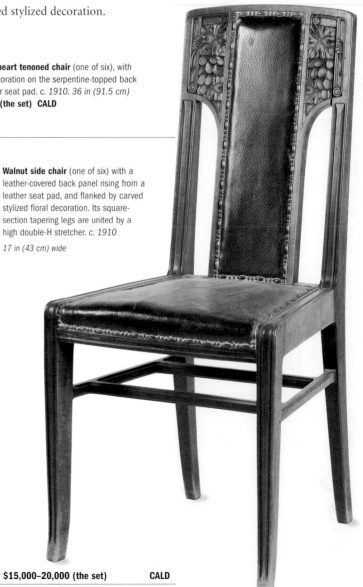

$15,000–20,000 (the set)   **CALD**

Austrian Furniture

As in Germany, furniture designers in Austria turned away from the florid marquetry confections of Emile Gallé and the flamboyant naturalism of Hector Guimard, favoring instead bold, classic, and functional designs in unconventional, modern materials such as laminated plywood, aluminum, and bent beechwood. Designers of the Vienna Succession and the Wiener Werkstätte—including Josef Hoffmann, Jacob and Josef Kohn, and Michael Thonet—forged a radical new path by creating fresh, original furniture in linear and geometric shapes that owed inspiration to the Scottish Arts and Crafts designer Charles Rennie Mackintosh.

Dark-brown stained-beech settle by J. & J. Kohn of Vienna. Its back splats are pierced with a panel of circles, and rise within a triple-arch framework. The arms are ball-bracketed to tapering legs. *c. 1905*
49½ in (125.5 cm) wide

$1,000–1,500   VZ

Pair of beechwood seats No. 725 designed by Josef Hoffmann. The frames have brass rivets and ball brackets, and hold leather seats and backs; the latter are tooled. *c. 1915*
34½ in (88 cm) high

$5,000–7,000 (the pair)   DOR

Nest of four dark-brown stained beechwood tables by Josef Hoffmann. With a rectangular top, side aprons, and slender tapering legs; the largest also has vertical side slats. *c. 1905*
29 in (74 cm) high

$3,500–4,500   DOR

Black stained-beech table made by J. & J. Kohn of Vienna. Its extendable rectangular top has rounded ends and is set on curved bentwood supports of stylized organic form. *1901*
52½ in (133.5 cm) wide

$5,000–7,000   DOR

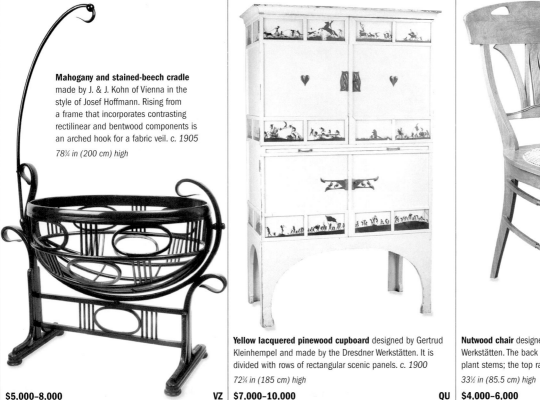

Mahogany and stained-beech cradle made by J. & J. Kohn of Vienna in the style of Josef Hoffmann. Rising from a frame that incorporates contrasting rectilinear and bentwood components is an arched hook for a fabric veil. *c. 1905*
78¾ in (200 cm) high

$5,000–8,000   VZ

Yellow lacquered pinewood cupboard designed by Gertrud Kleinhempel and made by the Dresdner Werkstätten. It is divided with rows of rectangular scenic panels. *c. 1900*
72¾ in (185 cm) high

$7,000–10,000   QU

Nutwood chair designed by Bernhard Pankok for the Vereinigte Werkstätten. The back slats are in the form of highly stylized plant stems; the top rail is pierced with leaf motifs. *c. 1900*
33½ in (85.5 cm) high

$4,000–6,000   VZ

Ebonized-beechwood chair made by Thonet of Vienna. Its legs are braced with curved supports, two of which sweep up into a U-shaped back with horizontal and vertical slats. The seat is covered in red leather. *c. 1905*

39 in (99 cm) high

$1,200–1,800   **VZ**

Pair of beech-frame armchairs made by Thonet of Vienna. Stained a red-brown mahogany, they incorporate bentwood side rails and arms, the latter curving into tapering legs. *c. 1905*

29½ in (75 cm) high

$2,000–3,000   **VZ**

Bentwood beech rocking chair by Thonet of Vienna, with scrolled and undulating arms and sides running into curved rockers. *c. 1890*

42 in (106.5 cm) high

$3,000–4,000   **QU**

Beech-frame armchair designed by Marcel Kammerer and made by Thonet of Vienna. The bentwood frame is stained mahogany. *c. 1910*

32 in (81.5 cm) high

$1,200–1,500   **DOR**

Adolf Loos

Moravian-born architect Adolf Loos (1870–1933) was a pivotal figure in the development of functionalism. In 1896, he settled in Vienna, where he contributed to a number of periodicals. Loos's writings denounced the use of ornament and proved to be of greater importance to the European movement than the simple, functional furniture he designed. Loos's approach placed him in opposition to Josef Hoffmann and the Wiener Werkstätte, but as his designs demonstrate, he was rather less restrained in practice than in theory, with a fondness for rich materials.

Adolf Loos maplewood folding table with a rectangular top and two pairs of serpentine X-frame legs united by plain, turned stretchers. *1898*

27½ in (70 cm) high

$7,000–10,000   **DOR**

Adolf Loos maplewood chair with pierced back slats, turned front legs, a serpentine top rail, a seat apron, and a canework seat. *1898*

34½ in (88 cm) high

$5,000–7,000   **DOR**

Adolf Loos three-legged footstand with a stained red bowl-like top, above splayed beechwood legs stained a brown-mahogany color. *c. 1905*

17¼ in (44 cm) high

$1,800–2,200   **DOR**

European and New World Furniture

The Wiener Werkstätte produced graceful, elongated furniture that owed a great debt to the Glasgow Four and Charles Rennie Mackintosh. The influence of Mackintosh can also be seen in the modern, uncompromising furniture designs of the Deutscher Werkbund, established in Munich in 1907 by Hermann Muthesius, Friedrich Naumann, and Henry van de Velde. Recognizing the importance of designing for mass production as well as for handcraft, designers such as Peter Behrens, Bruno Paul, and Richard Riemerschmid created clean-lined furniture—chairs, tables, and cabinets—that was both attractive and utilitarian.

Oak-frame armchair designed by Otto Eckmann of Hamburg, with square-section arms, rails, legs, and supports. *c. 1900*
37½ in (95 cm) high
$1,000–1,500   QU

Off-white painted softwood dresser attributed to Peter Behrens. The glass top doors have blue highlights; the splashback and base doors have dark-blue ceramic tiles. *c. 1900*
50 in (127.5 cm) wide
$4,000–6,000   QU

Oak dining table designed by Peter Behrens, with a six-panel circular top above an urn-shaped pedestal. Additional C-scroll supports form a circular base to a plain apron. *c. 1900*
40 in (102 cm) wide
$3,000–4,000   QU

Jarrah dresser by New Zealand craftsman J. W. Chapman-Taylor, made from hand-adzed wood and wrought iron. *c. 1910*
NPA   MNZ

Writing bureau from New Zealand with four legs supported by a central brace. The brace edges have been curved with notches, and diamond-shaped perforations decorate the top of the desk. *c. 1890*
NPA   MNZ

Cherrywood longcase clock by Adelbert Niemeyer. Raised on four feet, it has a fretwork panel near the base and a white-porcelain clock face framed in mahogany with painted purple-and-gold numerals. *1906*
78¾ in (200 cm) high
$3,000–5,000   VZ

Honey-brown oak chair designed by Gustave Serrurier-Bovy, with a leather-padded seat and a four-slatted back splat. *1899*

38¾ in (97 cm) high

$5,000–8,000   **VZ**

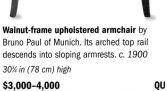

Walnut-frame upholstered armchair by Bruno Paul of Munich. Its arched top rail descends into sloping armrests. *c. 1900*

30¾ in (78 cm) high

$3,000–4,000   **QU**

Mahogany-frame armchair by Bruno Paul of Munich, with saber legs, scooped seat rails, ebonized arms, and an arched top rail. *c. 1900*

40¾ in (103.5 cm) high

$1,800–2,200   **QU**

Oak display cabinet by Bruno Paul of Munich, with glass-paneled doors set above two drawers with brass pulls. *c. 1910*

67¾ in (172 cm) high

$800–1,200   **QU**

The tops of the arms and back rest are decorated with brass inlay work in the form of highly stylized rose motifs.

Mahogany-frame armchair by Hans Christiansen with flat armrests and top rail, spindled sides, tapering legs with cuffed brass terminals, and an upholstered back rest and seat pad. *c. 1910*

28 in (71 cm) high

$2,000–3,000   **VZ**

Pale-hardwood armchair designed by Bruno Paul and made by the Deutsche Werkstätten. It has a canework back and seat. *c. 1935*

31½ in (80 cm) high

$300–500   **VZ**

Carl Malmsten

A designer who spent his whole life struggling for a more craft-oriented and functional approach to furniture was Carl Malmsten. A leading figure of the Functionalist movement that flourished in Sweden between 1930 and 1950, he also harbored progressive ideas about educational freedom. One of his greatest projects was the establishment of a residential craft school in Vickleby, along the lines of Ashbee's Guild of Handicraft. Malmsten's furniture harked back to the traditional forms of Swedish rural designs, which he modified with his brand of modern simplicity. The use of native blond woods is typical of his approach, which was respectful of natural form and color.

Carl Malmsten Swedish piano stool with a birchwood frame, turned and tapering legs, demilune arms (each with a vertical slat), and an upholstered drop-in seat pad. *c. 1920*

14¼ in (36 cm) wide

$800–1,200   **LANE**

Carl Malmsten Swedish open armchair with a birchwood frame. It has an upholstered, drop-in seat pad, openwork back and sides, and turned and tapering legs. *c. 1920*

23½ in (60 cm) wide

$2,000–3,000   **LANE**

Textiles

Spinning and weaving were changed almost beyond recognition by the Industrial Revolution, which slashed the time and cost involved in the manufacture of textiles and transplanted the enterprise from the cottages of rural England to new mills in towns and cities. The Arts and Crafts movement spurred the emergence of smaller studios specializing in hand-embroidered and loom-made textiles, with homey repeating patterns drawn from natural forms.

While many skilled workers were compelled to labor at repetitive tasks in poor conditions, companies like Morris & Co. and the Silver Studio in Great Britain allowed weavers to engage more fully with their trades, as well as work in more congenial surroundings. Hand-knotted carpets took the Arts and Crafts ideals of unhurried custom craftsmanship to a zealous (and costly) extreme. Designers and artisans across Europe and the United States produced tapestries and embroidery work of painstaking intricacy, inspired by the homespun philosophies of John Ruskin and William Morris.

As part of his grand design to recreate an idealized medieval interior, Morris began experimenting with embroidery while living at Red Lion Square in the late 1850s. He had recently returned from France, where he had been visiting Gothic cathedrals with his friend Edward Burne-Jones. The pair had also visited l'Hôtel de Cluny in Paris, where Morris was inspired by the fabulous medieval "Lady and the Unicorn" tapestries. He would later incorporate floral tableaux similar to those on display at Cluny into his own textile designs.

From his first experiments, Morris developed a passion for embroidery and weaving that was to last the rest of his life. He instructed his wife Jane in the art, as well as her sister Bessie Burden, who was later appointed chief instructor at the Royal School of Art Needlework. The family connection with textiles continued with Morris's daughter May, who was to take over the embroidery section of his company.

Central panel of the triptych tapestry *Greenery* by John Henry Dearle for Morris & Co. It is woven in colored wools and mohair depicting a wooded glade scene. *1892 181½ in (461 cm) wide* **$300,000–400,000 L&T**

MORRIS AND HIS INFLUENCE

Merton Abbey in Surrey became the focus of William Morris's textile venture, manufacturing woven and block-printed curtains and upholsteries to designs by Morris and John Henry Dearle among others. The pattern Strawberry Thief, depicting thrushes making off with strawberries from laden plants, was co-designed by Philip Webb. The subject matter was typical of Morris & Co. output, with its stylized foliage and verdant palette of peacock blue, sage green, and russet brown. This and other Morris & Co. designs, such as the popular favorite Bird, display a complex yet subtle symmetry in their repetition. Merton Abbey was also the scene of carpet tufting—a labor-intensive industry that put the finished product out of the reach of all but the wealthiest consumers. Cheaper machine-made carpets were manufactured on behalf of Morris & Co. by Wilton as part of its Axminster and Kidderminster ranges.

Where Morris led, others were bound to follow. The burgeoning popularity of embroidery led to the creation of the Royal School of Art Needlework in 1872, providing young women with suitable work and attracting the passing attentions of a string of artists and designers. From humble beginnings as a pursuit for genteel ladies, the art of embroidery rose to such prominence at the end of the 19th century that a host of gifted individuals at the top of their professions became involved. Many of them, including C. F. A. Voysey and M. H. Baillie Scott, not only designed textiles but also wrote on the subject. Arthur Silver established the Silver Studio in Hammersmith in 1880, overseeing its growth into a successful business. One of its main clients was Liberty & Co., the great retail champion of the Arts and Crafts scene. The Silver Studio produced cottons with repeating floral patterns, some of which were quite abstract, in a rich and deep palette.

A FLOURISHING MEDIUM

In Scotland, the Macdonald sisters enthusiastically took to embroidery after being trained by Jessie Newbery at the Glasgow School of Art. They truly adhered to Arts and Crafts ideals, displaying economy in their choice of fabrics: calico and linen were the favored backgrounds for their appliqué designs. A similarly humble aesthetic was being revived in Scandinavia through the efforts of Fanny Churberg's Friends of Finnish Handicrafts, established in 1879. Indeed, all

Morris & Co. woven woolen textile entitled Bird, designed by William Morris in 1878. It shows a symmetrical repeat image of birds resting and in flight amid dense foliage and flowers including sunflowers, in shades of red, beige, and olive green. *c. 1880* 29 in (73.5 cm) high **$600–900 PC**

KEY POINTS

The Arts and Crafts movement coincided with an explosion of interest in the crafts of needlework and embroidery. From crewelwork to tapestry, and from calico to silk, top-quality textiles of all descriptions flourished. Motifs were drawn almost exclusively from the natural world, as were the dyes used to illustrate them. The masses were catered to with machine-patterned versions of expensive hand-stitched designs.

Crewelwork bed cover embroidered with colored threads showing highly stylized flowerheads and leaves, emphasized with cross-hatched stitching, on broad sinuous stems interspersed with tiny red florets and leaves. The pattern also includes exotic birds in flight, exotic fruits, and acorns and oak leaves; on a pale linen background. *c. 1910* 98½ in (250 cm) wide **$600–900 ATL**

Printed linen design by C. F. A. Voysey, printed by G. O. and J. Baker, featuring scrolling leaves, flowers, and birds in muted organic colors, all against a dark blue ground. *1893.* **NPA V&A**

across Europe the textiles industry was flourishing. The Wiener Werkstätte, best known for its metalware, was enjoying great success with a range of beaded bags and lace, although it was not until 1910 that a specialized textile division was added. Dagobert Peche was instrumental in leading the Werkstätte down this avenue, and it is his abstract designs that have proved the most enduring. Some of Carl Otto Czeschka's designs are more aligned with

the British pastoral model, such as his Waldidyll pattern, which features fauns facing each other amid heavily stylized foliage.

STATESIDE TEXTILES

The Royal School of Art Needlework, such an important hub of the embroidery revival in England, provided the spark for a similar renaissance in the United States after an exhibit at the Philadelphia Centennial Exposition in 1876. Closely tied to the issue of women's emancipation, needlework was considered both an expedient means of decorating a home and a suitable channel for women to gain a little financial independence. Pillows picked out with aphorisms, Folk Art motifs such as shamrocks, and the ubiquitous floral motifs began to fill homes across the United States. Candace Wheeler founded the New York Society of Decorative Art and the Women's Exchange to encourage the manufacture and trade of objects crafted by American women.

Later, she joined Louis Comfort Tiffany's embryonic interior-decoration firm, heading its textile department. As part of her work there, Wheeler patented the process of "needleweaving" that gave her embroidered silks and other fabrics a delicate hand-painted aspect. Her clients at this time were drawn from the high society in which she circulated, high art being an expensive commodity.

A more egalitarian stance was taken by organizations such as the Society of Blue and White Needlework in Massachusetts, the members of which sought to keep alive the embroidery techniques of the first settlers.

Wiener Werkstätte silk appliqué textile entitled Mekka, designed by Arthur Berger, showing bell-shaped flowers with colored stamens or petals on sinuous stems from which sprout dark green leaves and tiny pale blue florets; on a light background. *1911–13 37½ in (95 cm) long* **$1,000–1,500 WROB**

Embroidered panel stitched in colored threads showing a pair of confronting peacocks with vivid plumage, their tail feathers sweeping behind their bodies. They flank a simplified flowering bush. The panel is stretched and mounted in a simple plain oak frame for use as a firescreen. *c. 1900. 33 in (84 cm) high* **$400–600 WW**

Length of woven cotton with a central repeat pattern of highly stylized plant forms arranged to form a visual grid and flanked by linear banding in olive green against a darker ground. Possibly Austrian. *c. 1910 57½ in (146 cm) long* **$700–1,000 WROB**

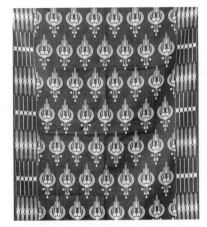

KEY FEATURES

Flat, bold, and closely integrated patterns featuring flowers, fruits, and foliage are typical of Morris's textiles, as well as bird and animal motifs and stylized figures.

Roses, honeysuckles, tulips, strawberries, and pomegranates are favored plants for Morris's decorative designs.

"Aesthetic" colors made from natural animal and vegetable dyes include russet brown, peacock blue, sage green, madder red, and a soft, subtle shade of yellow.

Signature textiles are rendered in colorful wools, printed cottons, linens, and handwoven silk, with delicate embroideries. Pictures, wall panels, and curtains are especially distinctive.

Morris & Co.

Rejecting the poor quality of machine-made textiles, Arts and Crafts pioneer William Morris looked to the past for inspiration, producing designs in vibrant colors that would change the face of home interiors.

The founding father of the Arts and Crafts movement, William Morris (1834–1896) felt an intense antagonism toward the commercial textile production of his day. He preferred to look back to the time-honored techniques of handcraftsmanship, paying tribute to the traditional role of the artist-craftsman.

In 1875, he established Morris & Co., which produced colorful embroideries, printed and woven textiles, wallpapers, carpets, and tapestries that celebrated the delights of the natural world. Morris forged a highly individual and recognizable style that boasted a vocabulary of flat, well-balanced, and integrated patterns of intertwined plants and foliage in a rainbow of rich, sumptuous hues.

Morris's unique, imaginative designs proved to be a pivotal influence on a number of textile designers. Responding to the new fashion for stylish interior decoration, Morris looked to designers such as Walter Crane and C. F. A. Voysey (*see p.26*) to supply the woven and printed textiles, carpets, wallpapers, and tapestries for the coveted "Artistic" home, which rejected the oppressive Victorian taste for heavy draping and gloomy interiors in favor of a light, clean, and less ostentatious style.

Morris's distinctive fabrics and wallpapers boasting complex patterns based on flowers, foliage, and animals became focal points of the Arts and Crafts home in both Europe and the United States. His experiments with natural animal and vegetable dyes resulted in "aesthetic" colors—such as peacock blue, madder red, soft yellow, russet brown, and sage green—that featured prominently in his dense and luxurious nature-inspired motifs.

Above: Strawberry Thief printed-cotton curtain (one of a pair) designed by Morris, with thrushes amid strawberry plants, flowers, and foliage. *c. 1890. 112½ in (286 cm) high* **$300–500 (the pair) L&T**

NATURAL IMAGERY

In the late 19th century, the natural world provided a fertile vocabulary of decorative motifs for wall hangings, carpets, upholstery fabrics, bed coverings, and curtains. William Morris and his followers, both in Europe and the United States, created a host of colorful and distinctive designs based on nature. These included bold renderings of stylized animals, fruits, and berries, luxurious intertwined foliage, birds, human figures, and a wide variety of garden flowers, such as the ever-popular tulips, peonies, and roses, which were arranged in flat, dense patterns.

Compton pattern printed-cotton curtain (one of a pair) designed by J. H. Dearle for Compton Hall, Wolverhampton. It depicts a dense mass of flowers and foliage including poppies, honeysuckle, and small florets. *c. 1900 53¾ in (135 cm) high* **$1,200–1,800 (the pair) L&T**

Evenlode printed-cotton curtain (one of a pair) designed by William Morris. It shows interwoven Persian-style flowerheads, stylized sunflowers, carnations, roses, and foliage. *c. 1900 83½ in (212 cm) high* **$300–500 (the pair) WW**

A CLOSER LOOK

A Garden Piece linen panel embroidered by May Morris in colored silks with trailing flowers and leaves; bearing a card with a signed inscription. *1938*

41 in (104 cm) wide

$500-700　　　　　　**BONM**

Tulip and Rose woven panel designed by Morris and registered as a fabric design in 1876. With a dense symmetrical image of stylized tulips, roses, and foliage. *c. 1885*

37 in (94 cm) long

$800-1,200　　　　　　**WROB**

Detail of the dresses is highlighted with metallic thread

Treatment of the birds and trees is very Scottish in style

Classical architectural columns are entwined with stylized ivy

Irises are symbolic of faith, valor, and wisdom

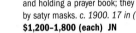

Embroidery (one of pair) believed to be by William Morris. It shows two women holding hands; the figures are thought to be Morris's wife Jane and one of his daughters. Both figures are wearing a medieval costume, and they are linked by garlands of roses and daffodils. *c. 1900. 17 in (43 cm) high*

$1,000-1,500 (each)　JN

Embroidery (one of pair) believed to be by William Morris, showing the two women of the item on the left later in life, after adopting a more pious attitude. Each figure is wearing a robe resembling a habit and holding a prayer book; they are flanked by columns surmounted by satyr masks. *c. 1900. 17 in (43 cm) high*

$1,200-1,800 (each)　JN

Vine and Pomegranate woven woolen curtain (one of a pair) designed by Morris or Kate Faulkner, with foliage and bunches of grapes and pomegranates. *c. 1890*

90 in (230 cm) long

$1,800-2,200 (the pair)　　**L&T**

Strawberry Thief printed-cotton curtain (one of a pair) designed by William Morris. It shows confronting thrushes, plants, and flowers. *c. 1900*

100 in (250 cm) long

$1,200-1,800 (the pair)　　**L&T**

Honeysuckle panel designed by William Morris in 1876, printed and embroidered in wool with honeysuckle, bell-shaped flowers, poppies, and meandering foliage. *c. 1900*

59 in (150 cm) long

$800-1,200　　　　　　**L&T**

Dove and Rose woven panel designed by Morris, in silk on woolen background with doves amid flowers and foliage. Discontinued c. 1905 due to high production costs. *c. 1890*

48 in (122 cm) long

$3,000-5,000　　　　　　**PC**

British Textiles

The use of natural dyes, flat patterns, and English floral motifs was championed by the Arts and Crafts pioneer William Morris, who helped rekindle interest in the "Olde English Garden" and influenced textile companies such as the Silver Studio and Alexander Morton. The botanical studies taught by Christopher Dresser were reflected in popular designs for textiles, carpets, and needlework, such as the embroidery created by Margaret Beale and her daughters. Brightly colored cottons featuring bold patterns of stylized flowers, foliage, birds, and geometric shapes were also favored for curtains and upholstery. British fabrics such as those sold through Liberty & Co. reached a worldwide audience and exerted a strong influence on both European and American textile designers.

Printed-cotton panel attributed to the Silver Studio, with a repeat pattern of stylized geraniums and foliage in shaded pinks and grays against a dark green ground. *c. 1900*

170 in (432 cm) long

$1,800–2,200　　　　　　　　**WROB**

Cotton furnishing fabric by the Silver Studio, with a repeat design of lush poppy blooms, scrolling foliage, and tiny florets in shaded pinks against a gray ground. *1890s*

89¾ in (228.5 cm) long

$1,000–1,500　　　　　　　　**WROB**

Cotton panel (one of a pair) printed in colors with a repeating design of a peacock perched among abundant daisies and leaves against a deep red ground. *1898–1900*

34 in (86.5 cm) long

$1,000–1,500 (the pair)　　　　　　　　**WROB**

Detail of a cotton-and-rayon panel attributed to Arthur Silver, with a tree and stylized stream motif formed as repeating hexagons, in shades of pink, mauve, and white. *c. 1920*

91 in (231 cm) long

$1,800–2,200　　　　　　　　**WROB**

Rectangular embroidered panel featuring a design attributed to Walter Crane and possibly made at the Royal School of Needlework. It is worked in ivory-colored silks, depicting three winged putti with various attributes—including a foliate branch, a dolphin, and a plumed bird—flanked by ribbons and foliage. *c. 1890*

51¼ in (130 cm) wide

$700–1,000　　　　　　　　**DN**

Detail of an Isphurhan velveteen-and-cotton curtain (one of a pair) by Alexander Morton, showing confronting images of birds in red or black flanked by stylized flowers and foliage in pale blue and gray with buff linen borders. *c. 1890*

$1,800–2,200 (the pair)   **L&T**

Crewelwork panel (one of three) worked in colored wools by Lady Phipson Beale, with a symmetrical design of formalized flowers and scrolling foliage against an unbleached linen ground. *c. 1880*

62½ in (159 cm) wide

$1,200–1,800 (the set)   **L&T**

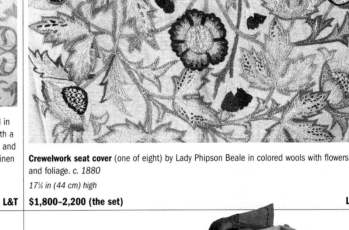

Crewelwork seat cover (one of eight) by Lady Phipson Beale in colored wools with flowers and foliage. *c. 1880*

17¼ in (44 cm) high

$1,800–2,200 (the set)   **L&T**

Donegal woolen carpet by Alexander Morton. With a symmetrical design (attributed to Gavin Morton) of geometric shapes and plant forms in greens, blues, and pale reds, against a madder red field. *c. 1890*

176¼ in (448 cm) long

$1,000–1,500   **L&T**

Scottish rectangular table runner in the manner of Ann Macbeth, worked with geometric linear forms and a checker design in black and white, pale blue, and red wools on an unbleached burlap ground. *c. 1900*

56 in (142 cm) long

$500–700   **L&T**

C. F. A. Voysey

Encouraged by his close friend A. H. Mackmurdo, C. F. A. Voysey designed wallpapers for the firm of Jeffrey & Co. His patterns make ample use of naturalistic flowers, birds, and trees, symbolizing his own deep religious convictions in the joy of pure, unspoiled nature. Voysey's textile designs in the Arts and Crafts style typically feature swans, owls, seagulls, flowers, and foliage in bold, stylized forms. Commercial companies such as Turnbull & Stockdale and Essex & Co. took full advantage of Voysey's design talent, as did the firm of Alexander Morton, who from 1895 hired him to furnish patterns for carpets and textiles.

Voysey Wilton woolen carpet retailed through Liberty & Co. The central symmetrical panel of flowers and foliage in olive greens, pale browns, and white is edged by a broad border of scrolling foliage. *c. 1890*

106¾ in (271 cm) long

$5,000–8,000   **L&T**

Voysey's Adam and Eve watercolor on paper textile design. Voysey's favorite motifs were birds and trees, which he believed symbolized unspoiled nature. *c. 1900*

NPA   **PC**

European and American Textiles

European artists such as Carl Otto Czeschka, Josef Hoffmann, Dagobert Peche, and Alphonse Mucha furthered the Arts and Crafts ideal through textiles. Austria's Wiener Werkstätte produced heavily decorated patterns for silk, cottons, linens, and wools that lent themselves to soft furnishings such as carpets, bed and table covers, draperies, and upholstery fabrics for chairs and sofas. At the same time, in the United States, designer Candace Wheeler founded the Society of Decorative Art. Joining forces with Louis Comfort Tiffany & Associated Artists, Wheeler was responsible for creating the company's colorful, nature-inspired textile patterns.

Waldidyll (Forest Idyll) cotton sample designed by Carl Otto Czeschka and possibly retailed through the Wiener Werkstätte. It shows a white deer crouching amid highly stylized flowering plants with circular and bell-shaped blooms with spiraling stamens, in autumnal colors against black. *1910–11*

15 in (38 cm) wide

$1,200–1,800 **WROB**

English heavy-cotton curtain printed with a symmetrical repeating pattern of formalized poppies and scrolling foliage against a rose-colored ground. *c. 1890*

120 in (305 cm) long

$1,000–1,500 **WROB**

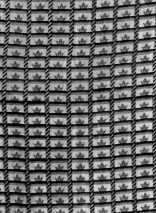

Austrian silk panel entitled Liszt, designed by Dagobert Peche for the Wiener Werkstätte, with stylized red leaves on white rectangles within a red-and-black grid. *1911–13*

40 in (101.5 cm) long

$1,200–1,800 **WROB**

English heavy-cotton curtain printed with a symmetrical repeating pattern of formalized poppies and scrolling foliage against a fuchsia-colored ground. *c. 1890*

65.5 in (166.5 cm) long

$800–1,200 **WROB**

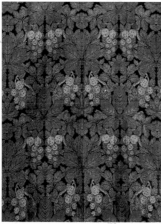

French silk panel woven with a symmetrical repeating image of horsechestnuts amid dense foliage with details highlighted with golden metallic thread. *c. 1900*

81 in (205.5 cm) wide

$3,000–4,000 **WROB**

Dutch mohair-velvet table carpet with a raised-pile pattern of stylized foliate forms in browns extending to yellow flowerheads. It also has a dense border of further floral clusters, as well as foliate and floret bands against an orange-red background. *1900–05*

110¼ in (280 cm) long

$800–1,200 **WROB**

Viennese fine-cotton panel attributed to the Wiener Werkstätte, with a brightly colored zigzag pattern in peach, yellow, and blue against a white background. *c. 1920*

41¾ in (106 cm) long

$2,000–3,000   **WROB**

American Folk Art hooked rug with an oval panel of a cat wearing a pink bow against a cream background; framed by a black border with colored floral decoration. *c. 1920*

32½ in (80 cm) wide

$300–500   **DRA**

American stenciled and embroidered pillow decorated along three edges with a blue, green, and yellow formalized design of dogwood flowers and leaves on linen. *c. 1900*

19½ in (49.5 cm) wide

$80–120   **DRA**

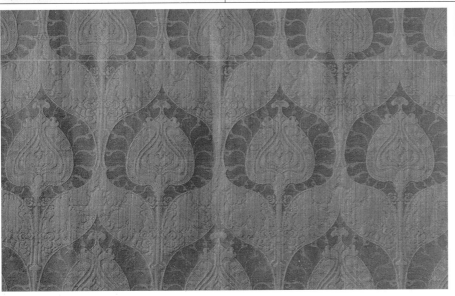

Silk-and-linen weave brocatelle panel with a repeating abstract design of almost heart-shaped motifs reminiscent of poppy flowers and foliage, in shaded reds and pinks. Possibly American. *c. 1900*

12 in (30.5 cm) long

$3,000–5,000   **WROB**

American stenciled and embroidered pillow with a design of a horseshoe and smoking accoutrements flanked by four-leaf clovers and the phrase "Smoke a Pipe for Luck." *c. 1900*

19½ in (49.5 cm) wide

$80–120   **DRA**

American embroidered pillow decorated in red, pink, and white with three stylized floral motifs resembling honeysuckle with slender stems on loosely woven ground. *c. 1900*

19½ in (49.5 cm) wide

$80–120   **DRA**

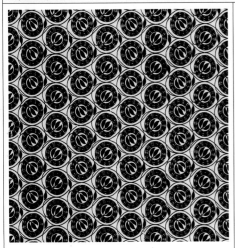

Printed cotton panel entitled Luchs (Lynx), by Josef Hoffmann, with a repeat pattern of black foliate roundels, each enclosing three leaves, against a white ground. *1910–12*

37 in (94 cm) long

$2,000–3,000   **WROB**

Velvet panel printed with a sinuous border of tulips and undulating foliage in soft colors with darker outlines against a peach-colored ground. *c. 1900*

118 in (300 cm) long

$2,000–3,000   **WROB**

American circular linen tablecloth embroidered with naturalistic red poppies in bloom, seed pods, and green foliage on an oatmeal ground; with a tasseled edge. *c. 1900*

39 in (99 cm) wide

$800–1,200   **DRA**

Ceramics

The principles of handcraftsmanship promoted by the Arts and Crafts movement were eminently applicable to the creation of ceramic objects. The motto coined by the successful American ceramicist Ernest Batchelder— "No two tiles are the same"—expressed a sentiment that even the largest ceramics factories were eager to embrace.

It was often the solitary artist, unfettered by the corporate machinery of a large organization, who came closest to achieving the Arts and Crafts ideal. In the United States, George Ohr personally carried out each stage of production at his pottery in Biloxi, from digging his own clay, to molding, firing, and decorating the finished product. In England, William de Morgan started his career as a potter by decorating mass-produced tiles, although he soon rejected this practice in favor of manufacturing his own biscuit. Like Ohr, he involved himself with every stage of the tile-decorating process.

Larger potteries, such as the Martin Brothers in Southall, tended to divide labor so that one person or a team of people could specialize in one aspect of production. Most Arts and Crafts ceramics studios followed this practice to a greater or lesser extent, since it allowed for a more economical use of resources and permitted craftsmen to develop their skills to a very high standard within a specific role. Rookwood built an extremely successful business on this model, employing designers, potters, and artists to work in turn on each of their products.

At the farthest end from the artist-potter ideal were large established firms that hired graduates from art schools in what was only a superficial homage to the Arts and Crafts philosophy. Hannah Barlow, who was employed by Doulton & Co., is a classic example of someone devoted to the Arts and Crafts idiom working under the auspices of a corporation that had little more than a commercial interest in the movement.

William de Morgan pottery tile painted with radiating flowers and leaves. Known as Bedford Park Daisy, this design was made for architect Norman Shaw's West London development.
c. 1885. 6 in (15 cm) square **$700–1,000 PC**

THEMES AND MOTIFS

As much as production methods and company structures differed, certain thematic currents can be traced through the various Arts and Crafts potteries. Sculpted and applied floral forms, for example, proliferated throughout the period, especially in the United States, where Roseville, Fulper, and Hampshire all produced various designs featuring flowers and plant forms in relief. Grueby is especially noted for the tooled and applied leaves that adorn many of its vessels. Rookwood developed this theme further, embossing vases and bowls with motifs as diverse as peacock feathers and seahorses.

Although figural ceramics did not sit well with the utilitarian disposition of the Arts and Crafts movement, the Martin Brothers became famous for creating grotesque birds, dogs, and fantastical creatures. By way of contrast, most of the brothers' vessels were comparatively pedestrian in their adherence to classical forms.

This renewed interest in classicism pervaded the decorative arts at the time and, merged with the Arts and Crafts ideals of individual craftsmanship, resulted in the artistic reinterpretation of time-honored

William Moorcroft Florian Ware ovoid vase tube-lined with stylized peacock feathers graduating in size. The eyes are surrounded by tiny florets and feathery plumage in dark and pale blues. c. 1900. 14¼ in (36 cm) high **$4,000–6,000 RUM**

shapes such as the baluster and the urn. George Ohr's pinched and twisted versions of archaic forms are a fine example of this attitude.

Other potters frequently used these classical shapes in their original state as canvases to showcase a glaze or a finish. Bright colors, such as the flambé glazes employed by Fulper and Moorcroft, and Pilkington's lustrous Lancastrian wares, provide a stark contrast to the more subdued and muted finishes used by the likes of Van Briggle and the Martin Brothers.

Numerous matt-finish glazes were developed during the period in which Arts and Crafts flourished, many of them particularly suited to either the forms they were applied to (the matt green on Teco's vegetal wares) or the subject matter of the decoration (the Vellum Glaze on Rookwood's misty landscapes). These matt glazes worked well with the soft grain and texture of much Arts and Crafts oak furniture. The incorrigibly contrary George Ohr eventually rejected the entire concept of glazing, or "adulterating," his work: "God put no color in souls so I'll put no color on my pots."

EASTERN INFLUENCES

The explosion of interest in glazes and finishes was, to some extent, the result of a new internationalism that was part and parcel of the Arts and Crafts aesthetic. The medievalism of William Morris had inspired an exploration of other feudal societies, such as Persia and Japan. Japanese art was also becoming increasingly available in the US following the end of the Edo period of Japanese isolation. Maria Longworth, founder of the Rookwood pottery, had been

KEY POINTS

Ceramicists working within the Arts and Crafts idiom focused a great deal of their attention on glazes. Developments in this field made a huge variety of textures, colors, and effects available to potters, from the rich luster of Pilkington's Lancastrian range to the more subdued matt greens of Grueby and Teco ware. Natural themes abounded, although they were subverted into grotesque caricatures by the Martin Brothers.

William de Morgan part-tile panel decorated in the Persian manner with fruiting trees, an arch, and a terrace. Designed as a frieze for the HMS *Arabia*, this panel was not used on the ship, which was torpedoed during World War I, and was probably made as a spare. c. 1890 34½ in (87.5 cm) high **$20,000–30,000 PC**

Pilkington Lancastrian vase designed by Gordon M. Forsyth. It is painted with foliage and what resemble stylized pomegranates in a silvery-gold luster against a flamelike orange-and-red ground. *1912 13½ in (34.5 cm) high* **$5,000–8,000 WW**

Martin Brothers stoneware model of a grotesque bird with a removable head. The creature rests on a circular base and has its beak open expectantly. Its plumage is decorated in green, brown, and ocher. *c. 1890. 7¾ in (20 cm) high* **$15,000–20,000 WW**

London house, he employed the talents of William de Morgan to augment the Persian wall tiles installed throughout the room. De Morgan's research into, and emulation of, Eastern ceramics led to some remarkable breakthroughs, not least his rediscovery of the technique of luster glazing.

LOOKING TO THE PAST

The medieval tenor at work in the distorted features of the Martin Brothers' birds, reminiscent of church gargoyles, is a manifestation of the atavistic tendencies so frequently exhibited in Arts and Crafts production. In the United States, a number of potters appropriated American Indian themes and styles to compensate for their historical exile from European heritage. Rookwood produced a number of wares with naturalistic portraits of native American subjects, and Clifton developed a range of wares with geometric patterning based on motifs used by various indigenous tribes, such as the Arkansas and Homolobi.

Alongside these tributary motifs, the most widespread decorative theme was the native flora and fauna of the North American landscape. American ceramicists wholeheartedly adopted the pastoral essence of British Arts and Crafts, resulting in a joyous celebration of the abundance and variety of the New World.

impressed by an exhibition of Japanese ceramics in Philadelphia in 1876, and this influence is clear in the wares produced by her company. Royal Worcester and Minton also experimented with the Japanese style at around the same time.

The "Hindoo style" of architecture and interior decoration had been growing in popularity in the West since the early 19th century, when John Nash's Brighton Pavilion became a benchmark by which high society measured chic. When Frederick Leighton, an avid Islamicist, built the Arab Hall within his

Rookwood Jewel porcelain tall and slender baluster vase painted by Carl Schmidt with tall naturalistic irises in soft pastel colors of lavender, white, and green against a shaded pale blue and white ground. *1925. 11¾ in (30 cm) high* **$20,000–30,000 DRA**

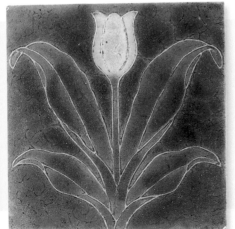

Grueby Pottery Cuenca tile with a textured oatmeal surface. The impressed design of a tulip is decorated with a pale yellow bloom flanked by leaves against a green ground. *c. 1905 6 in (15 cm) square* **$4,000–6,000 DRA**

George Ohr flambé glazed large globular teapot with a loop handle, a serpentine spout, and a drop-in cover with a pointed finial. The teapot is covered overall with a rich glaze shading from blood red through amber, white, and emerald green. *c. 1895 9 in (23 cm) wide* **$30,000–50,000 DRA**

KEY FEATURES

Fanciful and highly original salt-glazed stoneware creatures include birds and animals with human features; grinning, sneering, and grimacing human faces; menacing goblins; and mythical dragons.

A muted palette of cream, gray, brown, blue, and yellow is typical of Martin wares.

Ceramics made in Southall between 1882 and 1914 are nearly always incised "RW Martin & Brothers London & Southall," along with a number and date, while early pieces are signed "Martin."

Martin Brothers

The eccentric Martin Brothers created some of the most original and amusing pottery in the spirit of the Arts and Crafts movement to emerge from Great Britain in the second half of the 19th century.

Among the most creative and imaginative studio potteries working in the Arts and Crafts style was that established by the Martin Brothers in Fulham, London, in 1873. Led by Robert Wallace Martin (1843–1923), who studied at the Lambeth School of Art and began his career working as a freelance artist for the Doulton pottery (*see pp.90–91*), the Martin enterprise was a highly successful collaboration that produced a formidable range of fanciful and amusing salt-glazed stoneware objects.

Each brother contributed to an important aspect of the family business. Walter Frazer (1857–1912) was responsible for throwing pottery shapes, developing colored glazes, and creating much of the incised decoration. Chief decorator Edwin (1860–1915) specialized in marine scenes and aquatic motifs; and Charles (1846–1910) served as a part-time business administrator.

In 1877, the pottery moved to larger premises in Southall, Middlesex, where the Martin team continued to create a celebrated menagerie of finely modeled stoneware. Whimsical creatures—owls and parrots, toads, fish, hedgehogs, armadillos, and salamanders, often with grinning human features—were joined by an array of menacing goblins, dragons, and grotesque faces in a collection of imaginative vases, tobacco jars, water jugs, and punch bowls. Mottled "orange peel" salt-glazes in muted shades of cream, gray, brown, blue, and yellow were cleverly combined to create realistic surface effects.

The company also produced useful wares decorated with incised patterns of scrolling foliage that were inspired by the popular designs of William Morris (*see pp.72–73*). The Martin ceramics works closed in 1914.

Above: Salt-glazed stoneware grotesque modeled as a two-legged creature with a gargoylelike face, in shades of brown and blue. *1894 4¾ in (12 cm) wide* **$3,500–4,500 WW**

GROTESQUE IMAGERY

The taste for the bizarre motifs that characterize the salt-glazed stoneware objects created by the Martin Brothers has its origins in the decoration of the ancient subterranean ruins—or *grotte*—from Roman antiquity that were rediscovered during the Renaissance. In the 19th century, the fashion for Gothic style saw furniture, ceramics, and metalwork decorated with a variety of exotic, fanciful beasts. Robert Wallace Martin was a trained sculptor, and he was surely fascinated by the Neo-Gothic grotesque gargoyles and heraldic imagery he had seen as a stone-carver at London's Houses of Parliament.

Salt-glazed stoneware bird-jar from the grotesque aviary series. This late example, with a broad beak and squinting eyes, is incised and painted in shades of blue, ocher, and green. *1909 9¾ in (25 cm) high* **$15,000–20,000 WW**

THE MARTIN BROTHERS

Square-section stoneware vase with everted rim. Its body has sgraffito panels of exotic fish and other marine creatures painted in blues, greens, and browns on an off-white ground. *1903*

9½ in (24 cm) high

$4,000–6,000 L&T

Ovoid stoneware vase with sgraffito and painted Turk's-cap lilies in shades of green and brown on a mottled cream ground. *1885*

9½ in (24 cm) high

$2,500–3,000 WW

Salt-glazed stoneware vase of double-gourd form, with pierced center band, incised and painted panels of flowers, and scrolling foliage in shades of blue and brown. *1875*

16 in (41 cm) high

$5,000–7,000 WW

Stoneware gourd-shaped vase with a long neck and everted rim, vertically lobed in blue. Each panel is scalloped in black against a blue-gray ground. *1903*

7¼ in (18.5 cm) high

$800–1,200 DN

Stoneware seated Toby dog with a gargoyle-like face above a ruffled collar. It is incised and painted in mottled shades of green and blue. *1890s*

4¾ in (12 cm) high

$15,000–20,000 WW

Stoneware bird jar modeled as an owl with a short, hooked beak and rosette eye feathers. Painted in blues, greens, and ocher, and with a metal collar on the inside rim. *1899*

9¼ in (23.5 cm) high

$20,000–30,000 DRA

Stoneware bird jar modeled with a large beak and supercilious smiling expression. Naturalistically incised and painted in shades of blue, green, and brown. *1897*

11 in (28 cm) high

$30,000–40,000 WW

Stoneware Monk bird jar modeled with a shaved head and solemn expression. Painted in shades of blue, green, and ocher, and with a metal collar on the inside rim. *1905*

9½ in (24 cm) high

$15,000–20,000 WW

Moorcroft marks vary—from "W Moorcroft Des" or "WM des" on Florian ware from the MacIntyre period, to "Moorcroft Burslem," impressed with either "WM" or "W. Moorcroft" for wares produced in his own Burslem factory.

Tube-lined decoration was favored for much of Moorcroft's ceramic ware.

Pottery shapes were inspired by Persian, Iznik, classical Roman, Etruscan, and Far Eastern ceramics.

Stylized patterns of flowers, birds, peacock feathers, and landscapes rendered in vibrant colors are typical decoration, with the painting frequently extending over the vessel's rim.

Moorcroft

Following in the Arts and Crafts tradition established by William Morris, Staffordshire-born ceramicist William Moorcroft earned a reputation for his distinctive, exuberant, and colorful art pottery.

William Moorcroft (1872–1945) began his prolific career in 1897 as a designer for the firm of James MacIntyre & Co. in Burslem, Staffordshire, where he was soon appointed as director of the art-pottery department. His successful designs for practical tea- and tableware, along with a range of art-pottery vases, biscuit barrels, jugs and jardinières, found inspiration in the ceramics of Turkey, China, and Japan, and the Etruscan and classical Roman civilizations.

From the beginning, Moorcroft's earthenware pottery was embellished with stylized floral arrangements and landscapes painted in vivid shades of blue, yellow, and red.

Among his most distinctive designs were his Aurelian line of domestic wares—transfer-printed and colored with

red and blue enamels highlighted with gilding—and the celebrated range of handmade Florian vases, which were decorated with formal patterns of brightly painted flower blossoms, foliage, and peacock feathers. To add surface texture, Moorcroft lavishly employed the decorative technique known as tube-lining, in which creamy, semiliquid slip is piped in thin trails onto the body of a vessel to create ornamental relief patterns that can be filled in with colored glazes.

In 1913, Moorcroft left MacIntyre & Co. to set up his own ceramics factory in Burslem. He continued to expand his oeuvre to include an extensive assortment of designs—such as Pansy, Orchid, and Leaf and Berry—in a variety of bright colorways and including a popular range of wares decorated with a combination of sumptuous flambé glazes.

Above: Persian-style footed vase with oval body and cupped neck, and a Poppies & Forget-Me-Nots pattern in shades of blue, pink, yellow, and green. *c. 1905. 6 in (15.25 cm) high* **$3,000–4,000 RUM**

LIBERTY PIECES

The collaboration between Moorcroft and Liberty & Co. is almost as old as the firm itself. William Moorcroft's first range of Florian ware was retailed at the Regent Street store, and it was Liberty money that financed the construction of Moorcroft's Cobridge works in 1913. The Flamminian Ware range, with its use of Celtic roundels, was enthusiastically adopted by the department store as a typical exponent of the "Liberty style," while the Claremont pattern is so called due to Liberty's application of that moniker to the toadstool design.

Moonlit Blue–pattern vase with tall, leafy trees and rolling hills, characteristic of Moorcroft's later landscape patterns. It is rendered in shades of blue, green, and ocher on a mottled powder blue ground. *c. 1920 8½ in (21.5 cm) high* **$2,000–3,000 WW**

Claremont-pattern biscuit box of square section with twin strap handles and a loop-handled cover. Decorated with toadstools in lemon, red, violet, and olive green on a mottled olive green ground. *1903–13 6½ in (16.5 cm) high* **$3,000–4,000 DN**

Shouldered, tapering ovoid vase with a grapevine pattern in shades of pink, brown, blue, and green on an off-white ground. Designed for Liberty & Co. *1906–10*

4¾ in (12 cm) high

$1,800–2,200   **RUM**

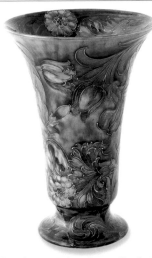

Footed, trumpet-shaped vase with a flowing, lively, floral-based Spanish pattern in rich reds, yellows, greens, and blues. Also made in other colors, notably greens and blues. *c. 1910*

8½ in (22 cm) high

$6,000–9,000   **RUM**

Moonlit Blue–pattern vase of baluster shape, depicting a landscape of tall, willowy trees and rolling hills in shades of blue and green on a powder blue ground. *c. 1920*

12½ in (31.5 cm) high

$6,000–9,000   **RUM**

Eventide-pattern ovoid vase in rich, warm shades of orange, red, and green. Like Moonlit Blue, this is one of the later landscape patterns. *c. 1925*

9¼ in (23.5 cm) high

$5,000–8,000   **RUM**

Chalicelike vase with everted rim, displaying an early Pomegranate. It is characterized by delicate slip trailing and a mottled green ground. Made for Liberty & Co. *1910–13*

6 in (15.25 cm) high

$1,800–2,200   **GORL**

Tudric Moorcroft preserve pot retailed by Liberty & Co., with a cover of Tudric pewter and a body with a Leaf & Fruit pattern under a light flambé glaze. *1920s*

4 in (10 cm) high

$500–800   **WW**

A CLOSER LOOK

Post-1916, Pomegranate has purple and blue grounds

Pattern is drawn in an exotic and sensual style

Richness of later Pomegranate colors is enhanced by a flambé glaze

Baluster-shaped, flambé-glazed Pomegranate vase in deep purples and blues. Made from 1910 until the late 1930s, Pomegranate was Moorcroft's most successful design. Drawn in an exotic, sensual style, earlier examples (such as the footed vase, *above left*) had mottled pale green or yellow grounds. *1916–20*

10 in (25.5 cm) high

$1,800–2,200 WW

Circular Flamminian Ware bowl with twin loop handles, retailed by Liberty & Co. Encircled by Japanese or Celtic foliate roundels, it is finished in a streaky, bright-red luster glaze. *1905–15*

7½ in (19 cm) wide

$400–600   **L&T**

KEY FEATURES

Decorative motifs on tiles and ceramics are typically embellished with rich colors—ruby red, soft golds and yellows, vivid purple, green, and turquoise blue.

Handmade works produced in the Merton Abbey workshops of William Morris boast the gold, red, and bluish-gray glazes found on 15th- and 16th-century Persian and Hispano-Moresque wares.

Flat patterns with stylized flowers and leaves, fish, birds, and mythical animals are painted to adapt to the shapes of vessels and tiles.

William de Morgan

The Arts and Crafts pioneer William de Morgan was instrumental in reviving handicrafts and elevating standards of decorative design with richly glazed, vibrantly colored tiles and ceramics inspired by the ancient past.

William de Morgan (1839–1917) was one of the most important and prolific pottery designers and a pioneer of the Arts and Crafts movement. He trained at the Royal Academy Schools before joining the influential circle of artist-craftsmen led by William Morris (*see pp.22–23*) and Edward Burne-Jones in the early 1860s. In London, at Morris & Co., de Morgan produced tiles and pottery with bird, animal, plant, and grotesque designs, and his early stained-glass work is reflected in the use of sumptuous, exotic colors—delicate golds, rich ruby reds, and the vivid purple, green, and turquoise blue found on 15th- and 16th-century Iznik and Persian ceramics.

By 1872, de Morgan had established his own pottery and showroom in Chelsea, where he experimented with enamel techniques and luster glazes. After moving to Morris's specially built Merton Abbey workshops in 1882, he specialized in handmade tiles and created a range of ceramics with gold, scarlet, and blue-gray glazes inspired by Hispano-Moresque and Persian wares. De Morgan proved to be an expert in harmonizing flat patterns to luxuriant effect, with individual motifs—leaves and flowers, mythical animals, fish, eagles, and peacocks—painted with great energy and well suited to the shapes of the vessels or tiles on which they are painted. These remain among his most memorable designs.

In 1888, de Morgan founded a pottery factory at Sands End, Fulham, in collaboration with Halsey Ricardo, and it was here that he produced some of his finest work, including his Moonlight and Sunlight series of ceramics embellished with double- and triple-luster effects. Ill health eventually drove de Morgan to Florence, where he set up a studio and supplied the Italian pottery Cantagalli with his imaginative designs.

Above: Ruby luster tile painted by Charles and Fred Passenger with fan-shaped flowers and foliage on a white ground. *1898-1907* *6 in (15.5 cm) wide* **$400–600 DN**

PERSIAN INFLUENCE

One of the most pivotal decorative influences on de Morgan's studio ceramics was pottery made in Persia (now Iran) from the 8th century onward. Persian pottery exercised considerable influence on Chinese porcelain, and the early blue-and-white wares of the Ming Dynasty in China were in turn much copied by Persian artisans. Both Turkish and European pottery drew inspiration from traditional Persian techniques, such as luster-painting and monochrome-glazed wares. Typical colors include cobalt blue, yellow, manganese purple, red, and green.

Iznik-style vase with cover, painted by Joe Juster with stylized flowers and leaves in strong Persian colors—blue, turquoise, and olive and pale green—on a white ground. *c. 1890. 10¾ in (27.5 cm) high* **$6,000–9,000 WW**

Persian-style vase painted by Joe Juster at the Sands End Pottery with bands of carnation sprays in pink and green on turquoise, between deep-blue foliage. *1888-98. 8¼ in (21 cm) high* **$2,000–2,500 WW**

Iznik-style glazed tile made at Merton Abbey with flower and leaf decoration in shades of green, blue, and white. *1882–88*

8 in (20.5 cm) wide

$700–1,000   **L&T**

Sands End tile (one of a set of eight) with Boston-design flowering sprigs in green and turquoise on a white ground. *1888–1907*

8 in (20.5 cm) wide

$1,200–1,800 (the set)   **L&T**

Rosettelike circular dish molded in relief with concentric bands of stylized petals under silver and copper luster glazes. *1891*

8¼ in (21 cm) wide

$1,000–1,500   **L&T**

Circular ruby luster charger painted with a fantastical fish and stylized scrolling foliage on a white ground. *1880s*

14¼ in (36.5 cm) wide

$3,000–4,000   **L&T**

Twin-handled urn in shades of turquoise, blue, and green, painted with birds perched among fruiting trees in a landscape; the cover is painted with flying birds. *1890s*

19 in (48.25 cm) high

$5,000–7,000   **L&T**

Deep, circular punch bowl decorated on the exterior with fan-shaped flowers and leaves in a pale ruby luster, and inside with a central rosette on a ruby luster ground. *1890s*

13 in (33 cm) wide

$600–900   **L&T**

Deep Iznik-style bowl decorated on the exterior with curled fronds, flowers, and leaves. The interior depicts tulip flowers within a blue stellar band. *1890–1907*

10¼ in (26 cm) wide

$3,000–5,000   **L&T**

Persian-style twin-handled vase with a conical body decorated in red luster with mythical feline beasts, flowers, and foliage on a white ground. *1890s*

7¼ in (18.5 cm) high

$1,200–1,800   **WW**

KEY FEATURES

A variety of shapes was produced by Pilkington and embellished with distinctive glazes, ranging from the celebrated Sunstone (1893) to Eggshell (1896) and luster glazes (1906).

The Royal Lancastrian range of ceramics—launched in 1903—looked for inspiration to natural forms, as well as to Greek, Persian, and Chinese pottery shapes.

Decorative patterns include flowers, foliage, and geometric designs, along with colorful interpretations of chivalric and romantic themes.

Pilkington

Pilkington's Royal Lancastrian Pottery and Tile Co., which was established in Clifton Junction, near Manchester, in 1892, became a byword for high-quality decorative pottery in the Arts and Crafts style.

The owners of glasshouses and coal mines, the Pilkington family collaborated with the Burton brothers—William, previously a chemist at the Wedgwood Factory, and Joseph, who was placed in charge of operations. Initially focusing on the production of architectural tiles, by 1897 the Pilkington factory had begun to experiment with decorative domestic ware embellished with animal, foliate, floral, and geometric patterns, and highlighted with richly colored glazes. The ceramics were shown to great acclaim at the 1900 Paris Exposition.

Until 1903, when the company started large-scale production, vases were mostly modeled on the factory premises; occasionally, however, they were made elsewhere and then brought to the Lancastrian factory to be glazed. Endless experiments eventually saw the Burton brothers develop a hard, richly colored transparent glaze that became the hallmark of the company, along with a new process for decorating in luster.

Decorative designs for dishes, vases, and tiles—with flat areas of color and simple asymmetrical forms—were furnished by the Arts and Crafts illustrator and decorator Walter Crane (1845–1915). Meanwhile, Morris disciples C. F. A. Voysey (1857–1941) and Lewis F. Day (1845–1910) were inspired by themes of romance and chivalry.

From 1903, Pilkington wares were sold under the title of Royal Lancastrian. The production of ornamental ceramics ceased in 1937, although tiles continued to be manufactured. The pottery reopened in 1948 and enjoyed nearly another decade of success, until 1957.

Lancastrian-range tile by Edmund Kent, tube-lined with a galleon at sea in shades of red, green, blue, and turquoise on a white ground. *1900-13. 4 in (10 cm) wide* **$180–220 WW**

LUSTER GLAZES

Celebrated on Hispano-Moresque pottery and Italian majolica, the shiny, iridescent metallic surface known as luster-glazing originated in Mesopotamia and Persia in the 8th century. It was created by painting a mixture of gold, silver, or copper pigments made from metallic oxides suspended in oil onto the face of a ceramic vessel. A thick coating of pigment resulted in the vessel resembling a piece of burnished copper, while thinner films produced more subtle iridescent effects. The ancient technique of luster-glazing was rediscovered in 19th-century England, most notably by William de Morgan and the Staffordshire potteries, before becoming a Pilkington hallmark.

Lancastrian-range vase by Gordon Forsyth. Of shouldered cylindrical form, it is luster-decorated with a winged classical figure and horses between cypress trees. *c. 1910 9 in (23 cm) high* **$1,800–2,200 WW**

Royal Lancastrian-range vase by Richard Joyce. Its footed, ovoid body is sgraffito-decorated and shows an ibex set against a streaked panel. *1913-20 6 in (15.5 cm) high* **$800–1,200 WW**

A CLOSER LOOK

Lancastrian-range vase designed by Annie Burton. Its footed ovoid body is decorated with flowers and foliage in polychrome luster glazes on a mottled ocher ground. *1908–14*

4 in (10 cm) high

$600–900 **WW**

Lancastrian-range vase designed by Walter Crane and painted by William S. Mycock. The frieze around its perimeter depicts lions en passant—a popular Arts and Crafts motif, along with knights and dragons. They are in gold luster on a uranium-red luster ground, a favorite Mycock combination. *1907–10*

5 in (13 cm) high **$2,000–3,000** **WW**

Alternating insect and floral motifs

From c. 1905 to c. 1914, Pilkington wares carried a seal mark "P" with two honeybees. Better pieces also bore a designer's and/or painter's mark(s); here, Walter Crane (left) and William S. Mycock (right).

Royal Lancastrian-range vase by Richard Joyce, modeled in low relief with a frieze of deer between trees painted in uranium orange-vermilion luster glazes. *1914–20*

8¼ in (21 cm) high

$400–600 **WW**

Royal Lancastrian-range vase designed by Edward Radford and painted by Gwladys M. Rogers. Its ovoid body is painted with a foliate-motif pattern. *1914–20*

9 in (23 cm) high

$120–180 **WW**

Lancastrian-range baluster-shaped vase by William S. Mycock, with cranes flying between foliage above a lake, in shades of pink, green, lavender, and orange on a blue ground. *1911*

8¼ in (21 cm) high

$1,000–1,500 **WW**

Royal Lancastrian-range vase modeled and painted by Richard Joyce, its ovoid body decorated with a simple geometric pattern under a mottled blue-green glaze. *c. 1920*

5 in (12.75 cm) high

$120–180 **WW**

Lancastrian-range box and cover by Dorothy Dacre. The cover shows a red Tudor rose set in an interlaced and scrolling ivy border in yellow on blue, which also decorates the sides. *1914–20*

4 in (10 cm) wide

$800–1,200 **WW**

Lancastrian-range vase painted by Charles Cundall, with a grapevine pattern in shades of copper, ruby, and gold luster on an underglaze green ground. *1909*

5¾ in (14.5 cm) high

$2,000–3,000 **WW**

Lancastrian-range vase designed by Walter Crane and painted by Richard Joyce, with a frieze of dancing maidens in polychrome luster glazes, including vivid turquoise. *1910–12*

9 in (23 cm) high

$2,000–3,000 **WW**

KEY FEATURES

Clean, simple pottery shapes are the backdrop for incised, modeled, or hand-carved decorative motifs, including animals, birds, beaded borders, flowers, and leaves.

The typical palette includes shades of green, blue, brown, and gray.

All Lambeth stoneware art pottery was unique, decorated by hand, and signed by the designer and/ or marked by the decorator.

The most successful artists at the Doulton factory specialized in particular decorative techniques, such as sgraffito, and their designs are easy to recognize.

Doulton

Like other ceramics manufacturers of the 19th and 20th centuries, the prolific and innovative Doulton & Co. took advantage of opportunities to collaborate with Arts and Crafts designers by establishing an art-pottery studio.

Doulton & Co. has enjoyed a long, distinguished history in the production of ceramics. Founded in 1815 in Lambeth, south London, by John Doulton (1793–1873), the factory initially specialized in utilitarian stoneware such as water filters, sanitation pipes, and chimney pots.

In a bid to emulate the success of the small craft studios that had grown up throughout Great Britain, John Doulton's son Henry (who took over the company in 1854) established an art-pottery studio around 1870 dedicated to handcrafted, hand-decorated ceramic ware. Collaborating with the nearby Lambeth School of Art, over the following decades, Doulton produced a range of decorated stoneware and a line of hand-painted faience. Several designers, painters, and sculptors (among them Frank Butler, Emily Edwards, George

Tinworth, and Arthur, Florence, and Hannah Barlow) contributed to the success of the Doulton studio. Every piece was unique, since the artists were free to choose the form and decoration of their vases, and all wares were signed. Simple shapes influenced by 16th- and 17th-century designs and incised, modeled, or hand-carved motifs featuring animals, birds, and abstract leaf and flower patterns were favored; glazes were typically in a subdued palette of brown, gray, blue, or green.

Doulton's art pottery met with great acclaim at the 1893 International Exhibition in Chicago. In 1877, Doulton assumed control of the former works of Pinder, Bourne & Co. in Burslem, where it produced art ceramics that were distinctly different from the Lambeth wares. The factory was renamed Royal Doulton in 1901.

Above: Lambeth stoneware bottle vase by George Tinworth, with an incised seaweed pattern in shades of blue and brown, and applied scrolling pearls. *1890s. 10½ in (27 cm) high* **$1,000–1,500 WW**

INCISED DECORATION

Favored by Doulton & Co., the practice of scratching into the body or paste of a ceramic vessel with a sharp instrument, such as a metal point, for decoration, or to record a name, date, or inscription, has roots in the pottery of classical antiquity. This decorative technique is commonly known as sgraffito. The design is scratched, or incised, onto the vessel through the slip before glazing in order to reveal the ceramic body beneath, although incising through the glaze will produce a similar effect.

Lambeth stoneware vase by Edith Lupton, incised with stylized foliate forms of Islamic inspiration in shades of brown, green, and white on a blue ground. *1888. 11¾ in (30 cm) high* **$1,200–1,800 WW**

A DOULTON FACTORY WORKER

Pair of Barbotine ovoid vases with *pâte-sur-pâte* wooded landscape patterns in shades of blue, green, and yellow against mottled pale-green grounds. *c. 1900*

8¾ in (22.5 cm) high

$1,000–1,500 (the pair)　　　　　　　　**DN**

Lambeth stoneware vase by Hannah Barlow, of footed and tapering cylindrical form with a sgraffito frieze of grazing goats, in a palette of browns, grays, blues, and greens. *1880–1900*

12 in (31 cm) high

$800–1,200　　　　　　　　**L&T**

Burslem floor vase on stand by Charles Noke. It is incised and painted with a monk strolling amid tall, stylized trees, in shades of green, yellow, and orange. *1900–10*

23¾ in (61 cm) high

$3,500–4,500　　　　　　　　**DRA**

Lambeth shouldered ovoid vase possibly by Edith Lupton, with incised and painted stylized foliate decoration of Islamic inspiration, in a subdued palette of blues and greens. *1886*

18 in (45.75 cm) high

$1,200–1,800　　　　　　　　**GORL**

Lambeth stoneware jardinière by Mark V. Marshall, incised with mythical beasts below a band of scrolling flowers and foliage. *1880s*

6½ in (16.5 cm) high

$1,200–1,800　　　　　　　　**WW**

The influence of Chinese ceramics can be seen in the shapes of Ruskin pottery.

Luster, crystalline, and high-fired glazes in rich, vibrant colors are the main methods of decoration for Ruskin ceramics.

Other glazing techniques employed to decorate Ruskin ceramic wares include "flambé," a lustrous rich crimson with streaks of turquoise blue, and the blue "soufflé." Both of these originated in China.

Ruskin

As the first decade of the 20th century dawned, the Ruskin Pottery of Smethwick produced ceramics in the Arts and Crafts style that challenged popular taste by relying only on elaborate glazing effects for decoration.

Established by William Howson Taylor (1876–1935) in 1898 in West Smethwick, near Birmingham, the Ruskin Pottery paid tribute to the Arts and Crafts champion John Ruskin.

Taylor's father was Edward Richard Taylor, the celebrated principal of the Birmingham School of Art. A friend of both William Morris (*see pp.72–73*) and Edward Burne-Jones, E. R. Taylor was renowned as a pioneer in the teaching of crafts skills. He provided a number of decorative designs for the Ruskin Pottery, while his son experimented with a new clay body for vases that were often rendered in Chinese-inspired shapes.

W. H. Taylor also energetically pursued the study of innovative glazing techniques—including luster, crystalline, and high-fired glazes in vibrant colors—and the mastering of such complex methods as "soufflé" and "flambé" glazes. He exhibited pieces around the world and won many prizes, most notably at the St. Louis Exhibition of 1904.

Although the Ruskin Pottery's achievements were internationally acclaimed, the factory was forced to close in 1935, when W. H. Taylor died and took the secrets of the glazes to his grave.

Above: High-fired stoneware stand of Oriental form, decorated with streaked lavender and sang-de-boeuf glazes over a silver ground. *Early 20th century.* 4¾ in (12 cm) high **$700–1,000** WW

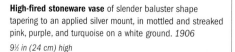

High-fired stoneware tig (a three-handled drinking vessel) decorated with mottled and lustrous sang-de-boeuf and lavender glazes on a white ground. *1933*

7¾ in (20 cm) high

$1,200–1,800 WW

High-fired stoneware vase of slender baluster shape tapering to an applied silver mount, in mottled and streaked pink, purple, and turquoise on a white ground. *1906*

9½ in (24 cm) high

$2,000–3,000 WW

Stoneware vase of ovoid shape decorated with speckled and splashed luster glazes, predominantly in tones of silver and gray, but also in blue and red. *1923*

6 in (15.5 cm) high

$800–1,200 WW

Elton

Although lacking formal training, Sir Edmund Elton managed to establish an influential Arts and Crafts pottery that married styles from past cultures with imaginative shapes and innovative techniques.

A self-taught art potter, Sir Edmund Harry Elton (1846–1920) founded the Sunflower Pottery at his Clevedon Court estate in Somerset, England in 1879. He enthusiastically embraced the Aesthetic movement, and his bold and original handmade Elton Ware—launched in 1882—reflects a broad range of influences, such as Renaissance Italy, ancient Greece, China, and Japan.

Elton is renowned for his vases decorated in relief with flowering branches, as well as for his imaginative pottery forms, which often boasted multiple handles or bizarrely shaped spouts.

He also developed a number of highly successful glazing techniques. Vases, cups, and jugs were often covered with platinum, silver, copper, or streaky gold glazes, or were glazed in several colors that were swirled to create a marbling effect and sometimes embellished with heavily enameled and incised decoration.

After 1902, the Sunflower factory introduced a range of metallic luster glazes over a heavily crackled surface. Elton Ware was exhibited at the Arts and Crafts Exhibition Society in London, and was widely celebrated throughout both Europe and the United States.

Above: Small loop-handled jug with a spout, decorated with medieval-style flowers, streaks, and splashes in blue, red, and green slips under a clear glaze. *c. 1910*
4¾ in (12 cm) high **$400–600 HBK**

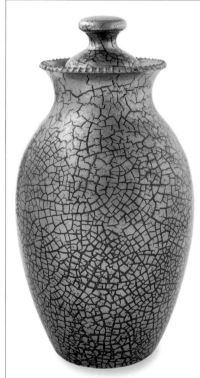

Shouldered ovoid vase and cover finished in a lustrous craquelé metallic glaze comprising a layer of high-fired liquid gold over liquid platinum. *1900–14*
10½ in (26.5 cm) high
$600–900 WW

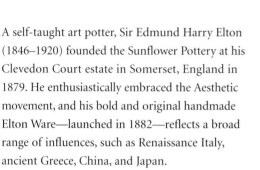

Shouldered ovoid vase with everted rim. The body is slip-decorated with red floral motifs on a mottled and streaked blue, green, and pink ground. *1890s*
9¾ in (24.5 cm) high
$400–600 CHEF

Ovoid vase with a wavy rim. It is slip-decorated with stylized red roses and green, budding stems against a streaked blue, gray, and olive-green ground, under a clear glaze. *1890s*
10¼ in (26 cm) high
$400–600 DN

British Ceramics

In Great Britain, a small but influential band of potters promoted the simple, functional designs championed by William Morris, as well as the elegant Japanese decorative style of the Aesthetic movement. Inspired by the individuality and high quality of their designs, along with a recognition that ceramics were an ideal medium for mass production, several British manufacturers—among them Foley Potteries, Linthorpe Pottery, and C. H. Brannam—produced art-pottery wares, while leading designers, such as Christopher Dresser and Frederick Rhead, experimented with new techniques of potting, glazing, and decorating.

Bernard Moore pottery plate with a portrait design, inspired by *The Laughing Cavalier*, in luster shades of red, orange, and turquoise against a mottled polychromatic ground. *1905–15*
8½ in (21.5 cm) wide

$700–1,000   **TCS**

Foley Potteries Intarsio-ware vase by Frederick Rhead. Its elongated tapering neck has four loop handles and depicts St. Cecilia and, on the sides, birds feeding on berries. *1890s*
16½ in (42 cm) high

$2,000–3,000   **WW**

C. H. Brannam Barum Ware vase with incised and painted slip floral decoration in shades of brown, yellow, and blue. *c. 1890*
7½ in (19.5 cm) high

$300–400   **ADE**

Della Robbia Pottery charger painted with a ship and "DR" in the center and geometric decoration around the edge. *c. 1900*

$3,000–5,000   **BRI**

Foley Potteries Intarsio-ware stick stand with panels of flowers and leaves in yellow, blue, green, and lavender. *1890s*
27¾ in (71 cm) high

$1,200–1,800   **WW**

Della Robbia Pottery vase with sgraffito and painted decoration. *1894–1906*
11 in (28 cm) high

$2,000–3,000   **V&A**

Stoneware charger by Alfred Powell painted with stems and leaves in turquoise and blue, encircled around the blue-lined rim by yellow fruits, all on a white ground. *c. 1900*

12¾ in (33 cm) wide

$800–1,200   WW

Johnson Brothers earthenware plate by J. Selwyn Dunn. Its center is painted with a galleon under full sail, encircled by a foliate border, all in blues and greens on a white ground. *1890s*

12 in (31 cm) wide

$100–200   WW

Christopher Dresser

A visit to Japan and training as a botanist were decisive influences on the ceramic designs of the multitalented Christopher Dresser (1838–1904). He was employed by a number of companies looking to capitalize on the art-pottery fashion, beginning with the commercial Minton concern at Stoke-on-Trent in the 1870s. By 1879 Dresser was art director of the newly established Linthorpe Pottery near Middlesbrough. His inventive and somewhat eccentric forms for Linthorpe wares looked to Japanese ceramics and pre-Columbian wares for inspiration. Dresser had moved on to the Ault Pottery at Swadlincote in Derbyshire by 1892, producing highly original designs for earthenware jugs, vases, and jardinières that were frequently enhanced with a shimmering aventurine glaze. Dresser's work remains the most highly sought after of all ceramics in the Arts and Crafts style.

Christopher Dresser Propeller vase designed for the Ault Pottery. Its fluid, dynamic form and its subtle combination of streaked and mottled blues, greens, and browns are characteristic of Dresser. *1890s*

13 in (33.5 cm) high

$1,800–2,200   WW

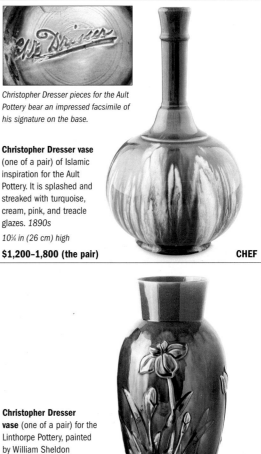

Christopher Dresser pieces for the Ault Pottery bear an impressed facsimile of his signature on the base.

Christopher Dresser vase (one of a pair) of Islamic inspiration for the Ault Pottery. It is splashed and streaked with turquoise, cream, pink, and treacle glazes. *1890s*

10¼ in (26 cm) high

$1,200–1,800 (the pair)   CHEF

Christopher Dresser vase (one of a pair) for the Linthorpe Pottery, painted by William Sheldon Longbottom, and with a molded iris pattern. Decorated in green, brown, and blue glazes. *c. 1880*

19 in (48.5 cm) high

$5,000–7,000 (the pair)   TCS

Brannam trumpet-shaped vase with seven loop handles, by James Dewdney. It features sgraffito and painted slip decoration of fish and aquatic foliage. *1901*

8½ in (22 cm) high

$500–700 DN

Brannam vase (one of a pair) of cylindrical shape with three loop handles, decorated in sgraffito and painted slips with a stork in flight. *c. 1900*

11¾ in (30 cm) high

$400–600 (the pair) DN

Large Brannam twin-handled vase by Frederick Braddon, decorated in sgraffito and painted slips with stylized birds and plant forms. *1904*

19½ in (50 cm) high

$1,200–1,800 PC

Massive Bernard Moore punch bowl of circular form. It is painted in red on a white ground with panels of interlaced Celtic motifs on the exterior, repeated on the interior with a dragon. *1910*

17¾ in (45.5 cm) wide

$1,800–2,200 L&T

Minton tile by John Moyr Smith, with a late medieval scene from Sir Walter Scott's novel *The Fair Maid of Perth* set within floral-motif borders and heraldic shields at two corners. *1880s*

8 in (20.5 cm) square

$120–180

WW

Minton polychrome charger decorated by Louis J. Rhead, with the profile of a young woman depicted in late medieval/early Renaissance style, and encircled by chrysanthemums. *c. 1880*

16¼ in (41.5 cm) wide

$7,000–10,000

L&T

Minton Secessionist-ware vase with tapering body and everted rim, ringed with stylized tree motifs rooted in the base, and tube-lined in brown and green on a blue ground. *c. 1910*

5¼ in (13.25 cm) high

$300–400

ADE

Hancock & Sons Morrisware

Hancock & Sons was a Hanley company founded in the mid-19th century, originally concerned with the production of mass-market home and hotel ware. The firm later began to experiment with art pottery and unveiled its Morrisware range to an approving press and public at the 1918 British Industries Fair. Decorated with a high-gloss glaze and tube-lined patterns, Morrisware is reminiscent of ceramics by Moorcroft, with which it may well have been meant to compete. Pieces are frequently signed by George Cartlidge, who worked on the range between 1918 and 1926, and by Edith Garter, who also contributed designs. Production was halted in 1937.

Hancock & Sons Morrisware vase by George Cartlidge, painted with purple poppies and yellow foliage on a mottled blue ground. *1918–26*

6¾ in (17.5 cm) high

$1,200–1,800

WW

Hancock & Sons Morrisware vase by George Cartlidge, painted with purple bell flowers and yellow leaves on a mottled blue ground. *1918–26*

14½ in (37 cm) high

$2,000–3,000

WW

Oriental shapes are typical, decorated with asymmetrical arrangements of flowers painted in underglaze colored slips on a dark shaded ground.

Sophisticated glazing techniques include the Vellum matt glaze, the Tiger-Eye crystalline glaze featuring flecks of gold, and several types of the Standard Glaze, including Sea Green and Iris.

Rare and distinctive decoration includes portraits of American Indians.

The factory name or an "RP" monogram with a flame feature on most Rookwood wares, as well as the date and the initials or signature of the decorator.

Rookwood

By far the largest and most influential pottery in the United States, Rookwood produced high-quality ceramics that embraced the Arts and Crafts style and enjoyed both critical and commercial success.

Founded in Cincinnati, Ohio, by Maria Longworth Nichols (1849–1932)—and named after the country estate of her father, art patron Joseph Longworth, who provided the capital for the venture—the Rookwood Pottery was established with the specific aim of producing handwrought and hand-decorated art wares.

From the beginning, the factory employed an exceptional team of talented artists and highly skilled technicians and prescribed extremely high standards of production. Rookwood fostered a "spirit of cooperation and good fellowship" among its workmen, according to the socialist writer Oscar Lovell Triggs, who in 1902 called the enterprise "an ideal workshop," where expressions of individuality, travel, study, and experimentation with different decorative styles and techniques were encouraged.

Rookwood earthenware designs embraced a variety of influences, not least the style and quality of Japanese ceramics. A visit to the Philadelphia Centennial Exposition in 1876 so impressed Mrs. Nichols that she invited the Japanese ceramicist Kataro Shirayamadani to join the firm. He became one of the company's most important designers, remaining until his death in 1948. Early Rookwood wares were heavily potted, slip-cast or thrown—often in Japanese-inspired forms—and painted with naturalistic decoration.

NEW GLAZES

Rookwood acknowledged the burgeoning interest in the Arts and Crafts movement and produced hand-carved wares boasting unusual, vibrant

Above: Early, rare portrait plaque made from red clay with an American Indian chief in a headdress painted in black and encircled by geometric motifs. *1881. 11 in (28 cm) wide* **$12,000–18,000 DRA**

AMERICAN INDIAN IMAGES

Many Rookwood wares feature portraits, including a series of vases depicting the Old Masters and another with images of African Americans, but it is the American Indian plaques and vases that are the most distinctive and popular. Usually sealed with Rookwood's trademark Standard Glaze, these portraits are exquisite in their detail and lend dignity to their subjects. Rookwood's best artists, including Grace Young and Matt Daly, contributed highly detailed and realistic portraits to the range. They reflect a growing appreciation of, and respect for, the indigenous cultures of the United States.

Exceptional Standard Glaze plaque painted by Grace Young, in its original frame. It depicts Chief High Hawk in a headdress and with a breastplate and tomahawk. *1903 14¾ in (37.5 cm) high* **$70,000–100,000 DRA**

PHOTOGRAPH OF YANKTON CHIEF

GLAZE DEVELOPMENT

The enduring success of the Rookwood Pottery was largely based on a creative spirit that continuously explored new decorative styles and techniques. Chief among the pottery's most celebrated innovations was a number of distinctive glazes. The earliest— a by-product of Victorian ware, called Standard Brown—featured hand-painted decorative patterns in slip relief beneath a lustrous, glossy finish. Vellum Ware, introduced ten years later in 1900, was celebrated for giving the painted decoration that it covered the soft, diffused look of an Impressionist painting. At about the same time, the company gave a nod to the Art Nouveau movement by developing the Iris Glaze, a clear glossy finish that made possible a sharp, highly realistic display of decorative motifs, including flowers, plants, and occasionally birds or animals.

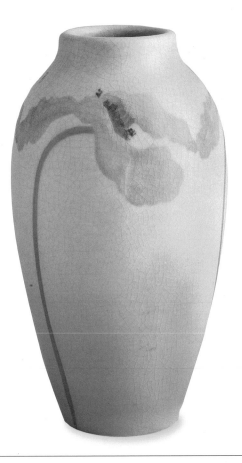

Vellum Ware vase by Sally Coyne, with a stone-gray ground. Its pink-poppy decoration is slightly diffused by the Vellum Glaze, giving it a subtle Impressionist appearance. *1908 2¾ in (7 cm) high* **$600–900 DRA**

matt overglazes. Quick to recognize the commercial potential created by the use of sophisticated glazing techniques, the company employed talented designers to experiment with richly colored, high-quality matt glazes. Among these artists was Artus Van Briggle (*see pp.116–17*), whose tenure at Rookwood spanned some 13 years before he left to set up his own studio.

CONTINUED INNOVATION

Rookwood pottery typically features a delicately applied slip in brown, yellow, and ocher on dark grounds, covered with a clear glossy glaze known as Standard Rookwood. Conceived by artist Laura Fry, the Standard Glaze saw color applied with an atomizer to give the ground a graduated shaded effect that moved from one tone to another. Several versions of the Standard Glaze were developed, including Sea Green, the muted gray Iris, and a mottled effect with streaks or flecks of gold known as Goldstone or Tiger-Eye.

The company continued to experiment, and in 1892, it introduced the decorative effect of silver appliqué, adding to its considerable output of useful wares, ceramic portraits, figures, animals,

birds, and tiles. In 1904, Rookwood patented a matt glaze called Vellum, which featured decoration of stylized flowers, as well as landscape, forest, and sailboat scenes.

HARDER TIMES

After winning a Grand Prix award at the 1900 Paris Exhibition, Rookwood pottery became ever more fashionable. By adapting to the times, the firm continued to flourish and grow, even surviving the Depression. Rookwood operated with a skeleton staff from late 1931 until the end of World War II, when it was taken over by new owners. However, the company's central focus on art wares had shifted, and it closed in 1967.

Early Japanese-style vase of cylindrical form with a flared rim. It is carved with script and an oriental peasant in high relief, in green, brown, and blue against a tan ground. *1882 11½ in (29.25 cm) high* **$3,000–4,000 DRA**

INSPIRATIONS

Rookwood's artists looked to the natural world for the bulk of their designs: flowers, birds, fish, and the American landscape were depicted in various forms. The Gothic sensibility prevalent at the turn of the 20th century was catered to by Rookwood's range of moody and haunting nursery tiles based on fairy tales and folklore.

THE JAPANESE CONNECTION

Japanese ceramicists used very fine glazes on their wares, a practice that Maria Nichols and Rookwood wholeheartedly embraced. Rookwood's potters adapted Japanese forms, and the artists used Japanese scenes, motifs, and text in their designs.

Standard Glazes

Among the earliest wares produced by Rookwood was the underglaze-painted line known as Standard Brown Glaze. The decoration of bowls, pitchers, vases, wall tiles, tea sets, and candlesticks centered mainly on floral patterns that were covered with a rich, limpid brown overglaze that lent all colors a brownish-yellow hue. The crisp, well-finished pottery was covered with hard and glassy glazes and with painting of the highest quality, and it helped to establish Rookwood's credentials as a well-respected art pottery. Later pieces of Standard Brown Glaze included highly original decoration featuring famous American Indians, historical figures, and American statesmen.

Unusual Standard Glaze basket painted by Harriet E. Wilcox with yellow buds and flowers and large green leaves. It is set in a silver mount by the Gorham Silver Co. *1893*

10½ in (26.5 cm) wide

$1,800–2,200   **DRA**

Baluster-shaped Standard Glaze vase modeled and painted by Kataro Shirayamadani with a panoramic view of two gray birds in flight above crashing deep-green waves, on a brown ground. *1898*

15½ in (39.5 cm) high

$6,000–9,000   **DRA**

Standard Glaze vase painted by Kataro Shirayamadani with orange and golden yellow chrysanthemums and green leaves. The silver mounts are by the Gorham Silver Co. *1898*

12 in (30.5 cm) high

$10,000–15,000   **DRA**

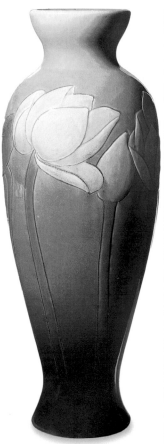

Baluster-shaped Standard Glaze vase by Matthew A. Daly, carved in sharp relief with yellow tulips and green stems. *1899*

14½ in (37 cm) high

$5,000–7,000   **DRA**

Unusual Standard Glaze vase of cylindrical form, painted by William P. McDonald with a nude woman with flowing hair. *1894*

14½ in (37 cm) high

$8,000–12,000   **DRA**

Sea Green Glaze

Introduced in 1894 alongside Aerial Blue and Iris, the Sea Green Glaze proved popular. The quality of the opalescent green-tinted glaze enhanced color and gave a sense of great depth to any surface it covered, usually slip-painted decoration of flowers or marine life, such as fish and water fowl. Like most of Rookwood's richly glazed lines, Sea Green was fraught with technical problems, the most obvious and commonplace being the fine cracks that appear in the glaze but do not penetrate the body—commonly known as crazing. By 1904, the high gloss of the popular Sea Green Glaze had been eclipsed by a new taste for matt glazes (*see p.102*).

Exceptional Sea Green Glaze vase painted by E. Timothy Hurley. It shows a large gray fish swimming in frothy white waves, set against a sandy ground. *1901*

8¼ in (21 cm) high

$15,000–20,000　　　　　　　　　　**DRA**

Sea Green Glaze vase painted by Matthew A. Daly with three large wading birds standing in tall grass against a green-and-brown ground. *1894*

7¼ in (18.5 cm) high

$4,000–6,000　　　　　　　**DRA**

Sea Green Glaze vase by Anne Marie Valentin. The rim and shoulders of its ovoid body are wrapped in a bronze, languid-nude mount with a verdigris patina. *1900*

5¼ in (13.25 cm) high

$12,000–18,000　　　　　　　**DRA**

Iris Glazes

Although the Iris line was officially introduced in 1894, its development had begun as early as 1889. The Iris Glaze was characterized by a clear glossy finish that allowed for a highly realistic display of decorative motifs. These mainly included patterns featuring flowers and plants, although occasionally bird, animal, landscape, and seascape designs were also produced. The background colors typically ranged from light to dark using shades of gray, cream, green, blue, yellow, and pink. A high point of Rookwood's ability to produce wares of unparalleled beauty and creativity, Iris Glaze wares also marked Rookwood's interpretation of Art Nouveau design—colorful and decorated with sinuous flowers that occasionally featured handcarved details.

Very rare Iris Glaze vase by Matthew A. Daly, with a slim, baluster-shaped body. It is carved with fleshy, burgundy-colored poppies, green stems and leaves, and turquoise pods, all set in high relief against a jet black ground. *1900*

13½ in (34.25 cm) high

$50,000–70,000　　　　　　　**DRA**

Iris Glaze landscape vase by Kataro Shirayamadani, with a tapering, cylindrical body. It is painted with a realistic panorama of tall trees and distant mountains around a lake, in celadon, gray, and pink. *1907*

9¼ in (23.5 cm) high

$15,000–20,000　　　　　　　**DRA**

Matt Glaze

For commercial reasons, the Rookwood Pottery paid tribute to the Arts and Crafts movement with its range of Matt Glaze wares introduced in 1901. Two distinct lines, comprising vases, bowls, and other domestic wares, used richly colored matt glazes to decorative effect. The wares were hand-carved in high relief, with flowers and foliage among the favorite decorative motifs, although the occasional sea creature or human figure appears. Another Rookwood Arts and Crafts innovation was the production of matt-painted wares, made by applying an overglaze to highlight the fine decorative detailing of floral and plant patterns.

Wax Matt vase by Albert Pons, with a squat, ovoid body painted with a maplike pattern in shades of green and purple on a pale, sea blue ground. *1907*

8½ in (21.5 cm) wide

$600–900   DRA

Matt Glaze vase by Harriet E. Wilcox, painted with large red chrysanthemums and green leaves against a dark gray and green ground. *1903*

9 in (23 cm) high

$7,000–10,000   DRA

Wax Matt vase by Elizabeth Lincoln, with an impressed floral frieze painted in blue and green below the rim, and a more abstract, orange floral pattern around the base. *c. 1905*

9 in (23 cm) high

$800–1,200   DRA

A CLOSER LOOK

Rare Matt Glaze vase by Kataro Shirayamadani, with an ovoid body modeled in relief with branches of ginkgo leaves and berries under a painted green-and-yellow matt glaze. Typically, the matt glazes impart not only a soft, hazy look to the underlying modeled decoration, but also a greater sense of depth. *1905. 10½ in (26.5 cm) high*
$10,000–15,000 DRA

Naturalistic modeling in relatively shallow relief

Matt glazes are rarely subject to crazing

Vellum Glaze

Introduced in 1900, Rookwood's Vellum Glaze diffused the painted decoration it covered, giving it a decidedly Impressionist appearance. Most pieces of Vellum ware were colored in shades of cream or blue, although a pastel palette including shades of pink, yellow, sky blue, and light green was also used. Most Vellum ware was decorated with flowers and occasionally landscapes, and a specialty product was wall plaques almost entirely glazed with Vellum and featuring river views and undulating, tree-filled landscapes. All pieces of Vellum ware are clearly marked with the company's Rookwood Pottery flame mark, dated in Roman numerals, and incised with a V to signify the Vellum Glaze.

Unusual Vellum Glaze vase painted by Carl Schmidt with different species of wild mushrooms in shades of brown, yellow, orange, and gray against a ground of blue graduating into celadon. *1906*

7 in (18 cm) high

$7,000–10,000

DRA

Vellum Glaze vase by Edith Noonan, painted with swimming trout on a shaded pink, ivory, and teal ground. *1908*

5 in (12.75 cm) wide

$1,200–1,800　　**DRA**

Scenic Vellum Glaze vase with a forest view painted by E. T. Hurley in mellow autumnal colors. *1908*

9 in (22.75 cm) high

$4,000–6,000　　**DRA**

Scenic Vellum Glaze plaque by Fred Rothenbush. In its original frame, and entitled *The Ravine*, it depicts a snowy landscape of a creek running through woods. *1913*

8 in (20.5 cm) high

$3,000–5,000　　**DRA**

Scenic Vellum Glaze plaque entitled *A Lake in the Mountain*, in its original frame. It depicts a tall tree on the banks of a lake, with snow-capped mountains in the distance. *1912*

8 in (20.5 cm) high

$2,000–3,000　　**DRA**

Vellum Glaze ovoid vase painted by Ed Diers, with clusters of blue berries hanging from delicate vines against a blush ground. *1908*

9¼ in (23.5 cm) high

$1,800–2,200　　**DRA**

KEY FEATURES

The soft, curvaceous lines found in peasant pottery and Oriental wares inspired the shapes of Newcomb College ceramics.

Typical decoration includes moonlit bayou scenes and the flora and fauna native to the American South: tobacco plants, cotton plants, lizards, and waterfowl.

A palette of yellow, blue, green, and black covered with a clear high glaze featured on early wares. After 1910, matt glazes in soft blues, whites, and creams were favored.

Newcomb pottery is marked with the firm's symbol, the cipher of the artist, the potter's mark, and a designated date.

Newcomb College

The ceramics created from 1895 by a talented group of female students at Newcomb College in New Orleans, Louisiana, remain among the most highly prized of all American art pottery produced during the Arts and Crafts period.

Founded in 1895 at H. Sophie Newcomb Memorial College—the women's division of Tulane University in New Orleans, Louisiana—Newcomb Pottery specialized in the production of vases decorated with imagery of the flora and fauna indigenous to the South. Ceramic shapes looked to Oriental and peasant pottery for inspiration, and decorative motifs included moonlit bayou scenes, native flora such as tobacco plants, cotton plants, and jonquils, lizards and waterfowl, and abstract Japanese-inspired Arts and Crafts designs.

Early wares feature shiny, luminous glazes in a distinctive palette of yellow, blue, green, and black, but from around 1910, a wider range of softly colored matt glazes was adopted.

Newcomb Pottery thrived under the direction of the highly skilled ceramic decorator and founder Ellsworth Woodward (1861–1939) and Mary G. Sheerer (1865–1954), and it attracted a team of talented designers and instructors, including Sadie Irvine, Harriet Joor, Anna Frances Simpson, and Henrietta Bailey.

The pottery began to market its wares as soon as it was established in 1895, ultimately receiving international acclaim at the Paris Exposition of 1900. The student artists were encouraged to sign their work and funded their tuition by selling the best examples in the gallery shop; all vases bore a label declaring that the "designs are not duplicated." Following Woodward's retirement in 1931, the quality of Newcomb College art pottery declined, and production finally ceased in 1940.

Above: Early tear-shaped vase painted by Mary Butler with stylized thistles in green and indigo on an ivory ground. *c. 1900*
4 in (10 cm) high **$7,000–10,000 DRA**

NEWCOMB POTTERY

The forward-looking H. Sophie Newcomb Memorial College established the Newcomb Pottery in 1895 as an educational enterprise. Faced with the decimation of the male population during the Civil War (1861–65), women were driven into the workplace and forced to take on jobs that traditionally had been held by men. Newcomb Pottery was instrumental in training women in the applied skills of ceramic decoration. Vases thrown by master potters were turned over to the young female students for decoration.

Ovoid vase by Henrietta Bailey, incised and surface-painted with cherries and leaves in indigo blue and dark green against white, and above mid-blue, grounds. *1904*
9½ in (24 cm) tall **$10,000–15,000 DRA**

WOMEN AT WORK

Candlestick with carved base by Leona Nicholson. It is decorated with white blossoms and green leaves, all under a soft waxy finish. *1912*

6¼ in (16 cm) high

$1,800–2,200   DRA

Scenic vase of slender oval form, carved and painted by Sadie Irvine with a view through tall pine trees on a shaded blue-green ground. *1915*

6½ in (16.5 cm) high

$4,000–6,000   DRA

Ovoid vase carved in relief and painted by Henrietta Bailey. It features paperwhites on green stems set against a matt blue ground. *1918*

6¾ in (17 cm) wide

$1,800–2,200   DRA

Early and unusual pitcher carved and painted by Harriet Joor. It has full-height branches and sprays of fruit in celadon on a glossy, indigo blue ground. *c. 1900*

8 in (20.25 cm) high

$4,000–6,000   DRA

Footed bowl of squat oval form, carved and painted by Alma Mason with light blue and white daffodils on a graduated blue-green ground. *1915*

7½ in (19 cm) wide

$1,800–2,200

DRA

A CLOSER LOOK

Early unsigned ovoid vase carved in relief, incised, and painted with stylized fern leaves in green on a cobalt blue and pale blue ground. The desirability of the vase is enhanced by the extent and crispness of the surface modeling and a harmonious use of color. *1902*
8¼ in (21 cm) high **$8,000–12,000 DRA**

Incised edges enhance the profile of the leaves

Newcomb's early grounds are mostly glazed in shades of blue

Early bell-shaped vase incised and painted by Sabina Wells with a highly stylized, geometric plant-form pattern in mottled indigo blue, light blue, and dark green. *c. 1900*

9½ in (24 cm) high

$15,000–20,000   DRA

Early bell-shaped vase incised and painted by Sabina Wells with large, stylized blossoms and leaves set on an ivory ground, above a mottled light blue lower half. *c. 1900*

9½ in (24 cm) high

$10,000–15,000   DRA

KEY FEATURES

Handmade earthenware vessels are covered with matt glazes in shades of brown and ocher, as well as a range of green hues—from the most characteristic moss green, to pale yellowish-green and the dark green of a cucumber skin.

Typical Grueby glazes are thick, opaque, and pitted with a matt effect that resembles the skin of a watermelon.

Decorative patterns inspired by nature—trees, leaves, plants, and flower blossoms—are often rendered in contrasting colors, such as yellow petals on a green background.

Art ware is usually marked with the name "Grueby" alongside a vegetal motif.

Grueby

Established in Boston, Massachusetts, in 1894, the Grueby Faience Co. produced award-winning ceramics renowned for their innovative matt green glaze and decorative motifs that looked to plant life for inspiration.

With his business initially dedicated to the manufacture of architectural bricks and tiles, William Henry Grueby (1867–1925) turned to the creation of art wares in 1897. He was influenced by the strong organic shapes found in the work of the French potter Auguste Delaherche (1857–1940).

Grueby pioneered the technique of covering ceramic vessels with thick, opaque matt glazes in rich shades of brown, ocher, or—especially—moss green, creating a surface texture that resembled the skin of a watermelon. Skillfully integrating a vessel's shape with its decoration, he embellished his hand-thrown earthenware with stylized hand-carved or relief patterns featuring flowers, grasses, leaves, and lotus blossoms. Many designs employed the Spanish Cuenca technique, in which patterns are impressed to form ridges that prevent colored glazes from intermingling.

Grueby declared in his company's brochure that "a fine piece of pottery is essentially an object of utility as well as of decoration." He also produced a collection of lamps in collaboration with the Tiffany Studios (*see pp.206–7*). The lamps— for both oil and electricity—consisted of a Grueby ceramic jar as the base and a leaded- or blown-glass Tiffany shade.

Produced at his studio in Boston, Grueby's highly prized ceramic wares received a gold medal, along with international acclaim, at the Paris Exposition of 1900. This success encouraged a host of imitators. By combining the techniques of mass production with those of handcraftsmanship—decorating simple hand-modeled vessels with standardized patterns, for example—Grueby's distinctive art pottery was destined to become a commercial success.

Above: Cuenca-decorated tile depicting a galleon in ivory and shades of brown against a teal-blue sea and sky. *c. 1900* *6 in (15.25 cm) square* **$1,200–1,800 DRA**

COLORED GLAZES

William Grueby is celebrated for his innovative matt glazes—in particular, a rich green color that drew inspiration from the flowers and plants of nature. The brochure published by the Grueby Faience Co. compared the "peculiar texture" of its rich, monotone glazed exteriors with "the smooth surface of a melon or the bloom of a leaf." Although moss green remains one of the most popular shades of green for Grueby pottery glazes, the color tones range from a pale yellowish-green to the rich, dark hue typical of the skin of a cucumber.

Single-color bulbous vase decorated with tooled and applied curling leaves. These are alternated with full-height buds on stems, under a mottled, vegetal-green matt glaze with white clay highlights. *c. 1905* *7½ in (19 cm) high* **$4,000–5,000 DRA**

Rare multicolored vase with a corseted neck ringed with yellow blossoms. The body features modeled, stylized leaf forms under a feathered, vegetal-green matt glaze. *c. 1905* *10 in (25.5.cm) high* **$10,000–15,000 DRA**

Rare multicolored advertising tile decorated in Cuenca. It shows a half-burned yellow candle in a matt, vegetal green glazed chamberstick, under the logo "Grueby Tile." *Late 1890s*

6 in (15.25 cm) high

$12,000–18,000 DRA

Cuenca-decorated tile with a stylized floral design, inspired by a Moorish tile in the Alhambra. It is glazed with oatmealed green, ivory, pale blue, and yellow. *c. 1900*

9 in (22.75 cm) square

$1,000–1,500 DRA

Multicolored Cuenca-decorated tile with stylized white and pale yellow waterlilies with matt, dark green leaves set against a paler, oatmealed matt green ground. *c. 1900*

6 in (15.25 cm) square

$3,000–4,000 DRA

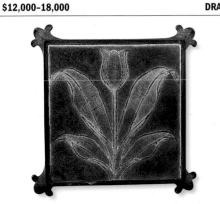

Cuenca-decorated tile by Marie Seaman mounted on a bronze trivet by Tiffany. It features a tulip with oatmealed pale green leaves on an oatmealed dark green matt ground. *c. 1905*

6 in (15 cm) square

$8,000–12,000 DRA

Extremely rare Cuenca-decorated tile designed by Addison LeBoutillier. It has an oak tree in oatmealed green glaze against paler green grass, ivory clouds, and a gray-blue sky. *c. 1905*

12¼ in (31 cm) square

$30,000–50,000 DRA

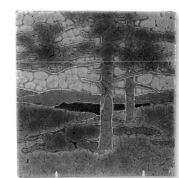

The Pines tile attributed to Addison LeBoutillier, with trees in brown and oatmealed matt green, against green grass and a lake, mountains, and sky in various tones of blue. *c. 1905*

6 in (15 cm) square

$3,000–4,000 DRA

A CLOSER LOOK

Tiffany leaded lamp in shades of green complements Grueby's naturalistic colors

Tiffany-shaded table lamp with a Grueby-made base. The latter is encircled by hand-modeled yellow flowerheads above trailing stems finished in and set against a matt, vegetal-green glaze. Both the green and yellow tones are echoed in the floral-, foliate- and mottled-pattern glass tiles of the made-to-match shade. *c. 1905*

21¾ in (55.25 cm) high

$150,000–200,000 GDG

Characteristic cucumber-green matt glaze

Cylindrical vase with tooled and applied leaves alternated, around the rim, with three scrolled handles, all finished in an oatmealed light green matt glaze. *c. 1905*

9¾ in (24.75 cm) high

$2,000–3,000 DRA

Bulbous, gourdlike vase by Wilhelmina Post, with tooled and applied leaves collaring and trailing from the neck. It is finished in a feathered, matt moss green glaze. *c. 1905*

7½ in (19.5 cm) high

$5,000–7,000 DRA

Ceramics are typically molded in architectural shapes with thickly potted walls, loop, or buttressed handles, and a minimum of decoration.

A high-quality matt glaze in a pale, silvery green color is a characteristic of Teco ware. This glaze is occasionally highlighted with a metallic black overglaze.

Teco ware is marked with a long-stemmed "T" with the letters "e," "c," and "o" arranged beneath each other.

Teco

The simplicity of the Arts and Crafts style resonated at the Teco Art Pottery, where the clean, architectural lines of its reasonably priced studio ceramics looked to the Midwest's Prairie School for inspiration.

Founded in Illinois by William Day Gates (1852–1928), the American Terracotta and Ceramic Co.—also known as Gates Potteries—initially produced bricks and architectural terra-cotta.

In 1902 Gates introduced a line of studio ceramics—vases, tiles, and garden ornaments—called Teco Art Pottery. Gates's aim was to bring "art pottery having originality and true artistic merit" to a wide audience at a relatively low cost, believing that anyone who appreciated art pottery should be able to own one or more pieces.

Influenced by the Prairie School movement of the American Midwest, Gates commissioned designs from architects Frank Lloyd Wright and William James Dodd, and appointed German sculptor Fritz Wilhelm Albert as chief designer. Most Teco stoneware and earthenware boast simple architectural shapes with looped or buttressed handles and thickly potted walls, although bulbous, organic gourdlike forms are not uncommon. Vessels were entirely molded and typically have a minimum of decorative detail, although handcrafted embellishments, such as impressed panels, were occasionally added.

A characteristic feature of Teco ware is a high-quality, pale, silvery green microcrystalline glaze with a matt effect—sometimes highlighted, or "charcoaled," with a metallic black overglaze. This was inspired by the matt glazes found on the French ceramics exhibited at the World's Columbian Exposition in Chicago in 1893.

The company's output included 500 different mass-produced shapes that were decorated with a variety of matt colors—mainly green, but also purple, rose, yellow, brown, blue, and gray. Earlier pieces with strong geometric shapes are particularly popular with collectors. The Teco Art Pottery ceased production in the mid-1920s.

Above: Twin buttress-handled vase of stylized organic form, finished in a fine matt green glaze with charcoaling on the handles. *1903–10. 8½ in (21.5 cm) high* **$1,800–2,200 DRA**

TECO STYLE

Early Teco wares were influenced by the Art Nouveau style, which had been brought from Europe to the factory by French sculptor Frederick Moreau. Ceramic shapes boast curved handles, whiplash buttresses, and embossed decoration of flowers or foliage. The Teco factory embraced a style characterized by clean, geometric lines and a silvery green matt glaze that was sometimes highlighted with a metallic black overglaze. Surface decoration was rejected in favor of form, color, and monumental architectural designs.

Rare organic-form vase with molded stylized tulip heads alternated with stylized full-height leaves, above a squat, curled leaf base, all finished in a fine, matt green glaze. *1903–10*
13¾ in (35 cm) high **$15,000–20,000 DRA**

Rare organic-form vase with eight leaf-shaped buttressed handles rising from the bulbous base to a lobed rim embossed with lotus blossoms. It is covered in a matt green glaze with charcoaled edges. *1903–10*
11½ in (29.25 cm) high **$20,000–30,000 DRA**

Double-gourd-shaped vase designed by W. B. Mundie, with four buttressed handles spanning the gourds, and finished in a fine matt green glaze with overall metallic-black glaze charcoaling. *1903–10*

6¾ in (17 cm) high

$4,000–6,000   DRA

Geometric vase of baluster shape with four full-height, rectangular buttressed handles, in a fine matt green glaze with selective metallic black glaze charcoaling. *1903–10*

7 in (17.75 cm) high

$3,000–5,000   DRA

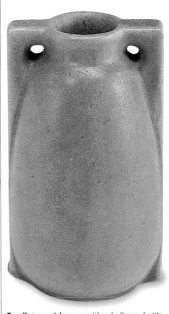

Small geometric vase with a bulbous, bottle-shaped body and two full-height buttressed handles, in a matt green glaze with selective metallic black glaze charcoaling. *1903–10*

5¼ in (13.25 cm) high

$1,800–2,200   DRA

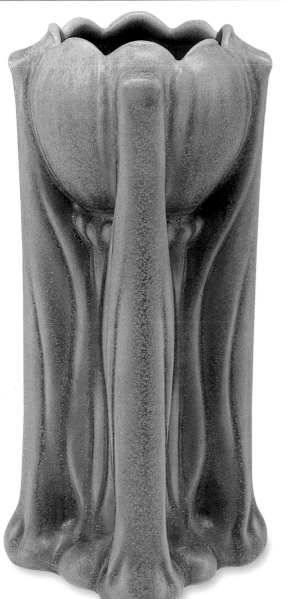

Tall organic vase in the form of a tulip flowerhead and stem with four full-height buttressed handles, in a matt green glaze with charcoaling in the crevices and on the edges. *1903–10*

12 in (30.5 cm) high

$5,000–7,000   DRA

Tapering vase with four buttressed handles spanning the pinched upper body and cupped neck, in a fine matt green glaze with some charcoaling on the handles. *1903–10*

10¾ in (27.25 cm) high

$3,000–4,000   DRA

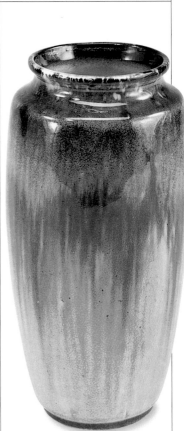

Rare shouldered ovoid vase with an everted rim, finished in a brilliant aventurine flambé glaze displaying streaked and mottled tones of red, tan, green, yellow, and gold. *1903–04*

8½ in (21.5 cm) high

$1,800–2,200   DRA

KEY FEATURES

Matt, gloss, metallic, or crystalline glazes in rich, muted colors frequently decorated Fulper's Vasekraft ceramics.

Glazes are often combined in unusual ways to produce distinctive and highly original effects on a single vessel.

Large table lamps—many in unusual shapes—boast both a ceramic base and a ceramic shade that has often been inset with glass panels.

Most art wares produced by the Fulper Pottery Co. were marked with a vertical impressed or printed "Fulper."

Fulper

Widely admired throughout the 19th century for its well-made, conventional utilitarian wares, the thriving Fulper Pottery Co. greeted the 20th century with a range of Arts and Crafts ceramics known as Vasekraft.

Established in 1805 in Flemington, New Jersey, the Fulper Pottery Co. initially produced simply shaped utilitarian ceramic wares. Just over a century later, to exploit the new fashion for art pottery and to coincide with the 1909 Christmas market, the company decided to introduce a line of artistic wares under the direction of the founder's grandson, William H. Fulper II, and his partner Martin Stangl. Known as Vasekraft, the relatively inexpensive range of table lamps and desk and smoking accessories was enthusiastically received by a discerning American middle class eager to acquire a fashionable piece of well-made art pottery.

Fulper's reputation as the maker of artistic wares was considerably enhanced by its pioneering experiments with a variety of glazing techniques. Once the pottery vessels—many in Japanese shapes—had been cast in molds, they were glazed individually by hand in a range of rich, subdued colors. A leader in the use of crystalline glazes, the Fulper manufactory also experimented with matt, gloss, flambé, and metallic glazes, which were combined or overlapped to achieve highly original effects.

Of particular note was Vasekraft's unusual line of large table lamps, distinctive because ceramic was used for both the lamp base and the shade; these were advertised as "art pottery put to practical uses." Among the most original were lamps shaped like toadstools decorated with irregular glazes and with glass panels set into the shades. The Fulper Pottery Co. closed in 1935.

Above: Early rare bulldog doorstop finished in mustard matt and Elephant's Breath flambé glazes. *c. 1905. 11 in (28 cm) long* **$1,000–1,500 DRA**

EXPERIMENTAL GLAZES

A distinctive feature of art ceramics produced in the early 20th century at factories across Europe and the United States was the innovative use of colored glazes. Commercial potteries such as Fulper turned organic vessels and practical wares into dazzling works of art thanks to the use of unusual and highly original decorative effects. Many looked to the past for inspiration—the lustrous glazes of Hispano-Moresque pottery of Islamic Spain or the Chinese-inspired crackle and flambé glazes.

Large shouldered ovoid vase of Oriental-inspired shape decorated with a flamelike pattern of thick and smoky gunmetal over mottled and swirling Chinese-blue crystalline glazes. *1909–14* *12 in (30.5 cm) high* **$2,000–3,000 DRA**

Large geometric vase with four buttresses rising from a squat, tapering base to the sides of a beakerlike body. Finished in a black-streaked green flambé glaze. *1909–14* *13½ in (34.25 cm) high* **$5,000–7,000 DRA**

A CLOSER LOOK

Vasekraft table lamp with a gently domed shade and tapering base, finished in a café-au-lait glaze. While some Fulper shades were made from an intricate network of colorful glass, others were mixed media: in this case, glazed earthenware with a ring of alternating L-shaped and rectangular inserts of hammered amber and opaque white leaded glass. *1910–15*
21½ in (54.5 cm) high
$10,000–15,000 DRA

Unusual and innovative use of glass and ceramic

Pottery color resembles metal, a material commonly used in fashionable Arts and Crafts lamps

Faceted oval vase with a simple molded geometric pattern around the rim. Finished in a robin's-egg blue crystalline glaze with mottled blues, greens, and browns. *1909–15*
7½ in (19 cm) high
$800–1,200   **DRA**

Shouldered bulbous oval vase with two loop handles flanking the collar rim. Finished in a frothy blue and olive green glaze dripped over a matt olive green ground. *1909–15*
8½ in (21.5 cm) high
$1,000–1,500   **DRA**

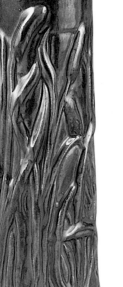

Rare candlestick bowl of circular form suspended on a tripod base rising to three candle cups. Finished in a mottled green crystalline glaze over a mottled blue-and-green ground. *1909–15*
11¼ in (28.5 cm) wide
$800–1,200   **DRA**

Bell pepper-shaped vase naturalistically molded and decorated with an unusual ocher crystalline matt glaze over a flowing blue-to-brown flambé glaze. *1909–15*
4½ in (11.5 cm) high
$600–900   **DRA**

Tall, cylindrical Cattail vase molded on the exterior with full-height, intertwined cattails and finished in a blue-gray and moss-green flambé glaze. *1909–15*
13 in (33 cm) high
$4,000–6,000   **DRA**

Squat, gourdlike vase with two angular and pierced buttressed handles. It is finished in a fine dripped and frothy cucumber-green matt glaze. *1909–15*
8 in (20.25 cm) wide
$600–900   **DRA**

Cylindrical hooded candle sconce finished in a rich ultramarine matt glaze, and with one rectangular and two triangular inserts of opaque off-white leaded glass. *1909–15*
10½ in (26.5 cm) high
$1,200–1,800   **DRA**

Small gourd-shaped vase with the mottled and swirled abstract pattern of a fine Leopard Skin crystalline glaze combined with a lustrous Elephant's Breath flambé glaze. *1909–15*
5½ in (14 cm) high
$600–900   **DRA**

KEY FEATURES

Ohr's pottery is lightweight, thinly potted, and brittle.

Eggshell-thin pots of red earthenware are pinched, twisted, crushed, folded, and pressed into bizarre sculptural shapes.

Rich lustrous glazes in a range of hues cover Ohr's hand-thrown pots. Green, brown, blue, bronze, black, salmon, and orange glazes frequently combined to produce mottled, speckled, metallic, and crystalline effects.

Most Ohr pottery is signed and impressed "G.E. Ohr Biloxi Miss," while later examples usually bear an incised facsimile signature.

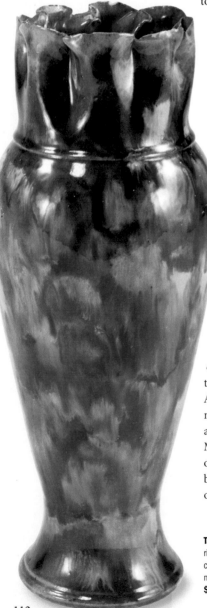

George Ohr

Although never a commercial success during his lifetime, eccentric American art potter George E. Ohr—nicknamed "the Mad Potter of Biloxi"—made some of the most original pottery of the Arts and Crafts period.

A prolific potter with unconventional ideas, George Ohr (1857–1918) established a small studio in the artist's colony of his home town of Biloxi, Mississippi, in 1883. During his career he made more than 10,000 pots—or "mud babies"—of exceptional virtuosity, which he displayed for sale in his shop called Pot-Ohr-E to a curious public. Most Ohr ware available to collectors today comes from his personal collection of more than 6,000 pieces that remained unsold during his lifetime. This remarkable cache of pottery—packed away in barrels in the family attic as a legacy left to his children—was finally recovered from storage in 1972.

Apart from a brief association with Newcomb College (*see pp.104–5*) in New Orleans in the mid-1890s, Ohr worked alone from 1883 until 1907. Using local clay that he dug himself from a nearby riverbank and hauled to his studio in a wheelbarrow, Ohr created paper-thin pottery vessels of extraordinary quality and imagination. He made nearly every piece by hand from start to finish and believed that each vessel should be distinctly different.

BIZARRE PIECES

Sometimes called the father of the studio-pottery movement, Ohr used a wheel and a wood-burning kiln—which he built himself—to produce hand-thrown wares in startling designs that indeed resemble early studio pottery. Ohr's pots, almost exclusively in red earthenware, tend to be thinly potted with a lightweight, brittle body, which he then manipulated by pinching, folding, crushing, twisting, and pressing into

Above: Bulbous in-body twisted vase with a pinched and pleated rim, in a rare blue and lavender glaze with green sponging. *1890s 4¾ in (12 cm) high* **$20,000–30,000 DRA**

A COLORFUL CHARACTER

George Ohr was a man of eccentric lifestyle, rebellious spirit, and unusual appearance, and he cultivated this colorful image, turning his cleverly named shop, Pot-Ohr-E, into a tourist attraction. Ohr relished his role as flamboyant entertainer and local curiosity, appearing at exhibitions where he demonstrated to audiences his skill in manipulating clay, turning, twisting, and firing vases in a portable kiln. Although he gave the impression of having received no formal training as a potter, in fact he had begun an apprenticeship in 1879 with the ceramicist Joseph Meyer in New Orleans before leaving to establish his own studio in 1883. While Ohr left contemporary critics bewildered, most would agree that his work was that of an unequaled and highly original creative talent.

Tall baluster-shaped vase with a pleated rim, decorated with a rare and vibrant combination of red, blue, amber, and white mottled glazes. *1890s. 10¼ in (26 cm) high* **$20,000–30,000 DRA**

GEORGE OHR

POTTERY FIRE

George Ohr's genius as an artist-potter is illustrated by the extraordinary breadth of his ceramic creations, his determination to push boundaries with new ideas, and his uncanny ability to turn something bizarre and even grotesque into a highly original work of art. A fitting example of this unusual talent can be seen in the wake of the devastating fire that swept through his Biloxi pottery in October 1893, damaging his building and kiln and destroying much of his inventory. It is a true measure of Ohr's rebellious nature and creative genius that he turned disaster into triumph. Rather than discarding the blackened pots covered with charcoal shards, Ohr called them his "burnt babies" and promoted them as yet another unorthodox range of art pottery.

Burnt Baby bulbous vase with a torn rim, its original finish disfigured by, and submerged in debris from, the 1893 fire at Ohr's pottery. *1893. 4½ in (11.5 cm) high* **$500–700 DRA**

VIRTUOSO POTTER

Without a doubt, George Ohr wears the mantle of quintessential Arts and Crafts potter. During his lifetime, he channeled his talent and imagination into one-of-a-kind ceramic vessels unlike any that had been produced before or, indeed, since. His hands-on determination to fashion a pot from start to finish, to realize his vision, and to ensure the high quality of the final product looks back to earlier traditions of craftsmanship.

PIONEERING SPIRIT

By digging his own clay, making his pots by hand, and even selling them in his shop, Ohr—perhaps without even realizing it—embraced the aesthetic values promoted by Arts and Crafts pioneers such as William Morris and C. F. A. Voysey. The simplicity and honesty of Ohr's work are reflected in his statement that "God put no color in souls so I'll put no color on my pots."

---

bizarre and highly unusual shapes. This bold handling of clay was complemented by a mastery of daring and unusual glazing techniques—another extraordinary dimension of Ohr's considerable craft. He mixed his own glazes, which are exceptionally lustrous, mottled, and made up of rich green and brown tones. Other favorite colors include red, blue, bronze, purple, black, and orange. Ohr frequently combined different mottled or speckled glazes, occasionally using two completely different glazes on opposite sides of a pot or vivid colors dappled over the surface of a vessel.

REMARKABLE OUTPUT

After 1900, Ohr lost interest in glazing, preferring to focus mainly on the simplicity and honesty of his work in the time-honored Arts and Crafts tradition. A significant portion of his later work—known as bisque ware—was severely manipulated into pinched, asymmetrical sculptural shapes and left unglazed. While many of Ohr's pots were relatively plain, he occasionally made wares with applied decoration, such as spikes and snakes.

Although Ohr's remarkable output throughout his career included both practical and ornamental ware, he sold hardly a single piece during his lifetime. He closed his studio in around 1907, leaving behind an extraordinary legacy of wares that, while out of step with the American south of the early 1900s, remains some of the most exceptional and highly prized pottery to emerge from the Arts and Crafts movement.

Bisque vase with folded rim, deep in-body twist, dimpled center, and notched wave and geometric patterns to the base and neck. Incised on the base: "Mary had a little Lamb & Ohr has a little Pottery." *1903 9 in (23 cm) high* **$20,000–30,000 DRA**

Scrolling ribbon-handled vessel with a bell-shaped top half on a pyramid base, with a gunmetal, indigo, and green glaze. *1890s*

6¾ in (17 cm) high

$15,000–20,000 DRA

Long-necked vase with a pinched and twisted rim, finished in a white, turquoise, and amber glaze over a raspberry ground. *1890s*

4¾ in (12 cm) high

$4,000–6,000 DRA

Ovoid vase with a pinched neck, decorated in a green, gunmetal, indigo, and raspberry glaze sponged over a white ground. *1890s*

5½ in (14 cm) high

$6,000–9,000 DRA

Tapering footed cylindrical vase with dimpled sides and a twisted wave-scroll rim. Finished in a mottled, glossy amber glaze. *1890s*

4 in (10 cm) high

$3,000–5,000 DRA

Footed bulbous ovoid vase with a bird's-throat neck and two scrolled handles. Its marbleized clay body is glazed in four panels: brown and green; caramel; gunmetal; and bottle green. *1890s*

8¼ in (21 cm) high

$10,000–15,000 DRA

Waisted and footed ovoid vase with a deep in-body twist and a pinched and folded rim. Decorated in a speckled brown, gunmetal, and dark-green glaze. *1890s*

6¼ in (15.75 cm) high

$3,000–5,000 DRA

Slim, footed cylindrical vase with a bulbous base, tapering body, and pinched, twisted, and folded rim. Decorated in a speckled brown and black glossy glaze. *1890s*

7¾ in (19.5 cm) high

$6,000–9,000 DRA

Highly sculptural vase of clamlike form with abstract imagery beneath the lower lip. Its mottled glaze is in shades of green, brown, gunmetal blue, and fleshy pink. *1890s*

8 in (20.25 cm) wide

$6,000–9,000 LG

Red bisque clay vase of footed cylindrical form. The body is pinched and folded and has oxidization on one side. *c. 1905*

4¾ in (12 cm) wide

$2,000–3,000   **DRA**

Pale-beige bisque vessel of footed, oval form with a broad rim. Its in-body twist is a particularly deep example of Ohr's twisted and tortured style of modeling. *c. 1905*

3 in (7.5 cm) high

$5,000–7,000   **DRA**

Scroddled clay bisque pitcher with deeply pinched and folded sides and spout. Blended from red and beige clays to create a marbleized finish. *c. 1905*

6 in (15.25 cm) high

$6,000–9,000   **DRA**

Pale-beige bisque mug of tiglike form, with one loop and two serpentine-profile handles of varying size spanning the corseted waist of its body. *c. 1905*

8½ in (21.5 cm) high

$2,000–3,000   **DRA**

Terra-cotta bisque cabinet vase of corseted form, with a central knop and a twisted and folded rim. It features selective oxidized coloring across its surface. *c. 1905*

4½ in (11.5 cm) high

$2,000–3,000   **DRA**

Most of Ohr's bisque clay pieces are marked with his large script signature.

Scroddled clay bisque face vase of footed, squat oval form with a folded petal rim, pinched nose, and applied eyes. *c. 1905*

5½ in (14 cm) wide

$3,000–5,000   **DRA**

Squat ovoid bisque vessel with a deep, swirling twist around its shoulder. Made from pale-beige clay and incised "Mud from N.O. [New Orleans] Street." *1905*

4¾ in (12 cm) wide

$5,000–7,000   **DRA**

Pale-beige clay bisque vase with a circular base beneath a dimpled, pinched, and folded body of triple-lobed, tulip, or podlike forms. *c. 1905*

5¼ in (13.25 cm) wide

$3,000–5,000   **DRA**

Organic shapes are commonly decorated with flower blossoms and leaf patterns, although molded figures of women, men, and animals occasionally feature.

The finest-quality ceramics produced by the factory are considered to be those made between 1902 and 1904, under the direction of Artus.

Van Briggle vessels are typically marked at the bottom with an incised "AA" symbol, representing the well-known founding couple.

Pieces made before 1908 have an incised four-digit date beneath the company's mark.

Van Briggle

Tucked into the mountainous terrain of Colorado, the husband-and-wife team of Artus and Anna Van Briggle brought the simple philosophy of Arts and Crafts design to their celebrated American art pottery.

Artus Van Briggle (1869–1904) and his wife Anna founded the Van Briggle art pottery in Colorado Springs, Colorado, in 1899. The Van Briggles had been lured to Colorado by the mountain climate, which they hoped would ease Artus's tuberculosis.

Having worked as a decorator at the Rookwood Pottery (*see pp.98–103*) in Cincinnati, Ohio, Artus—who spent three years studying in Paris in the 1890s—brought to the new enterprise a taste for organic-shaped slip-cast ceramic vessels decorated with sumptuous matt glazes. A favored Van Briggle decorative technique used an atomizer to spray colored glazes onto clean-lined pots.

The company's output varied widely, ranging from high-quality innovative studio wares to ordinary commercial merchandise. Vases were typically molded and decorated with embossed patterns featuring stylized Art Nouveau flowers and leaves or American Indian designs. Occasionally the factory produced vessels that were embellished with molded animals or human figures—the best known being Despondency and the celebrated Lorelai vases.

The Van Briggle pottery produced its finest work before the death of Artus in 1904. However, until Anna sold the factory in 1912, the company continued to create quality art wares in a variety of distinctive hues that looked back to the early period—the characteristic golds, cucumber and lime greens, purples and mauves, turquoise blues, and deep, burgundy reds—as well as looking ahead to the natural, Colorado-wilderness shades of ocher, white, pink, and black. The success of the pottery, which remains in operation today, largely depends on copies of the wares originally created by Artus Van Briggle.

Above: Turquoise-and-blue glazed center bowl in the form of a crouching maiden overlooking a pond with a frog on a flower. *c. 1910* *15 in (38 cm) wide* **$300–500 DRA**

MATT GLAZES

In 1893, while studying in Paris, Artus Van Briggle first encountered the Chinese Ming Dynasty matt glazes that would launch his quest for their formula. Back in Cincinnati in 1896, he set to work on this task. Van Briggle first exhibited his matt-glaze vases at the Paris Exposition Universelle in 1900 as part of the Rookwood display. The wares caused such a sensation that William Taylor, the president of Rookwood, wrote to Van Briggle asking for his glaze formula. Matt green is the most common color on early pieces, followed by tones of blue, then maroon. Occasionally, multiple glazes are employed. Rarer still are the iridescent finishes, used mainly during 1904 and probably from a single kiln test.

Cylindrical vase with a flared rim, embossed with peacock-feather motifs and finished in a blue-green, purple, gold, and mauve luster glaze on a purple ground. *1908–11* *10 in (25.5 cm) high* **$3,000–4,000 DRA**

Shouldered ovoid vase with a collar rim, embossed with alternating, full-height dogwood blossoms and leaves under a mottled and spotted matt green glaze. *1906* *8 in (20.5 cm) high* **$1,200–1,800 DRA**

Squat, waisted cylindrical vase embossed with full-height, stylized tulips, under a frothy light-blue glaze with raised edges of underlying beige clay ghosting through. *1908–11*

5¾ in (14.5 cm) high

$1,000–1,500 DRA

Early slender ovoid vase with two small, pierced, buttressed handles, with a deep red glaze graduating into lime green. *1903*

7¾ in (19.5 cm) high

$1,800–2,200 DRA

Waisted bulbous-shaped vase embossed with blossoms, stems, and leaves, under a feathered glaze with beige clay highlights. *1908–11*

7½ in (19 cm) high

$1,000–1,500 DRA

Shouldered cylindrical vase embossed with poppy pods and stems, under a green glaze with beige clay highlights. *1908–11*

7 in (17.75 cm) high

$1,000–1,500 DRA

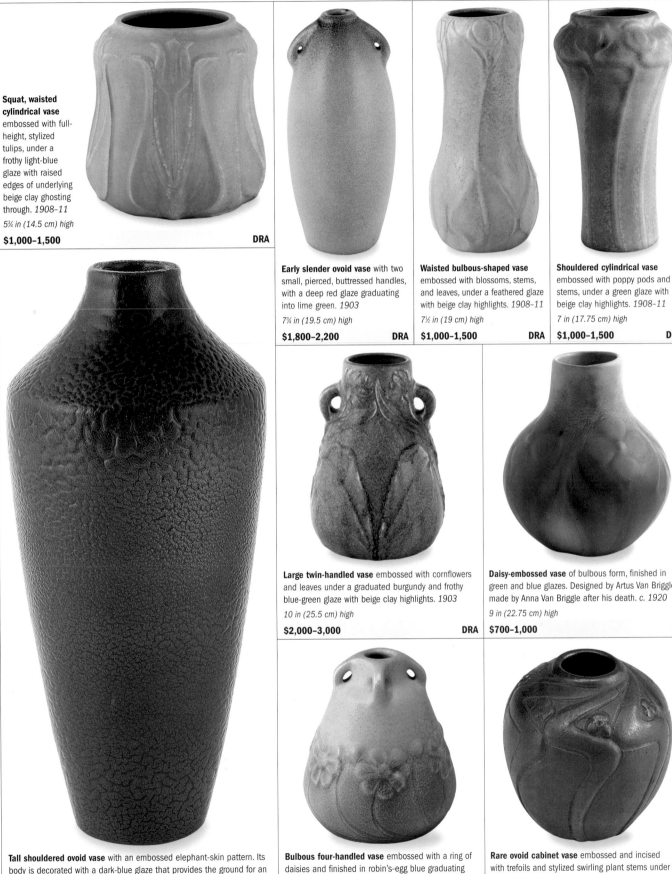

Large twin-handled vase embossed with cornflowers and leaves under a graduated burgundy and frothy blue-green glaze with beige clay highlights. *1903*

10 in (25.5 cm) high

$2,000–3,000 DRA

Daisy-embossed vase of bulbous form, finished in green and blue glazes. Designed by Artus Van Briggle; made by Anna Van Briggle after his death. *c. 1920*

9 in (22.75 cm) high

$700–1,000 LG

Tall shouldered ovoid vase with an embossed elephant-skin pattern. Its body is decorated with a dark-blue glaze that provides the ground for an additional purple glaze over the neck and shoulders. *1906*

11½ in (29.25 cm) high

$1,800–2,200 DRA

Bulbous four-handled vase embossed with a ring of daisies and finished in robin's-egg blue graduating into a speckled purple-blue glaze. *1903*

5 in (12.75 cm) high

$2,000–3,000 DRA

Rare ovoid cabinet vase embossed and incised with trefoils and stylized swirling plant stems under a mottled, copper metallic finish. *c. 1910*

3 in (7.5 cm) high

$700–1,000 DRA

KEY FEATURES

The Rozane art-pottery range is made from molded stoneware and typically features richly colored glazes over painted, incised, or embossed decoration of flowers, fruit, or foliage.

Roseville pottery is generally unmarked, although the Rozane range boasts a stamped seal.

Small vases and bowls are the most common Rosewood vessel forms; the least common are hanging baskets, tea sets, sand jars, wall pockets, and jardinière and pedestal sets.

Copies of Rookwood Pottery designs include a range of Standard Glaze, Azurean-replicated Iris Glaze, and Aerial Blue Glaze.

Roseville

Although the Ohio-based Roseville Pottery Co. excelled in producing useful ceramic wares at reasonable cost, it earned a reputation for its richly glazed art pottery in the Arts and Crafts style.

First established in Roseville, Ohio, in 1890—and later located in the nearby town of Zanesville—the Roseville Pottery Co. produced basic, utilitarian stoneware under the directorship of George F. Young. Although the factory's output centered on the production of lesser-quality useful wares, it earned a solid reputation for its art ware, which was created from 1900 until 1920. Roseville was widely considered to be the finest of the "second-tier" companies working in the Arts and Crafts style.

Roseville's line of art vases—marketed as Rozane Ware—was characterized by painted, incised, or molded decoration of flowers, fruit, and leaves and typically covered with luminous, richly colored glazes. A significant portion of Roseville's art ceramics comprised faithful—albeit less expensive—copies of the ceramic range made famous by the rival Rookwood Pottery (*see pp.98–103*).

The renowned British potter Frederick Hurten Rhead (1880–1942), who held the post of art director at Roseville from 1904 until 1908, designed the celebrated Della Robbia range, which proved the company's ability to produce well-designed, high-quality ceramic wares. Rhead was succeeded as art director by his brother Harry G. Rhead (1881–1950), although the company's fortunes had begun to wane by 1910, when only the plant in Zanesville continued to operate.

With the onset of World War I, the market for art ware diminished and the company shifted to the more commercially viable molded wares; by 1920, mechanical processes were being employed to add decorative details. The Roseville Pottery ceased production in 1954.

Above: Approximately 60 percent of Rozane Ware pieces made prior to 1907 were marked. This example, from the vase shown opposite (*top right*), also carries a specific range mark: "Woodland."

ROZANE WARE

While Roseville's mass-produced pottery enjoyed great success, it was a growing demand for decorated art pottery that prompted the company to introduce hand-painted art ware at the beginning of the 20th century. Under art director John Herold and the banner Rozane—fusing the Roseville and Zanesville names—Roseville looked to emulate the popularity and success of the Rookwood Pottery of Cincinnati, initially producing decent-quality, underglaze slip-painted stoneware that copied the Rookwood designs. By 1905, however, the Zanesville plant had become more creative, tapping the design talents of English potter Frederick H. Rhead and Frank Ferrell and introducing imaginative ranges of art pottery such as Della Robbia, Fudji, Crystallis, and Woodland.

Bottle-shaped Fudji-range vase conceived by Gazio Fudjiyama. Its molded oriental form is squeeze-bag-decorated with a stylized floral and foliate design. *c. 1910. 8½ in (21.5 cm) high* **$2,000–3,000 DRA**

Fudji-range cylindrical vase of waisted form, squeeze-bag-decorated with full-height poppies, stems, and leaves in shades of red and green on a graduated pink-beige-blue bisque ground. *c. 1910. 10¼ in (26 cm) high* **$700–1,000 DRA**

Baluster-shaped pitcher with a ring handle, molded with stylized plant forms, under a semimatt green glaze. *c. 1905*

7½ in (19 cm) high

$400–600 DRA

Della Robbia-range bottle vase modeled and incised with a sewn-leather and bunches-of-grapes design. *c. 1905*

10 in (25.5 cm) high

$2,000–2,500 DRA

Baluster-shaped floor vase slip-decorated in relief with tall trees and a river in mottled greens and blue on a blue-beige ground. *c. 1915*

18 in (45.75 cm) high

$1,200–1,800 DRA

Woodland-range ovoid vase incised and painted with large chrysanthemum blooms in shades of red, with yellow-green foliage, on a mottled beige bisque ground. *c. 1915*

15 in (38 cm) high

$2,000–2,500 DRA

A CLOSER LOOK

Della Robbia-range vase of slender, cylindrical form, with a cavalier standing among trees, set between bands of tulips and spade-shaped leaves. Typical of this up-market range, the hand-painted decoration—in shades of green, blue, yellow, orange, and pink—is also incised and excised, rather than molded. *c. 1905*

18½ in (47 cm) high

$8,000–12,000 DRA

Colorful cavalier reflects fashion for theatrical imagery

Made under Frederick Rhead's direction, this vase displays techniques of high-end pottery

Tall Woodland-range vase of slim cylindrical form, incised and painted with hanging branches of white blossoms and green leaves on a matt beige ground. *c. 1915*

15 in (38 cm) high

$1,000–1,500 DRA

Rozane Ware tear-shaped vase with twin D-loop handles and a circular foot. It is decorated with a high-gloss, burnt orange glaze with selective burnt umber highlights. Heavily restored. *1920s*

6 in (15.25 cm) high

$80–120 DRA

Painted or incised designs—including stylized flowers, sailing ships, geometric patterns, animals, birds, fish and insects, and American Indian motifs—adorn simple, elegant, hand-thrown vessels.

Matt glazes feature a soft, muted color palette of blues, gray, rose, yellow, green, and brown, with several colors sometimes combined on a single vessel.

Pottery is usually marked with the impressed outline of a ship accompanied by the initials "MP," all enclosed within a circle, and sometimes including the initials "AEB" and/or "HT" (for Arthur E. Baggs and Hanna Tutt).

Marblehead

The picturesque New England coastal town of Marblehead, Massachusetts, was home to a small American pottery that produced a range of high-quality handcrafted wares in the Arts and Crafts style.

Founded in 1905 in the small fishing village of Marblehead by Dr. Herbert J. Hall, the Marblehead Pottery was conceived as a craft-therapy program to provide "quiet manual work" for convalescing "nervously worn-out patients." By 1915, Dr. Hall's Handcraft Shops, which also included metalwork, woodcarving, and weaving, had been transformed into a commercial enterprise, having been purchased by Arthur Eugene Baggs (1886–1947), who remained as director until the company closed in 1936.

Guided by Arts and Crafts philosophy, the Marblehead Pottery specialized in hand-thrown matt-glazed ware in simple,

well-designed, and elegant shapes. Tiles, vases, jars, garden ornaments, and bowls were individually decorated with incised and painted geometric patterns, stylized flowers, animals, birds, insects and fish, and occasionally American Indian motifs by a team of artists led by Hanna Tutt. A soft, muted color palette boasted harmonious tones such as blue, warm gray, wisteria, rose, yellow, green, and tobacco brown.

After 1936, Baggs served as professor of ceramic arts at Ohio State University until his death.

Above: Small polychromatic tile with a stylized basket of fruit and flowers in blues, greens, red, and yellow on a speckled pink ground. *c. 1910. 4½ in (11.5 cm) square* **$300–500 DRA**

Tall cylindrical vase with the simple, clean lines of its hand-thrown body highlighted by a smooth, semigloss enameled glaze of mottled yellow-ocher hue. *c. 1915*
10 in (25.5 cm) high
$1,800–2,200 DRA

Earthenware vase by Hanna Tutt, with floral incised and glazed decoration. The artist modeled the design into the vessel's surface, and the multicolored decoration makes the piece both rarer and more valuable. *c. 1908*

NPA CHR

Rare seven-piece cider set by Arthur Baggs. Finished in a speckled matt green glaze, with its original hammered-copper tray by Gustav Stickley. *1915–20*
Tray: 16 in (40.5 cm) wide
$5,000–7,000 DRA

Pair of bookends with a different, molded tall ship on each. The decoration is rendered in shades of blue and green on a white ground. *1920s*
5½ in (14 cm) high
$1,000–1,500 DRA

Clifton

Although a relatively small enterprise, the Clifton Art Pottery produced a collectible range of decorative wares and pioneered the creation of vessels inspired by American Indian designs.

Founded in Newark, New Jersey, in 1905 by William A. Long (1844–1918) in collaboration with chemist Fred Tschirner, the Clifton Art Pottery enjoyed a brief but productive tenure. It created a range of designs and experimented with a variety of decorative techniques.

Molded from dense, white Jersey clay, the company's most celebrated line—the Crystal Patina ware—featured dazzling microcrystalline glazes in vibrant hues of green, amber, cream, and brown that resembled the green oxidation of bronze, and that were sometimes enhanced with a thin silver overlay. A small number of vessels were produced with orange, rich brown, and gold flambé glazes. Although most were molded smooth, some were embossed with decorative motifs such as fish, birds, or flower blossoms.

Clifton also produced a popular line of vases—Indian Ware—inspired by the forms and decoration of American Indian pottery, with a red clay body, incised decoration featuring Indian motifs, and a glossy black glaze.

After Long's return to Ohio in 1909, Clifton produced decorative wares for two more years before turning to tile manufacturing.

Above: Indian Ware bottle vase incised and painted with American Indian motifs and swirls in black and ivory on a terracotta ground. *1905-08. 12¼ in (31 cm) high* **$800–1,200 DRA**

KEY FEATURES

Small-sized vessels boasting clear glazes, underglaze decoration, and American Indian motifs are the main features of Clifton pottery.

There are four main types of Clifton ware: Crystal Patina (the most avidly sought), Tirrube, Indian Ware, and Robin's-Egg Blue.

Smooth-molded vessels are most common, although occasionally Clifton wares feature embossed decoration of flower blossoms, birds, or fish patterns.

Pieces tend to be marked with an incised or impressed "Clifton" or "Clifton Pottery Newark," usually with the "CAP" cipher and often bearing a die-stamped shape number. Indian Ware may also refer to the Indian nation from which the form originated.

Squat and footed ovoid vase with a fine Crystal Patina glaze in soft but lively tones of yellow and chartreuse flowed over a celadon ground. *1906*
7 in (17.75 cm) wide
$800–1,200   **DRA**

Gourd-shaped Indian Ware vase with geometric motifs derived from an Indian design, in ivory on a red clay ground. Slight glaze flakes. *1905-08*
6½ in (16.5 cm) wide
$500–700   **DRA**

Rare Crystal Patina vase with a bulbous base and long, wide neck. Its stylized floral pattern is augmented with silver-deposit decoration. *1906*
6¾ in (17 cm) high
$800–1,200   **DRA**

Baluster-shaped Tirrube vase superbly slip-decorated in shallow relief by Albert Haubrich with a white heron and palm fronds set against a dark terra-cotta bisque ground. *1905-08*
12 in (30.5 cm) high
$1,000–1,500   **DRA**

KEY FEATURES

Incised decoration and a soft palette of matt colors—yellow, blue, green, white, brown, and gray—are hallmarks of the ceramic wares produced by the Saturday Evening Girls Club.

A high-gloss glaze featuring bold shades—from jade to metallic black—was occasionally used.

Lamps and candlesticks, bowls, bookends, vases, tiles, and a range of dinner sets were among the items produced.

Children's breakfast sets were often decorated with fanciful animal motifs.

Wares are typically signed with an impressed or painted mark featuring Paul Revere on horseback over the words "The Paul Revere Pottery Boston," and the letters "SEG" or "PRP," often with the year.

Saturday Evening Girls

The brainchild of the entrepreneurial Mrs. James J. Storrow and Edith Brown, the Paul Revere Pottery of Boston built its reputation on the hand-decorated ceramics created by the Saturday Evening Girls Club.

The idea behind the Saturday Evening Girls Club of Boston, Massachusetts, was to have a group of immigrant girls gather on a weekly basis to decorate pottery that could then be sold in support of their settlement-house activities. The girls studied the basics of ceramics and, with a small kiln purchased by the Club's benevolent patron, Mrs. Storrow, learned how to glaze and fire their wares with the help of an experienced potter.

What had begun in 1906 as a relatively modest experiment at the settlement house grew into such a highly successful enterprise that two years later the pottery moved to larger premises, adopting the name of the Revolutionary War hero Paul Revere. The Saturday Evening Girls Club

continued to train young women to work as ceramic decorators, although the pottery was rarely profitable. Further expansion to a specially designed building modeled on Cincinnati's Rookwood Pottery (*see pp.98–103*) saw the company broaden its range of wares to include candlesticks, lamps, vases, bookends, and paperweights—as well as tiles, tea wares and dinner sets, and a popular line of children's breakfast sets that were fancifully decorated with playful motifs such as rabbits, chicks, and ducks.

Director Edith Brown died in 1932 and the onset of the Great Depression sounded the death knell for the Paul Revere Pottery, which was forced to close in 1942, two years before the death of Mrs. Storrow.

Above: Cuerda-seca-decorated bowl with pairs of yellow roosters ringed above the motto: "Early to Bed & Early to Rise Makes a Child Healthy Wealthy and Wise." *1915–20*
6 in (15.25 cm) wide **$3,000–4,000 DRA**

SOPHISTICATED SIMPLICITY

The art pottery hand-decorated by the Saturday Evening Girls Club was admired for its simplicity and charm. Decorative motifs including landscapes and woodland scenes were complemented by engaging designs featuring farm animals, witches on broomsticks, and windmills. A palette of soft, pretty colors and smooth, silky finishes in matt or glossy glazes enhanced the decorative patterns, giving these wares a lighthearted yet elegant quality. Many pieces are decorated with the "cuerda seca" technique, where the design is drawn on the piece using wax. During the firing process, the glaze beads up against the wax barrier, creating subtle flooded areas.

Bullet-shaped wall pocket decorated in cuerda seca with a ring of stylized yellow poppies set against white and lime green grounds. *c. 1915*
6 in (15.25 cm) high **$2,000–3,000 DRA**

Squat, spherical bowl decorated in cuerda seca around the upper body, with stylized blue blossoms and brown leaves set on a green ground. *1910–20*
8 in (20.25 cm) wide **$1,500–2,000 DRA**

Cuerda-seca-decorated bowl with a Greek-key band below the rim rendered in taupe and ivory against white-and-brown semimatt grounds. *c. 1920*

6 in (15.25 cm) wide

$1,000–1,500   DRA

Dinner plate (one of a set) decorated in cuerda seca with a border of white lotus blossoms set on a blue-gray semigloss ground. *1915–25*

10 in (25.5 cm) wide

$500–700 (plate only)   DRA

Cuerda-seca-decorated bowl of flat, spherical form with golden nasturtium blossoms and green leaves on blue-and-green matt grounds. *1908–15*

8½ in (21.5 cm) wide

$1,800–2,200   DRA

Shallow serving bowl with a yellow soft-gloss glaze, separated from a beige tone rim on the inside by a thin, black cuerda-seca band. *1922*

8½ in (21.5 cm) wide

$120–180   DRA

Hampshire Pottery

Another New England pottery working in the Arts and Crafts style was the Hampshire Pottery. Established by James S. Taft in 1871 in Keene, New Hampshire, it grew into a thriving enterprise under the direction of Englishman Thomas Stanley. He expanded the range of household ceramic wares to include a line of high-glaze majolica tableware, and souvenir plates and jugs with transfer-printed decoration. The pottery also specialized in the production of a wide variety of matt glazes.

Hampshire Pottery loop-handled water pitcher with a molded body embossed with leaf-form decoration, its exterior under a matt glaze, and its interior with a semigloss one. *c. 1910*

8¼ in (21 cm) high

$100–150   DRA

Hampshire Pottery gourd-shaped vessel with a molded body decorated with a speckled glaze. Its interior features a nacreous black glaze. *c. 1910*

4½ in (11.5 cm) wide

$300–400   DRA

Hampshire Pottery molded twin-handled cup (or cylix) of ancient Greek form, with embossed leaf decoration on the body and foot, and finished with a speckled green matt glaze. *c. 1910*

8 in (20.5 cm) wide

$500–800   DRA

American Ceramics

In the United States, the art-pottery movement gained considerable momentum following the 1876 Centennial Exhibition in Philadelphia, which had highlighted the dismal quality of American industrial ceramics. During the 1880s and 1890s, an art-pottery industry developed across the country, and by 1900, more than 200 companies producing decorative wares—from large kiln works to small studio ventures—were established. Although early American art pottery was relatively plain and essentially derivative, potters eventually developed their own style, experimenting with innovative glazing techniques and modeling methods.

Three nursery-rhyme tiles by the Mosaic Tile Co. mounted in an Arts and Crafts hardwood frame: Puss in Boots, Little Miss Muffett, and Humpty Dumpty. *1940s*

4 in (10.25 cm) square

$600–900   DRA

Rare Losanti Ware vase by Mary Louise McLaughlin, with carved and grain-of-rice blossoms; white glaze, oxblood flashes. *c. 1900*

4¾ in (12 cm) high

$20,000–30,000   DRA

Unusual tapering vase by the Arequipa Pottery, embossed with branches of fruits and leaves. *c. 1915*

6 in (15.25 cm) high

$5,000–7,000   DRA

Walrath Pottery baluster vase decorated with a fine crystalline glaze in mottled and "cratered" tones of amber and celadon. Incised "Walrath 1907."

9 in (23 cm) high

$4,000–6,000   DRA

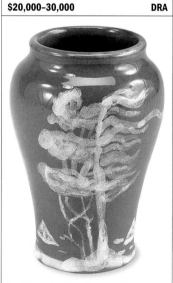

Small baluster-shaped vase by Denver White, painted with trees and sailboats in an opaque white glaze on a blue-gray ground.

5¼ in (13.5 cm) high

$400–600   DRA

Walrath Pottery baluster vase with stylized orange blossoms on brown and light green stems, on a green, matt glaze ground. *c. 1905*

6 in (15.25 cm) high

$4,000–6,000   DRA

Hand-thrown Merrimac Pottery humidor with three small handles on the body and a button-handled cover. Finished in a mottled green, semigloss glaze. *1902–08*

6½ in (16.5 cm) high

$800–1,200   **DRA**

Acorn-shaped cabinet vase by the Hampshire Pottery, embossed with Grueby-style leaves under a leathery ocher glaze. *c. 1910*

3½ in (9 cm) high

$500–800   **DRA**

Mission-ware vase by the Niloak Pottery, with a marbleized, internally glazed body of brown, blue-gray, ivory, and terra cotta. *1911–28*

7½ in (19 cm) high

$400–600   **DRA**

Bulbous Arequipa Pottery vase carved with a stylized vegetal design, under a gunmetal-black, semimatt glaze. *c. 1910*

4¾ in (12 cm) high

$3,000–5,000   **DRA**

Dedham Pottery Crackleware pitcher with stenciled geometric- and rabbit-pattern bands on white, under a clear crackle glaze. *c. 1920*

9 in (22.75 cm) high

$700–1,000   **DRA**

Chelsea Keramic

From 1875, the Massachusetts-based Chelsea Keramic Art Works owned by the Robertson family began producing art pottery. Copies of ancient Greek vases were among the first decorative wares to be made, but the influence of Chinese ceramics took hold from 1884, when Hugh Cornwall Robertson (1844–1908) assumed control, producing vibrant monochrome and flambé glazes. Although forced to close in 1888 due to a lack of funds, the company was revived in 1891 under the new name Chelsea Pottery US. In 1895, the factory changed location and began trading as Dedham Pottery. It closed in 1943.

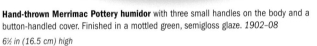

Chelsea Keramic Art Works scroll-footed pillow vase carved with blue violets and mottled green leaves on a bottle green ground and under a transparent glaze. *c. 1880*

4¼ in (10.75 cm) high

$800–1,200   **DRA**

Chelsea Keramic Art Works twin-handled rectangular vase with lion-paw feet, molded with a sunflower design. *Early 1880s*

8¾ in (22.25 cm) high

$1,000–1,500   **JF**

Salesman's sample of Batchelder tiles in a metal frame with diverse plain monochrome and patterned examples—the latter mostly stylized floral designs, with some in Cuenca. *1920s*

13½ in (34.25 cm) square

$1,800–2,200 DRA

Unsigned 12-tile panel squeeze-bag-decorated with an autumnal landscape of trees, a river, and distant hills, in matt and semimatt polychrome glazes. *1920s*

24 in (61 cm) wide

$4,000–6,000 DRA

Rare University City vase almost certainly incised by Frederick H. Rhead with stylized trees in matt gray on a mottled, matt green ground. *1911*

6½ in (16.5 cm) high

$4,000–6,000 DRA

Hartford Faience Co. mosaic tile by Francis G. Plant. Its Eventide design depicts a Pre-Raphaelite-style maiden holding flowers, surrounded by a green brick border. *c. 1910*

13 in (33 cm) high

$12,000–18,000 DRA

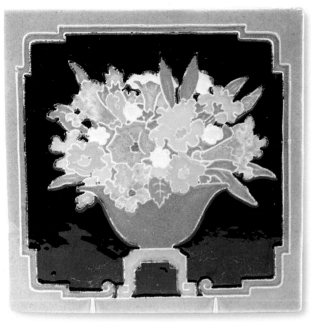

Claycraft Potteries Co. tile decorated in Cuenca with a brilliant turquoise bowl of yellow, pink, lilac, and white flowers, against a glossy black, turquoise-bordered ground. *1920s*

7¾ in (19.5 cm)

$600–900 DRA

High-fired porcelain tile by Adelaide Robineau, decorated in Cuenca with a rooster in brown, cobalt, yellow, and green crystalline glaze, on a semimatt blue-green ground.

6½ in (16.5 cm) square

$6,000–9,000 DRA

Weller

Established in 1871 in Zanesville, Ohio, by Samuel Weller (1851–1925), the Weller Pottery exploited the prevailing fashion for hand-thrown ceramics and the international Arts and Crafts style. In 1894, Weller purchased the Lonhuda Pottery works of Steubenville, transferring it to Zanesville in 1895. The company developed a version of Lonhuda's slip-painted ware, which it marketed as Louwelsa between 1895 and 1918, while other wares mirrored popular styles produced by Roseville and the Rookwood Pottery. Weller employed a number of distinguished designers and decorators, including Frederick H. Rhead, Charles Babcock Upjohn, Albert Haubrich, and the French potter Jacques Sicard (1865–1923). The latter was responsible for a range of handsome vases covered with a glittering iridescent glaze very similar to one produced by Tiffany & Co. between 1901 and 1907, which the Weller concern called Sicardo Ware. The company closed in 1948.

Weller Pottery vase by Jacques Sicard, of tapering cylindrical form and decorated with full-height pine branches and needles in iridescent shades of green, yellow, orange, and red on a copper-gold ground. *c. 1905*

9 in (22.5 cm) high

$1,800–2,200 LG

Weller Pottery bullet-shaped vase by Jacques Sicard, decorated with full-height pine trees in front of a mountain lake, in shades of gray against bands of iridescent yellow and red. *c. 1905*

6 in (15.25 cm)

$500–800 DRA

European Ceramics

All across Europe, from Paris to Vienna, pottery artists such as Peter Behrens, Henry van de Velde, Clement Massier, and Richard Riemerschmid embraced the new, organic style for their ceramic wares, which they decorated with plants, flowers, birds, and insect motifs. Designs were typically applied by hand-painting, transfer-printing, or slip-trailing and embellished with colorful glazes such as Clement and Jean-Baptiste Massier's luster glazes. In France, these ceramic designs tended to be more florid and flamboyant than the stylized and restrained German and Austrian examples, which have more in common with the contemporary Arts and Crafts ceramics produced in Great Britain and the United States.

Glazed earthenware ovoid vase by Boch Frères Keramis of Belgium. It is enameled with a tulip pattern against a mottled pale-brown and yellow ground. *c. 1920*

12 in (30.5 cm) high

$700–1,000　　　　　　　　**FRE**

Glazed earthenware bulbous ovoid vase by Boch Frères Keramis of Belgium. It is thickly enameled with stylized flowerheads and undulating bands of hatching. *c. 1920*

7¾ in (19.5 cm) high

$400–600　　　　　　　　**FRE**

Twin-handled porcelain vase of waisted bulbous form by Delphin Massier of Vallauris, France. It is hand-painted with birch trees in a rural landscape. *c. 1900*

5¼ in (13.5 cm) high

$600–900　　　　　　　　**DRA**

Conical earthenware vase by Clément Massier of Golfe-Juan, France. The square rim flares to a round base with four small handles. Finished in streaked luster glazes. *1890s*

4 in (10 cm)

$100–150　　　　　　　　**WW**

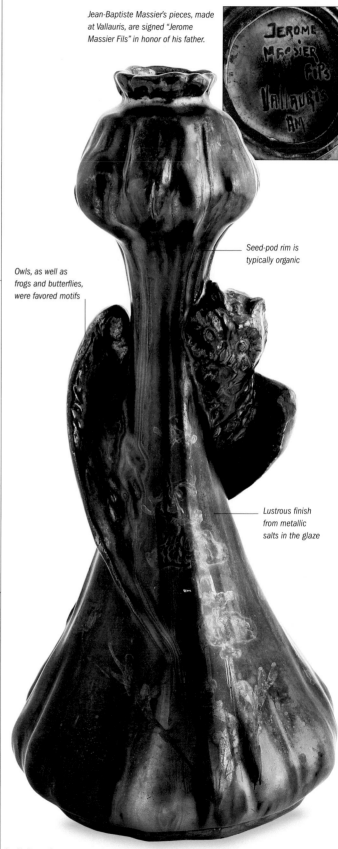

Jean-Baptiste Massier's pieces, made at Vallauris, are signed "Jerome Massier Fils" in honor of his father.

Seed-pod rim is typically organic

Owls, as well as frogs and butterflies, were favored motifs

Lustrous finish from metallic salts in the glaze

La Nuit earthenware vase by Jean-Baptiste Massier. Its fluted and ribbed organic form rises, via an applied resting owl, to a poppy seed-pod head. Both bird and plant are emblematic of the night, a symbolism enhanced by an all-over lustrous, nocturnal-like glaze. *c. 1900*

10¼ in (26 cm) high

$7,000–10,000　　　　　　　　**MACK**

Slender ovoid vase by Max Lauger. It is tube-lined with delicate, full-height grass forms in shades of green, applied over a very dark blue-black glazed ground. *1890s*

14¼ in (36 cm) high

$1,800–2,200   **WW**

Tubular earthenware vase by Henry van de Velde. Its ribbed and folded body rises to a loop-handled rim, and is finished in streaked orange and green glazes. *c. 1900*

11¼ in (28.5 cm) high

$7,000–10,000   **MACK**

Twin-handled stoneware vase by Henry van de Velde. Made by R. Merkelbach, it has a domed lid and stylized leaves. *1902*

13½ in (34.5 cm) high

$10,000–15,000   **VZ**

Twin-handled earthenware vase by Gouda, with a squat round base rising to an elongated neck with flowers and leaves. *c. 1910*

9½ in (24 cm) high

$500–700   **DRA**

Shallow stoneware washbowl designed by Peter Behrens and made by R. Merkelbach. Its white body is tinted green and decorated with blue-glazed, abstract wave forms. *c. 1900*

11½ in (29 cm) wide

$7,000–10,000   **VZ**

Shouldered ovoid lidded vase by Zsolnay (pronounced "Jerni") of Pecs, Hungary. It is painted with butterflies and stylized and naturalistic foliage in luster glazes. *c. 1900*

6¾ in (17 cm) high

$3,000–4,000   **WW**

Long cylindrical-necked vase with a squat, bulbous base by Zsolnay of Pecs, Hungary. It is finished with an iridescent glaze shading from petroleum green to blue and purple. *c. 1900*

18¾ in (47.5 cm) high

$5,000–7,000   **VZ**

Glazed earthenware vase by Richard Riemerschmid. Rising from a squat, globular body, its long tubular neck is slip-trailed with stylized plant forms. *c. 1905*

16½ in (42 cm) high

$2,000–3,000   **QU**

Large Amphora Ware vase of slender ovoid form, with applied and painted flowering thistles in shades of pink, brown, yellow, and green against a pale blue ground. *c. 1905*

17¼ in (44 cm) high

$2,000–3,000   **TEL**

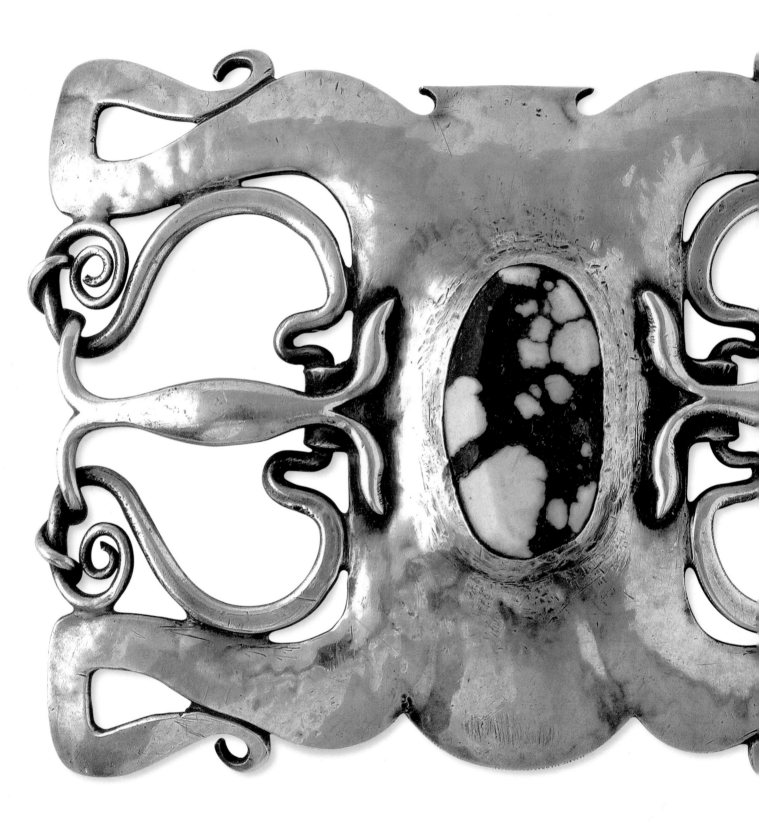

Jewelry

While the Victorians believed that the value of an item of jewelry was determined by the presence of stones and precious metals, the Arts and Crafts metalsmiths focused on the quality of craftsmanship. The worth of a necklace, brooch, or bracelet was linked to its workmanship, and its beauty admired for an imaginative design and the way in which the materials were used.

In the late 19th century, jewelry design underwent changes not unlike those being made in interior design and other branches of the decorative arts, such as ceramics and metalwork.

Inspired by the teachings of the Arts and Crafts father figure William Morris, jewelers reacted against the excesses that were typical of Victorian taste. The fashion for cluttered, showy ornaments was rejected in favor of jewelry characterized by simplicity and restraint. Clean, pure lines and decorative motifs based on nature, including flowers, birds, and butterflies, superseded the ostentatious, artificial, and sentimental themes that had held sway with the Victorians. The value of a piece of Arts and Crafts jewelry was no longer dictated by how many flashy precious stones were used to embellish it, but by the way in which the craftsman handled his materials and by the artistic integrity of the design.

In the spirit of the Arts and Crafts movement, artisans looked to the past and revived ancient jewelry-making techniques, such as the Renaissance art of enameling. A wide variety of colorful semiprecious stones—pearls, moonstones, opals, coral, malachite, and turquoise, to mention a few—were popular, often used in unusual combinations with unconventional materials such as horn, shagreen, ivory, and mother-of-pearl.

It was C. R. Ashbee at the Guild of Handicraft who paved the way for the new style of jewelry. His unpretentious and versatile items boasted simple, pure lines and naturalistic forms that looked back for inspiration to Renaissance masters such as Benvenuto Cellini.

Liberty & Co. silver two-piece buckle the design of which is attributed to Oliver Baker. It is centered with a turquoise matrix plaque flanked by pierced and applied wirework scrolls. *1900. 2¾ in (7 cm) wide* **$1,800–2,200 VDB**

THE BRITISH STYLE

Led by C. R. Ashbee, British craftsmen such as Archibald Knox, Alexander Fisher, John Paul Cooper, Edith and Nelson Dawson, and Arthur and Georgina Gaskin took up the baton and created modern, inspired designs for pendants, bracelets, earrings, rings, brooches, and buckles. Craftswomen—including Phoebe Stabler, Jessie M. King, Phoebe Traquair, and the Chicago-based Clara Barck Welles—also played a pivotal role in jewelry design, creating sophisticated items for a largely female market.

The prevailing fashion for clothes featuring simple, uncluttered lines supplied a decorous backdrop for crisp, modern ornaments set with semiprecious cabochon stones or colorful enamels. The 17th- and 18th-century fashion for buckles was also revived by the Arts and Crafts practitioners, who hand-hammered metal into a wide variety of shapes that incorporated intricate decorative patterns—such as trailing scrolls, Celtic interlacing, or stylized floral and foliate motifs—and set them with brightly hued enamels and semiprecious stones.

In the typical Arts and Crafts tradition, many jewelry designers were also architects and expert metalworkers. Among the ancient artistic techniques that were revived was "Limoges"

enameling, which was the specialty of Alexander Fisher, who taught at London's Central School of Arts and Crafts. His experiments with firing techniques resulted in metal jewelry embellished with vibrant, multicolored enamels.

A center of the metalwork trade from the 18th century, Birmingham was home to a number of silversmithing workshops and art schools that had built a reputation for excellence in jewelry design. The influential Arthur Gaskin, who headed the Vittoria Street School, and his wife Georgina created original but simple handcrafted gold and silver jewelry featuring delicate floral patterns highlighted with pale opaque enamels or colorful semiprecious stones.

With artists such as Henry Wilson, who favored Byzantine and Gothic designs, and the multitalented John Paul Cooper, British Arts and Crafts jewelry scaled new heights and became widely admired for its virtuosity of craftsmanship and breathtaking imagination.

COMMERCIAL WARES

As in other areas of decorative wares—pottery and metalwork, for example—commercial firms were quick to capitalize on the fashion for the simple, distinctive, and hand-hammered designs created by Arts and Crafts jewelry craftsmen. London's leading retailers, such as Liberty & Co. and Murrle Bennett, specialized in mass-produced pendants, necklaces, bracelets, and brooches of variable quality. Such items often featured an imitation hammered finish but boasted outstanding design, thanks to the creativity of talented but unacknowledged artists including Archibald Knox and Kate Harris.

Guild of Handicraft silver necklace designed by C. R. Ashbee. A butterfly-shaped pendant with blue enameled wings is centered with a turquoise matrix cabochon, set with further turquoise stones and with turquoise drops. The suspension chains are similarly decorated. *c. 1900* *11½ in (29 cm) long* **$6,000–9,000 VDB**

KEY POINTS

Silver was the material of choice for Arts and Crafts jewelry designers. As well as precious stones like opals, a whole gamut of semiprecious stones, such as chrysoprase and peridot, was employed as decoration. Other natural materials, including mother-of-pearl and abalone, provided further visual interest. Enamel and plique-à-jour were often used to depict landscapes, stylized floral designs, and geometric patterns.

W. H. Haseler silver pendant the design of which is attributed to Archibald Knox. The cruciform shape is cast with Celtic knots and set with plaques of abalone shell. Probably retailed through Liberty & Co. *c. 1900. 2 in (5 cm) high* **$2,000–3,000 VDB**

Liberty & Co. silver pendant with a winter-landscape plaque enameled in colors by Charles Fleetwood Varley within an enameled mount designed by Jessie M. King. *c. 1910* *18 in (46 cm) long* **$2,000–3,000 VDB**

Liberty & Co. silver two-piece rectangular buckle with flared petal-like panels and Celtic-inspired roundels picked out with shaded blue-and-green enameling. Stamped with maker's marks for Birmingham. *1911 3 in (7.5 cm) wide* **$1,200–1,800 VDB**

INFLUENCES AND DEVELOPMENTS

The decoration of the Arts and Crafts style coalesced around themes inspired by the natural world. While French jewelry designers such as René Lalique, Georges Fouquet, and Eugène Feuillatre favored a sinuous, florid interpretation in sumptuous materials, German and Austrian artists—such as Joseph Maria Olbrich, Richard Riemerschmid, Carl Otto Czeschka, and Dagobert Peche—took jewelry design in a different direction, choosing restrained, linear, geometric forms decorated with highly stylized, abstract motifs based on nature that reflected the influence of Charles Rennie Mackintosh and the Glasgow School.

The Europeans parted company with their British Arts and Crafts counterparts by their willingness to embrace modernity—not just in their designs but also in the use of materials such as chromium and in their appreciation of the advantages offered by the machine.

In the United States, the premier manufacturer of Arts and Crafts jewelry was the renowned Tiffany Studios, which tended to favor a flamboyant strain of design and decoration. Jewelry-making workshops run by influential luminaries—including Frank Gardner Hale, Edward E. Oakes, and Clara Barck Welles at her all-female Kalo Shop—created pieces in the new taste, which was widely celebrated and highly prized for quality and craftsmanship.

Their lead was also followed by small independent concerns established by creative designers such as Josephine Hartwell Shaw, Mildred Watkins, and James Winn.

Rokesley Shop of Cleveland silver pendant of waisted shape, pierced and embellished in shallow relief with an iris bloom and leaves picked out with blue-green enameling. With a freshwater-pearl drop. *c. 1910. 1¾ in (4.5 cm) high* **$3,000–4,000 CHI**

German silver pendant with an oval cabochon of chrysoprase set below an openwork frame of a stylized rose flanked by foliage and set with a half-pearl. It also has a freshwater-pearl drop. *c. 1905. 2¼ in (6 cm) long* **$300–400 RG**

Heinrich Levinger silver and *plique-à-jour* brooch of winged organic shape, cast with fine veins and stylized stems and enameled in translucent pale mauve. The open center is set with an oval opal cabochon. *c. 1900. 1½ in (4 cm) long* **$2,000–3,000 VDB**

KEY FEATURES

Colored enamels or cabochons, amethysts, turquoise, pearls, or opals, and Celtic interlacing are typical decorative details of Murrle Bennett jewelry.

Jewelry shapes were either sinuous and edged with tendrils or geometric and linear.

Long necklaces embellished with blue-green enamels and stylized leaves were among the most popular items.

Finely hammer-textured surfaces are often adorned with small bumps simulating rivets.

Pieces are usually marked "MB" or "MB & Co," although even unmarked jewelry can often be attributed to Murrle Bennett due to its distinctive designs.

Murrle Bennett

By marrying exceptional design with commercial sense, Murrle Bennett & Co. produced a range of decorative jewelry inspired by a variety of styles, including Arts and Crafts, with its emphasis on craftsmanship.

Established in 1884 by the German Ernst Murrle in collaboration with an elusive Englishman called Mr. Bennett, the London-based retail company of Murrle Bennett specialized in affordable gold and silver jewelry in a host of popular styles. Designs were inspired by the abstract, geometric style of the German Jugendstil, the Cymric range of silver sold by Liberty & Co., and the English Arts and Crafts technique in which rivets and joints were boldly highlighted and sometimes even faked for artistic effect.

Like many other commercial firms, in an effort to imitate the Arts and Crafts style of heavily hammered silverwork and translucent enameling, Murrle Bennett evolved a type of silverwork, often with a spurious "hand-worked" hammered finish, that was decorated with panels of shaded enamels. Although quality-wise Murrle Bennett mass-produced jewelry tended to be

rather perfunctory, it stands out for its highly innovative and distinctive designs. Two designers associated with the firm—F. Rico and R. Win—never signed their individual work.

Typical Murrle Bennett items are gold pendants and necklaces boasting a sumptuous matt sheen and frequently inset with colorful turquoise, amethysts, and mother-of-pearl. Other techniques find gold or silver wires entwined around a pearl or turquoise, creating a cagelike structure similar to the designs of the Austrian Wiener Werkstätte (*see pp.198–99*).

Different styles coalesced in the jewelry manufactured by Murrle Bennett. The fluid outlines characteristic of nature-inspired Art Nouveau jewelry were complemented by pendants and brooches featuring the rectilinear shapes typical of contemporary German designs.

Above: Fifteen-carat gold brooch of sinuous outline set with an oval turquoise cabochon and with a freshwater-pearl drop. *c. 1900* 1¼ in (3 cm) long **$1,200–1,800 VDB**

NATURAL AND GEOMETRIC DESIGN

Companies such as Murrle Bennett capitalized on the mercurial tastes of the public and created jewelry in a number of fashionable styles. The sinuous, fluid lines found in nature that were key to the Art Nouveau style, the strong geometric shapes typical of German and Austrian design, and the simplicity and handcraftsmanship that lay at the heart of the Arts and Crafts movement all found their way into the designs for mass-produced jewelry. Bracelets, pendants, and brooches could be bold and angular with abstract motifs, or styled with an eye to nature, featuring soft, flowing outlines, and stylized floral or foliate patterns highlighted with colored enamels or cabochons.

Hammer-textured silver necklace mounted with an enameled plaque showing a sailboat in naturalistic colors. It is suspended from chains with enameled spacers and has a pearl drop. *c. 1900.* 18½ in (47 cm) long **$1,800–2,200 VDB**

Geometric-shaped silver brooch with textured surface and rivet decoration. It is set with three opal cabochons, one on a panel hanging on rings, and has two more opal drops. *c. 1900.* 1¼ in (3.5 cm) long **$500–700 VDB**

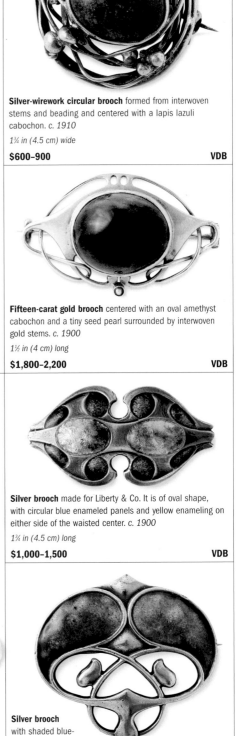

Silver-wirework circular brooch formed from interwoven stems and beading and centered with a lapis lazuli cabochon. *c. 1910*

1¾ in (4.5 cm) wide

$600–900   **VDB**

Circular silver pendant with a central mother-of-pearl plaque and embellished around its outer edge with flowers in blue and green enameling. It is suspended from a chain and stamped with the maker's mark. *c. 1900*

1 in (2.5 cm) wide

$500–700   **WW**

Fifteen-carat gold brooch centered with an oval amethyst cabochon and a tiny seed pearl surrounded by interwoven gold stems. *c. 1900*

1½ in (4 cm) long

$1,800–2,200   **VDB**

Silver brooch made for Liberty & Co. It is of oval shape, with circular blue enameled panels and yellow enameling on either side of the waisted center. *c. 1900*

1¾ in (4.5 cm) long

$1,000–1,500   **VDB**

Open-teardrop gold necklace with heart-shaped motif and tendrils, set with a plaque of turquoise matrix suspended from a spacer and chain. *c. 1900*

Pendant: 1¾ in (4.5 cm) long

$2,000–3,000   **VDB**

Silver necklace of openwork circular shape with rivet decoration, a central amethyst, and an amethyst drop. Another amethyst is set on the spacer. *c. 1900*

Pendant: 1¾ in (4.5 cm) long

$700–1,000   **VDB**

Oval gold pendant with a turquoise matrix cabochon in a caged mount and interwoven knot decoration. With three freshwater-pearl drops. *c. 1900*

1¾ in (4 cm) long

$1,800–2,200   **VDB**

Silver brooch with shaded blue-and-green teardrop-shaped panels extending into interwoven stems. With a freshwater-pearl drop. *c. 1900*

1¼ in (3.5 cm) long

$1,200–1,800   **VDB**

KEY FEATURES

Colorful semiprecious stones—
rubies, amethysts, pearls, emeralds,
and occasionally diamonds, which
were typically left natural—were
used to embellish finely crafted,
handmade jewelry.

Moonstones, turquoise, opals,
aquamarine, mother-of-pearl, and
topaz were also popular materials
for brooches, pendants, and
necklaces—as well as enamels
in a variety of hues.

Forward-looking designs are
typically rendered in silver or gold.

Jewelry boasts clear, simple lines
along with decoration featuring
naturalistic motifs such
as flowers, birds and butterflies,
and Celtic interlaced patterns.

Guild of Handicraft

At the celebrated Arts and Crafts institution the Guild of
Handicraft, founder C. R. Ashbee introduced a range of
innovative jewelry that looked back to the Renaissance for
inspiration, yet was a leader in trendsetting modern design.

The gifted and influential Arts and Crafts
designer and silversmith Charles Robert
Ashbee (1863–1942) encouraged the romantic
ideal of the artist-craftsman, and at his Guild
of Handicraft he established a studio dedicated
to producing high-quality, well-made jewelry.

Although imbued with a medieval and
Renaissance spirit, the Guild's innovative
jewelry items confirmed its reputation for
trendsetting, modern design. Ashbee upheld
the Arts and Crafts conviction that a jewel's
value depended not on the cost, but on the
handling of the materials and on the artistic
integrity of the design.

Ashbee's straightforward,
expressive silver and gold

jewelry boasted simple lines and naturalistic
decorative motifs, including flowers, birds, and
butterflies. Necklaces, brooches, and pendants
were typically decorated with colorful
semiprecious stones—rubies, emeralds,
amethysts, and pearls—or with less expensive
aquamarines, moonstones, opals, and topaz.

The Guild's jewelry was eventually eclipsed
by the burgeoning dominance of Liberty & Co.,
since Ashbee's venture was unable to compete
with the London retailer's aggressive investment
in jewelry production. The Guild closed in 1907.

Above: Hexagonal silver brooch designed by C. R. Ashbee, with a
circular agate cabochon surrounded by eight pale blue enameled
sections, each with a yellow foliate motif. *c. 1902*
1¾ in (4.5 cm) wide **$5,000–8,000 VDB**

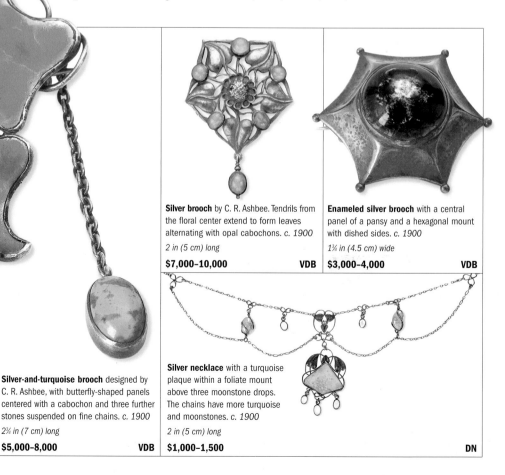

Silver brooch by C. R. Ashbee. Tendrils from
the floral center extend to form leaves
alternating with opal cabochons. *c. 1900*
2 in (5 cm) long

$7,000–10,000   **VDB**

Enameled silver brooch with a central
panel of a pansy and a hexagonal mount
with dished sides. *c. 1900*
1¾ in (4.5 cm) wide

$3,000–4,000   **VDB**

Silver-and-turquoise brooch designed by
C. R. Ashbee, with butterfly-shaped panels
centered with a cabochon and three further
stones suspended on fine chains. *c. 1900*
2¾ in (7 cm) long

$5,000–8,000   **VDB**

Silver necklace with a turquoise
plaque within a foliate mount
above three moonstone drops.
The chains have more turquoise
and moonstones. *c. 1900*
2 in (5 cm) long

$1,000–1,500   **DN**

Bernard Instone

A Birmingham native, Bernard Instone was closely linked with the promotion of the jewelry trade in that English town throughout his career. His personalized jewelry designs display the values of an artisan of the old school.

Thanks to a scholarship, Bernard Instone (1891–1973) went to study at Birmingham's Central School of Art when he was still only 12 years old. It soon became clear that he possessed a rare talent, and his training continued on Vittoria Street, in the heart of Birmingham's jewelry district. There followed some years as a journeyman, very much in the mold of the medieval European craftsman. During this period, Instone spent time with Emile Lettré on Berlin's fashionable Unter den Linden Boulevard and then with John Paul Cooper in Kent. After fighting in World War I, he returned to the West Midlands, where he established the Langstone Silver Works in 1920.

Although the Langstone Works produced tableware, jewelry was always Instone's forte. He liked to design for individual clients, so he could tailor the shape, form, and color of his creations to their individual look.

His tireless efforts on behalf of the business community saw him become a liveryman of the Worshipful Company of Goldsmiths and, in 1937, president of the Birmingham Jewelers' Association. Instone worked hard to democratize his art, educating his clients as well as his apprentices, and striving to keep his jewelry affordable. An economy of materials is evident, for example, in the use of semiprecious stones rather than more valuable gems.

Above: Silver brooch set with a cornelian cabochon within a silver wreath of eight small florets and tangled leaves. *c. 1900* *1¼ in (3 cm) wide* **$180–220 AVW**

KEY FEATURES

Wheatsheaves and berries often decorate Instone's jewelry, whose designs frequently refer to the English countryside.

Every piece is individual, a testament to Instone's practice of customizing his jewelry for specific clients.

The use of vine motifs and continental-stone inclusions reveals a European influence.

Silver is the predominant metal, although Instone also worked with gold.

The vast array of stones used speaks of Instone's attempts to find colors ideally suited to different skin tones.

Silver lady's ring set with an oval Swiss lapis cabochon framed with a mount of tiny florets and leaves. *c. 1900*
1 in (2.5 cm) wide
$800–1,200   **AVW**

Silver lady's ring centered with a square amethyst within a mount embellished with interwoven leaves and florets. *c. 1900*
1 in (2.5 cm) wide
$800–1,200   **AVW**

Silver brooch with a central faceted citrine within a mount of leaves and tendrils punctuated with three peridots. *c. 1920*
1¼ in (3 cm) long
$300–500   **DN**

Silver brooch with a central faceted citrine flanked by a border of swirling leaves and faceted smoky quartz. *c. 1920*
1½ in (4 cm) long
$500–700   **PC**

Elaborate silver necklace with seven large faceted amethysts within foliate mounts. The stones alternate with square openwork plaques set with chrysoprase cabochons amid leaves. It is linked by loops that resemble three-petaled florets. *c. 1930*
20½ in (52 cm) long

$3,000–4,000   **VDB**

Liberty & Co.

By striking a balance between innovative designs and commercial concerns, London retailer Liberty & Co. succeeded in bringing art jewelry of exceptional quality to the general public. Liberty employed several leading British Arts and Crafts designers—although they worked under the Liberty & Co. name—including Archibald Knox (1864–1933), Jessie M. King (1876–1949), and Oliver Baker (1856–1939), to create stylish jewelry in quality materials for industrial production. Liberty & Co. was celebrated for decorative jewelry that was at once artistic, well made, enduringly appealing, and widely affordable.

Silver-and-enamel buckle with two circular sections cast with a forest scene against a background of enameled green and blue. *1904*

1¼ in (3.5 cm) wide

$300–500   **WW**

Silver buckle designed by Oliver Baker, with a central plaque of mother-of-pearl flanked on either side with stylized floral interwoven scrollwork; marked "Cymric." *c. 1900*

4½ in (11.5 cm) wide

$3,000–4,000   **VDB**

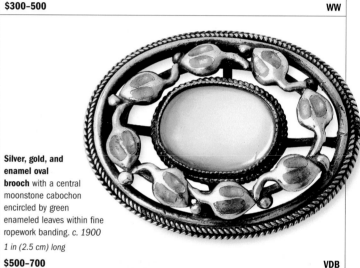

Silver, gold, and enamel oval brooch with a central moonstone cabochon encircled by green enameled leaves within fine ropework banding. *c. 1900*

1 in (2.5 cm) long

$500–700   **VDB**

Silver two-piece buckle with heart-shaped sections enclosing four stylized mythical beasts with tails that extend to form a complex design of Celtic knots and swirls. *1906*

4¼ in (11 cm) wide

$300–400   **DN**

Gold necklace by Archibald Knox, with a winged-shaped pendant set with pink tourmalines, and freshwater pearls and a peridot suspended on chains. *c. 1900*

2¾ *in (7 cm) long*

$5,000–8,000   **VDB**

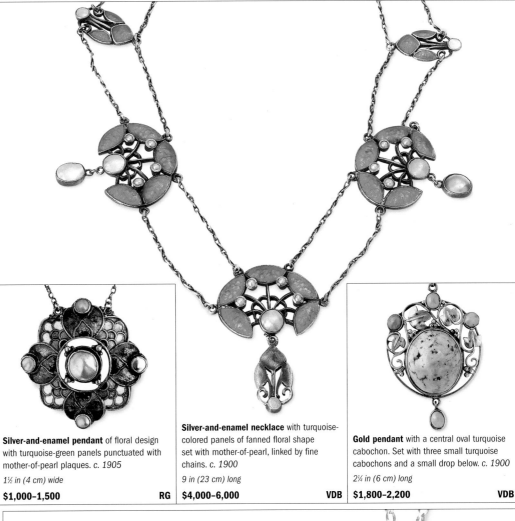

Silver-and-enamel pendant of floral design with turquoise-green panels punctuated with mother-of-pearl plaques. *c. 1905*

1½ *in (4 cm) wide*

$1,000–1,500   **RG**

Silver-and-enamel necklace with turquoise-colored panels of fanned floral shape set with mother-of-pearl, linked by fine chains. *c. 1900*

9 *in (23 cm) long*

$4,000–6,000   **VDB**

Gold pendant with a central oval turquoise cabochon. Set with three small turquoise cabochons and a small drop below. *c. 1900*

2¼ *in (6 cm) long*

$1,800–2,200   **VDB**

Gold necklace by Archibald Knox, with a pendant set with pearls and a turquoise matrix; the chain has turquoise pebbles and two gold plaques with pearls *c. 1900*

19¼ *in (49 cm) long*

$5,000–8,000   **VDB**

W. H. Haseler

A small gold and silversmithing company established in Birmingham in 1850, W. H. Haseler forged a partnership with Liberty & Co. in 1899 and became the sole supplier of the celebrated Cymric range of silverware. In 1901, the companies merged to create Liberty & Co. Cymric Ltd., registering the mark in 1903. The venture lasted until 1927. In addition to metalware, Haseler produced a line of colorful jewelry bearing the company's own mark. Haseler jewelry was largely the handwork of its chief silversmith Harry C. Craythorn (1881–1949) after Celtic-inspired designs created in the Arts and Crafts style by Archibald Knox.

Haseler 9-carat gold brooch designed by Archibald Knox, formed by sinuous interwoven tendrils, with a green enameled heart-shaped leaf and punctuated by three small pearls. *1905*

1¼ *in (3.5 cm) long*

$1,000–1,500   **RG**

Haseler enameled silver pendant in blue and turquoise, with a three-pronged spray resembling a fleur-de-lys. *c. 1905*

1¼ *in (3.5 cm) long*

$600–900   **DN**

British Jewelry

British jewelry really excelled in exploring Arts and Crafts themes, such as the use of simple floral, foliate, and figural patterns for decoration, along with motifs inspired by Celtic art. Led by C. R. Ashbee, British craftsmen such as John Paul Cooper, James Fenton, George Hunt, and the Gaskins reacted against flamboyant Victorian taste by choosing affordable materials, such as horn, for their necklaces, brooches, buckles, and pendants. Metals were finely hammered to create a soft, matt appearance, with richly colored enamels, semiprecious cabochon stones, and inexpensive materials assembled into intricate, delicate designs. Many artists—among them Archibald Knox, Jessie M. King, and Murrle Bennett—also supplied jewelry to commercial companies such as Liberty & Co.

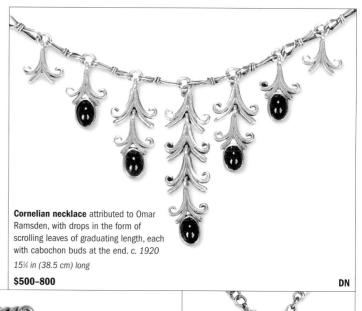

Cornelian necklace attributed to Omar Ramsden, with drops in the form of scrolling leaves of graduating length, each with cabochon buds at the end. *c. 1920*

15¼ in (38.5 cm) long

$500–800   DN

Heart-shaped gem-set clip by Dorrie Nossiter, with golden wirework scrolls flanked by garnets, turquoise cabochons, and half-pearls. *c. 1920*

1½ in (3.5 cm) long

$500–800   DN

Gold-and-citrine brooch attributed to Dorrie Nossiter, with a central faceted oval citrine nesting within intertwined wirework tendrils, golden leaves, and beading. *c. 1920*

1½ in (3.5 cm) wide

$300–500   DN

Silver-and-enamel pendant by Omar Ramsden, its central panel enclosed by thorny tendrils; with three tassel drops below. *c. 1930*

1½ in (4 cm) long

$2,500–3,000   VDB

Green enameled silver necklace by Bertha L. Goff, depicting Leda and the Swan, suspended on an elaborate chain. *1902*

14½ in (37 cm) long

$4,000–6,000   VDB

Silver-and-moonstone drop necklace by Katie Eadie, of intricate foliate and floral design with mother-of-pearl decoration. *1900–10*

19 in (48 cm) long

$7,000–10,000   VDB

Silver heart-shaped openwork pendant by Child & Child. Scrolling bands have citrines and aquamarines; with a citrine drop. *c. 1890*

12 in (30.5 cm) long

NPA   VDB

Enameled quatralobe pendant by Phoebe A. Traquair, depicting two angels embracing; with an enameled drop below. *c. 1905*

1½ in (4 cm) long

$12,000–18,000   VDB

Enameled brooch by George Hunt depicting a woman within a scrolling mount of enameled leaves and moonstone cabochons. *c. 1930*

2½ in (6 cm) high

$2,000–3,000 VDB

Enameled brooch by George Hunt, depicting a dark-haired girl within a green enameled foliate mount with moonstones. *1932*

2¾ in (7 cm) long

$1,800–2,200 VDB

Clip brooch with an oval lapis lazuli cabochon flanked by golden beading, two leaves with wirework stems, and a pearl cabochon. *c. 1930*

1½ in (3.5 cm) long

$300–400 DN

Enameled silver rectangular brooch by George Hunt, depicting in naturalistic colors a windmill in a landscape at dusk. The mount has a beaded edge. *c. 1930*

1½ in (4 cm) long

$500–700 VDB

Gem-set brooch by Dorrie Nossiter, arranged around the outer edge with citrines and other stones of autumnal colors. *c. 1920*

1½ in (4 cm) wide

$700–1,000 PC

Large moonstone-and-amethyst brooch with five large oval moonstone cabochons and three round amethysts. *c. 1900*

4½ in (10.5 cm) long

$400–600 RP

Arthur and Georgina Gaskin

The Birmingham-based silversmith Arthur Gaskin (1862–1928) designed innovative jewelry in a successful partnership with his wife Georgina (1868–1934). In contrast to indifferently designed commercial Victorian jewelry, the Gaskins' silver and gold jewelry—decorated with pale opaque enamels or set with small colored stones—was hailed for its simplicity and exceptional craftsmanship. Less-than-perfect semiprecious stones frequently formed the centerpiece of a Gaskin design, especially when set in silver mounts with plain borders composed of flowers and leaves that ultimately focused attention on the stone and the beauty of its imperfections.

Gaskin silver brooch of oval form set with plaques of opal interspersed with pink tourmalines, peridots, birds in flight, and florets. Stamped "G." *c. 1915*

1½ in (4 cm) wide

$1,200–1,800 L&T

Gaskin silver pin with oval openwork plaque embellished with leafy branches and florets. It is set with four bright green pastes, three of which are tear-shaped, the other square. *c. 1910*

3 in (7.5 cm) long

$1,200–1,800 VDB

Gaskin silver-and-amethyst necklace with a central oval cabochon set within a foliate mount flanked by small plaques of mother-of-pearl. Signed with a "G." *c. 1900*

2 in (5 cm) long

$1,800–2,200 PC

Silver-and-citrine domed brooch centered with a faceted stone flanked by foliage, stems, and berries. *c. 1910*

1½ in (4 cm) wide

$300–400   DN

Heart-shaped cornelian-drop earrings by Sibyl Dunlop, suspended from floral wirework panels set with amethysts, moonstones, and other colored chalcedonies. *c. 1930*

1¼ in (3.5 cm) long

$5,000–7,000   VDB

Enameled gold oval wreath brooch by Harold Stabler. The enameled green leaves are punctuated with garnets and pearls. Converted from a pendant. *1913*

2 in (5 cm) long

$1,800–2,200   DN

Silver-and-moonstone pendant with a central cabochon flanked by four moonstones held within a wirework scroll. *c. 1900*

1½ in (4 cm) long

$300–500   DN

Octagonal silver brooch with a central cornelian cabochon; the mount is embellished with studs and wirework. *c. 1910*

1¼ in (3.5 cm) wide

$70–100   DN

Oval silver brooch with a central plaque of blister pearl encircled by an openwork band of foliate branches. *c. 1900*

1¼ in (3 cm) wide

$80–120   AVW

Silver-and-amethyst brooch with a central square stone within a mount of golden thistles and silver leaves, flanked by two further amethysts set in silver mounts. *c. 1900*

2 in (5 cm) wide

$180–220   AVW

Silver necklace with a fan-shaped pendant that is set with green and white pastes and foliate motifs. *c. 1910*

2 in (5 cm) long

$600–900   DN

Lozenge-shaped silver-fronted brooch embossed in shallow relief with floral and foliate motifs, flanking a blue-glazed Ruskin Pottery plaque. *c. 1900*

2½ in (6.5 cm) wide

$70–100 AVW

Silver-and-aquamarine ring with a central cushion-shaped stone within a mount of interwoven foliate stems punctuated with golden berries. *c. 1900*

1 in (2.5 cm) wide

$800–1,200 AVW

Pentagonal silver-and-chalcedony pendant with foliate stems and berries encircling the green oval cabochon. *c. 1920*

1½ in (4 cm) long

$300–500 DN

Silver pendant formed as a stylized flowerhead. With faux pearls in the center, and enamels of mauve and pearly white. *c. 1900*

1¾ in (4.5 cm) long

$300–400 DN

Silver bar brooch with a central oval cabochon of turquoise matrix within an oval textured mount. The bar has textured and studded decoration. *c. 1900*

3 in (7.5 cm) wide

$80–120 AVW

Silver-and-chalcedony bar brooch featuring three lilac-colored cabochons and embellished with floral stems interspersed with golden foliage and beading. *c. 1900*

3 in (7.5 cm) wide

$400–600 AVW

Silver-and-aquamarine pendant attributed to Rhoda Wager. The rectangular faceted stone is held within a foliate mount. *c. 1900*

1 in (2.5 cm) long

$300–400 TDG

Gem-set pendant with a heart-shaped rock crystal suspended from a foliate wirework mount with chalcedony cabochons. *c. 1890*

3 in (7.5 cm) long

$600–900 TDG

Silver pendant necklace by Henry William King, with a panel of vivid blue butterfly wing within an openwork flower-form mount. *c. 1905*

12 in (31 cm) long

$300–300 AVW

Silver Crafts pendant enclosing a plaque of blister pearl embellished with foliate stems. It has a Swiss-lapis cabochon drop. *c. 1900*

Pendant: 2 in (5 cm) long

$300–500 DN

Silver brooch of winged form, with overlapping bands against a ground of blue and green enameling set with seed pearls and a mother-of-pearl plaque and drop. *c. 1900*

1¼ in (3.5 cm) wide

$300–500 AVW

Enameled silver pendant by James Fenton, with a central heart-shaped panel flanked by curved stems and a drop. *1908*

2 in (5 cm) long

$300–500 RG

Enameled silver necklace by James Fenton, with a turquoise enameled pendant with foliate decoration and drop. *1909*

2¼ in (5.5 cm) long

$600–900 RG

Enameled pendant by James Fenton, with stylized foliate detail, suspended from chains with enameled spacers. *1909*

1½ in (4 cm) long

$500–700 RG

Enameled necklace by Charles Horner, featuring an elliptical pendant with an openwork winged top and an enameled drop and spacer; marked. *1908*

2¾ in (7 cm) long

$700–1,000 DN

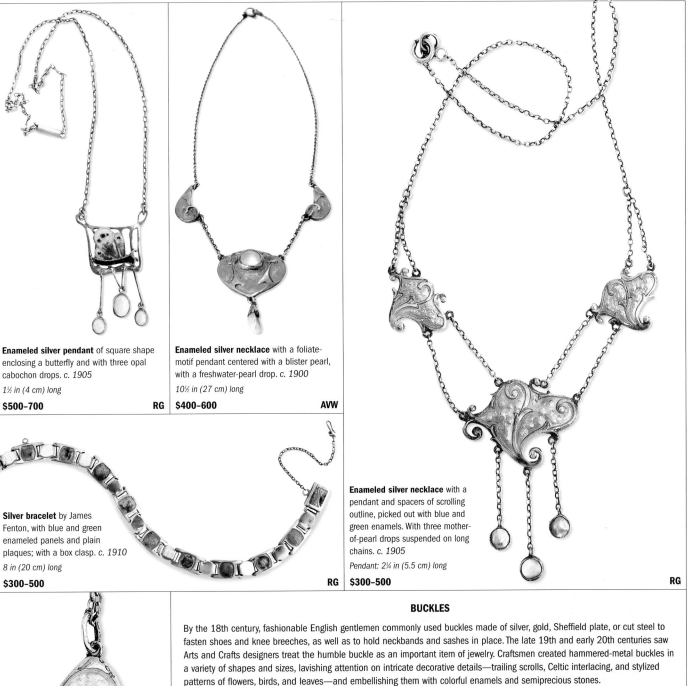

Enameled silver pendant of square shape enclosing a butterfly and with three opal cabochon drops. *c. 1905*

1½ in (4 cm) long

$500–700   **RG**

Enameled silver necklace with a foliate-motif pendant centered with a blister pearl, with a freshwater-pearl drop. *c. 1900*

10½ in (27 cm) long

$400–600   **AVW**

Silver bracelet by James Fenton, with blue and green enameled panels and plain plaques; with a box clasp. *c. 1910*

8 in (20 cm) long

$300–500   **RG**

Enameled silver necklace with a pendant and spacers of scrolling outline, picked out with blue and green enamels. With three mother-of-pearl drops suspended on long chains. *c. 1905*

Pendant: 2¼ in (5.5 cm) long

$300–500   **RG**

Silver pendant by James Fenton, formed by three overlapping elliptical loops, enameled yellow-green and blue; on a fine chain. *1909*

1½ in (3.5 cm) long

$300–500   **RG**

BUCKLES

By the 18th century, fashionable English gentlemen commonly used buckles made of silver, gold, Sheffield plate, or cut steel to fasten shoes and knee breeches, as well as to hold neckbands and sashes in place. The late 19th and early 20th centuries saw Arts and Crafts designers treat the humble buckle as an important item of jewelry. Craftsmen created hammered-metal buckles in a variety of shapes and sizes, lavishing attention on intricate decorative details—trailing scrolls, Celtic interlacing, and stylized patterns of flowers, birds, and leaves—and embellishing them with colorful enamels and semiprecious stones.

Silver belt buckle of shaped outline with hammer-textured surface applied with whiplash tendrils and centered by a turquoise. Hallmarks for Birmingham. *1901*
4 in (10 cm) wide **$300–500 L&T**

Silver two-piece buckle by W. H. Haseler, with each part enclosing highly stylized florets with embossed detail on the petals. Marked "W.H.H." for Birmingham. *1902*
3¾ in (9.5 cm) wide **$300–400 DN**

KEY FEATURES

Handcrafted jewelry was usually rendered in silver, although sometimes gold was used.

Nature-inspired motifs such as flowers, fruit, and foliage patterns are typical, but stylized geometric designs are also featured.

A hammered, pierced and chased surface texture is common on brooches, necklaces, pendants, bracelets, and earrings.

Semiprecious stones were often used to embellish Kalo Shop jewelry.

Kalo Shop

With boundless enthusiasm, the indefatigable Clara Barck Welles established the Kalo Shop in Chicago, with an all-female staff creating simple, elegant, award-winning jewelry in the American Arts and Crafts style.

A graduate of the Art Institute of Chicago and a champion of women's causes, Clara Barck Welles (1868–1965) established the Kalo Shop in 1900. The name derives from the Greek word *kalos*, meaning "beautiful," and the studio's motto was "Beautiful, Useful, and Enduring." From the beginning, it was Welles's intention to establish a business that would both teach and train young women who had an interest in arts and crafts.

Her all-female workshop was initially dedicated to creating leather goods and weaving, but following her marriage to amateur metalworker George Welles in 1905, she organized the Kalo Arts-Crafts community as both a studio and a school.

In addition to producing a range of widely acclaimed silver tableware, Welles and her students—

known as "Kalo girls"—added a line of simple and elegant handcrafted jewelry to their repertoire. The brooches, pendants, necklaces, bracelets, and earrings that were designed by the Kalo Shop typically favored both stylized geometric shapes and naturalistic decorative motifs. These included lush foliage such as oak leaves with acorns, vine leaves, seed-pods, and flower blossoms.

Kalo Shop jewelry was usually in silver, but gold was employed occasionally. Many popular designs are embellished with semiprecious stones, such as moonstones, cornelians, and pearls, and they boast a handwrought, hammered surface texture inspired by the work of C. R. Ashbee (*see p.160*). After a long and prolific tenure, the Kalo Shop closed its doors in 1970.

Above: Eye-shaped brooch made in sterling silver with a variegated green and reddish brown oval stone cabochon at its center. *c. 1915* *3 in (7.75 cm) wide* **$800–1,200 CHI**

NATURALISTIC DESIGNS

Like many American metalwork and jewelry firms specializing in the Arts and Crafts tradition, the Kalo Shop of Chicago looked to the natural world for inspiration. The flowing lines reflected in nature were adopted for a variety of silver and gold designs for brooches, bracelets, necklaces, earrings, and pendants. Flower blossom and foliage designs were handcrafted and often set in the middle with bezel-set semiprecious stones. Patterns featuring flower blossoms, lush foliage, and fruit are among the most popular.

Sterling silver pendant necklace with a paperclip chain. The pendant features a blister pearl wreathed with flowers, beneath additional linked flowers and above two small silver pearl drops. *c. 1915* *Pendant: 1¼ in (3.25 cm) long* **$4,000–6,000 CHI**

Sterling silver flowerhead brooch set in a pierced and chased oval frame. It has six handwrought and chased petals around a cluster of seed-pods and a bezel-set, oval moonstone cabochon. *c. 1935.* *2¼ in (5.75 cm) wide* **$800–1,200 CHI**

Sterling silver bar pin with cut-out sides ending in demi-arrowheads. The central, bezel-set bloodstone cabochon is flanked by applied flowers. *c. 1920*

2¾ in (7 cm) wide

$800–1,200   **CHI**

Sterling silver bracelet with handwrought and chased flowerheads with round, bezel-set cornelian cabochons, ending in a pearl-shaped V-spring box clasp with a safety chain. *c. 1935*

7½ in (19 cm) long

$2,000–3,000   **CHI**

Sterling silver bar pin with cut-out and interlaced geometric-pattern side, flanking a large, square, bezel-set citrine-colored stone. *c. 1915*

1¾ in (4.5 cm) wide

$800–1,200   **CHI**

Unusual sterling silver belt with 14 twin cherry-and-leaf motif links alternated with 14 twin leaf motif links. All are handwrought and chased within pierced frames. *c. 1935*

35 in (89 cm) long

$2,000–3,000   **CHI**

Pair of sterling silver earrings handwrought and chased as curvaceous leaf forms. With screw-clip backs. *c. 1935*

1 in (2.5 cm) high

$180–220   **CHI**

Sterling silver brooch of round shield shape with a plain, crimped border encircling a handwrought and chased oak-leaves-and-acorns pattern in deep relief. *c. 1935*

2¼ in (5.75 cm) wide

$300–500   **CHI**

Shield-shaped gold pendant on a paperclip chain, with a large blister pearl framed by applied flowers and vines, all above a baroque pearl drop. *c. 1910*

Pendant: 2¼ in (5.75 cm) long

$7,000–10,000   **CHI**

Sterling silver necklace featuring three bezel-set, oval lapis stones in handwrought and chased frames, above three lapis teardrops with scalloped silver tops. *c. 1910*

17 in (43.25 cm) long

$7,000–10,000   **CHI**

American Jewelry

The Arts and Crafts tradition of craftsmanship was embraced by American jewelry-makers, and by the end of the 1800s, metalsmiths such as Clara Barck Welles at the Kalo Shop, Frank Gardner Hale, Edward E. Oakes, Peer Smed, and Robert Jarvie were creating quality handcrafted jewelry in silver, gold, or a combination of metals. Two main centers of mass production—Newark, New Jersey, and Providence, Rhode Island—turned out pieces for the fashion-conscious middle classes. Flowers, scrolling foliage, and Celtic interlaced designs were the favorite decorative patterns, embellished with colored enamels or semiprecious stones.

Handwrought brooch by Clemens Friedell of Pasadena. It is made of delicately hammered silver and is in the shape of a California poppy, with one large and one small blossom, one bud, and stems and leaves. *c. 1920*

4 in (10 cm) long

$3,000–5,000 (with matching earrings)   CHI

Sterling silver floral brooch designed, handwrought, and chased by Peer Smed in the form of a lily with a beaded stamen. *c. 1930*

2½ in (6.25 cm) long

$600–900   CHI

Circular shield-shaped brooch made by the Panis Gallery of Falmouth, Massachusetts, in sterling silver. It is handwrought, pierced, and chased with a thistles-and-leaves pattern. *1940s*

1½ in (4 cm) wide

$180–220   ARK

Sterling silver brooch by Vivien Lyke with a heart-shaped stone in shades of purple, mauve, red, and black. It is framed by a large, curling leaf with a spiraling stem and berries. *c. 1945*

2 in (5 cm) wide

$180–220   ARK

Rare Robert Jarvie pendant necklace with a paperclip chain, made from handwrought sterling silver with a large, oval, bezel-set chrysoprase stone flanked by, and above, smaller chrysoprase stone drops. *c. 1915*

Pendant: 2 in (5 cm) long

$7,000–10,000   **CHI**

Pendant necklace by James Scott of the Elverhoj Craft Colony, with a stone in a silver frame with leaf and berry motifs. *c. 1925*

1¼ in (3 cm) long

$500–700   **ARK**

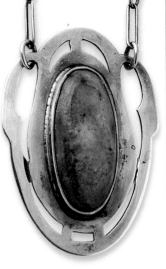

Shield-shaped pendant necklace by the Art Silver Shop of Chicago. The cut-out pendant is centered with a dyed agate cabochon. *c. 1920*

1½ in (4 cm) long

$500–700   **CHI**

Sterling silver bar pin by the Art Silver Shop of Chicago, its bow-tie-shaped frame hammered, and with chased and applied leaves flanking a bezel-set light blue-gray cabochon. *c. 1920*

2¼ in (5.75 cm) wide

$600–900   **CHI**

Frank Gardner Hale

While working in Great Britain with Ashbee's Guild of Handicraft (*see p.136*), US artist Frank Gardner Hale was steeped in the Arts and Crafts aesthetic. On his return to the US, he established a studio in Boston, where he took on apprentices of his own, including Edward E. Oakes (*see p.151*). Hale drew praise for the practical nature of his settings and links—an area where other practitioners of the Arts and Crafts style had been found wanting. This is all the more remarkable considering that every piece of his jewelry was made by hand. The skillful use of enamels and semiprecious stones is a hallmark of Hale's work and one that ensures its continued popularity.

Frank Gardner Hale shield-shaped necklace featuring a sterling silver pendant with handwrought scrolls and beads; set with a garnet cabochon and four bezel-set blister pearls, above a garnet drop. *c. 1915*

Pendant: 2 in (5 cm) long

$7,000–10,000   **CHI**

Frank Gardner Hale sterling silver brooch chased and pierced with plant-form motifs framing the center. *c. 1915*

1½ in (4 cm) wide

$1,000–1,500   **ARK**

Frank Gardner Hale sterling silver ring with a large, oval variegated turquoise cabochon flanked by applied leaf and berry motifs in gold. *c. 1920*

¾ in (2 cm) wide

$2,000–3,000   **CHI**

Shield-shape brooch designed by George Frost of the Frost Arts and Crafts Workshop, in Dayton, Ohio. It is made of hand-hammered copper with a central acid-etched leaf pattern, and marked on the reverse with a triangle encompassing the company's initials. *1908–15*

2½ in (6.5 cm) wide

$180–220   **ARK**

Unsigned Arts and Crafts brooch of rectangular shieldlike form made from handwrought nickel (or "German silver"). Within a plain border, it is decorated with an acid-etched pattern comprising a stylized bowl of flowers flanked by stylized leaves and berries. *c. 1905*

2½ in (6.5 cm) wide

$200–300   **ARK**

Unsigned American bar pin of elongated oval form. It features a central, variegated blue-green oval opal set in a similarly shaped 14-carat gold frame. The latter is handwrought with interlaced and curling leaf forms. *c. 1915*

1¾ in (4.5 cm) wide

$600–900   **ARK**

Unsigned American bib necklace with a paperclip chain. The handwrought and chased sterling silver bib has linked leaf and fruit forms, with the fruits represented by malachite cabochons. *1907*

Neckpiece: 4 in (10 cm) wide

$700–1,000   **ARK**

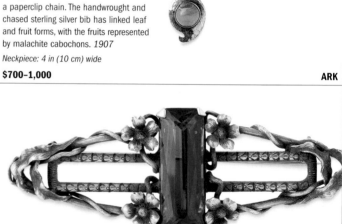

Unsigned American Arts and Crafts pin with a handwrought gold frame configured as staves and climbing-plant stems, terminating in four flowerheads, flanking a baguette-cut green tourmaline stone. *c. 1920*

2¼ in (5.5 cm) wide

$1,800–2,200   **ARK**

Gold, jade, and pearl brooch by Potter Mellen, Inc. of Cleveland, Ohio. Its 14-carat gold frame is handwrought in the form of leaves and plant stems and set with pearls of graduated size; it encloses hand-cut jade green and white plant forms. *c. 1940*

2½ in (6.5 cm) wide

$1,800–2,200

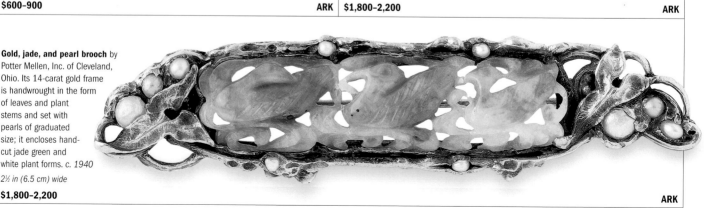

ARK

Bracelet with bezel-set onyx stones with 18-carat gold links and settings, by Margaret Rogers of Boston. The stones are flanked by gold fleur-de-lys and alternated with bezel-set pearls. *c. 1920*

7¼ in (18.5 cm) long

$7,000–10,000 **CHI**

Handwrought 18-carat gold bracelet by the Rokesley Shop of Cleveland, Ohio. It comprises four linked swollen rectangular plaques with water-chestnut and swirling-branch motifs. *1910*

7½ in (19 cm) long

$7,000–10,000 **CHI**

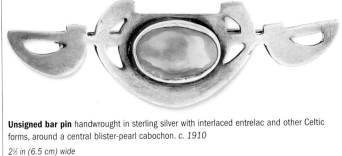

Unsigned bar pin handwrought in sterling silver with interlaced entrelac and other Celtic forms, around a central blister-pearl cabochon. *c. 1910*

2½ in (6.5 cm) wide

$200–300 **ARK**

Carence Crafters designed and made many high-quality examples of Arts and Crafts jewelry, most notably in sterling silver. Its company mark is a pair of interlaced "C"s set in a rectangle.

Sterling silver brooch by Carence Crafters of Chicago. It is handwrought in an unusual plaque- or pillowlike form, with Celtic-style interlacings at its base, and its center is set with a rectangular block of variegated yellow, green, and brown agate. *1907*

1½ in (4 cm) wide

$800–1,200 **ARK**

Edward E. Oakes

Born in Massachusetts in 1891, Edward E. Oakes was a "second-generation" Arts and Crafts master who studied and worked with Frank Gardner Hale and Josephine Shaw. In 1923, he won a medal at the Society of Arts and Crafts, Boston. He worked independently from around 1915 onward, and his imaginative and award-winning jewelry designs looked to nature for inspiration, featuring small leaves and flowers, tendrils, coils, and beads. They were handcrafted and used decorative techniques such as fine wirework, sawing, carving, and chasing. Like many Arts and Crafts jewelers, Oakes favored colorful semiprecious stones, and his play with a wide range of hues was reminiscent of Impressionist painting.

Edward E. Oakes unsigned gold bracelet with bezel-set and faceted rectangular golden topaz, alternated with rectangular plaques of handwrought and chased leaf forms, all with 14-carat gold links and settings. *Early 1920s*

6¾ in (17.25 cm) long

$7,000–10,000 **CHI**

Edward E. Oakes signed gold ring made in 18-carat gold with handwrought and chased scrolling leaf and flower forms, set with pearls and faceted blue zircons of graduated size. *1925–30*

½ in (1.25 cm) wide

$7,000–10,000 **CHI**

KEY FEATURES

Silver and low-carat gold are the metals of choice for Fahrner jewelry pieces.

Blue and green color schemes are frequently featured in bracelets, pendants, and rings.

Jewelry is typically embellished with marcasites, colorful semiprecious stones, and enameled designs.

Bold, abstract, and geometric designs are in keeping with the style favored by the Wiener Werkstätte and the designers of the German Jugendstil.

Theodor Fahrner

A pioneer of affordable art jewelry on a mass scale, the German designer Theodor Fahrner looked for inspiration to a group of Jugendstil artists to create his abstract, modernistic pieces.

Much of the inexpensive commercial jewelry sold in Great Britain—pendants, earrings, bracelets, and brooches—was produced by the imaginative designer Theodor Fahrner (1868–1928) at his factory in Pforzheim, Germany.

Fahrner carved a niche for himself in the world of jewelry-making by producing inexpensive but stylish items made from silver or gold highlighted with marcasites and embellished with a variety of colorful semiprecious stones, such as blue chalcedony, topaz, and orange cornelian. Pieces were artistically designed and made in limited runs, but industrial methods were used for their production. Fahrner, who won a silver medal at the 1900 Paris World Fair, believed that the worth of a piece lay in the success of its design rather than the monetary value of the materials used.

Fahrner's association with the group of avant-garde designers working at the artists' colony in nearby Darmstadt encouraged him to produce bold, abstract, modernistic jewelry items in geometric shapes, a fashion that at the time was widely popular in Germany and Austria. Known as Jugendstil, this style found its way via catalogs and through retailers such as Murrle Bennett (*see p.134–35*) and Liberty & Co. (*see p.138–39*) to Great Britain, where it was enthusiastically taken up and integrated into British Arts and Crafts jewelry design.

Sold in 1919, the factory continued to thrive until the 1950s as Gustave Braendle-Theodor Fahrner Nachf, before finally closing its doors in 1979. Pieces produced by Fahrner were marked with "TF" from 1901; the "Fahrner Schmuck" trademark was introduced in 1910. A marked piece is desirable among collectors and equivalent unmarked items can command as much as 75 percent less.

Above: Silver two-piece buckle of organic outline with wavelike banding, set with green-stained agate cabochons and rows of green-enameled florets. c. 1900. 3¼ in (8.5 cm) wide **$3,000–4,000** VDB

MODERNIST DESIGNS

The jewelry produced by Fahrner drew inspiration from the minimalist, abstract, geometric style featured in the items of celebrated Wiener Werkstätte designers such as Koloman Moser and Josef Hoffmann. It was also influenced by the German Jugendstil style favored by the avant-garde metalworkers at the artists' colonies in Darmstadt and Munich. Rejecting the fluid, flamboyant French Art Nouveau style, Fahrner answered the demand for affordable and fashionable jewelry. His pendants, brooches, and bracelets were designed with an eye for the modern taste for decorative motifs based on an abstract interpretation of nature.

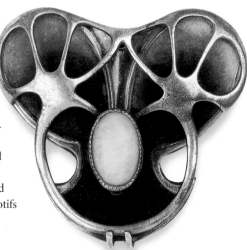

Flared silver pendant enameled in shaded blue and green, applied with stems and a cagelike mount set with turquoise matrix cabochons. With a further turquoise drop suspended from a chain. c. 1900. 2¼ in (6 cm) long **$3,000–4,000** VDB

Silver brooch of trefoil shape, applied with an organic webbed mount revealing the shaded blue-and-green enameled surface beneath. It is set with an oval opal cabochon. c. 1900 1¼ in (3.5 cm) wide **$3,000–4,000** VDB

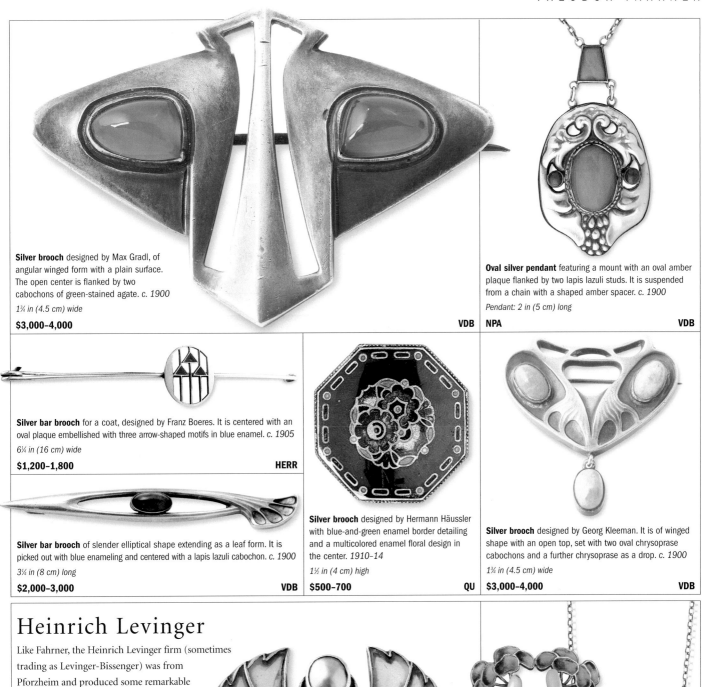

Silver brooch designed by Max Gradl, of angular winged form with a plain surface. The open center is flanked by two cabochons of green-stained agate. *c. 1900*

1¾ in (4.5 cm) wide

$3,000–4,000   VDB

Oval silver pendant featuring a mount with an oval amber plaque flanked by two lapis lazuli studs. It is suspended from a chain with a shaped amber spacer. *c. 1900*

Pendant: 2 in (5 cm) long

NPA   VDB

Silver bar brooch for a coat, designed by Franz Boeres. It is centered with an oval plaque embellished with three arrow-shaped motifs in blue enamel. *c. 1905*

6¼ in (16 cm) wide

$1,200–1,800   HERR

Silver bar brooch of slender elliptical shape extending as a leaf form. It is picked out with blue enameling and centered with a lapis lazuli cabochon. *c. 1900*

3¾ in (8 cm) long

$2,000–3,000   VDB

Silver brooch designed by Hermann Häussler with blue-and-green enamel border detailing and a multicolored enamel floral design in the center. *1910–14*

1½ in (4 cm) high

$500–700   QU

Silver brooch designed by Georg Kleeman. It is of winged shape with an open top, set with two oval chrysoprase cabochons and a further chrysoprase as a drop. *c. 1900*

1¾ in (4.5 cm) wide

$3,000–4,000   VDB

Heinrich Levinger

Like Fahrner, the Heinrich Levinger firm (sometimes trading as Levinger-Bissenger) was from Pforzheim and produced some remarkable designs for jewelry and buckles at the turn of the 20th century. Levinger jewelry typically incorporates silver, pearl, and *plique-à-jour* enameling, and is sometimes marked with the initials "HL." One of the most prominent designers working for Levinger was Otto Prutscher (1880–1949), who experimented with both organic and geometric designs.

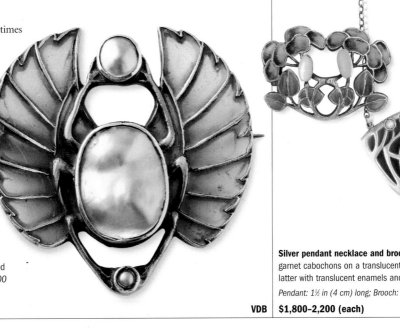

Silver and *plique-à-jour* brooch designed by Otto Prutscher as a scarab with translucent green enameled wings and a plaque of blister pearl as its body. *c. 1900*

1¼ in (3 cm) long

$3,000–4,000   VDB

Silver pendant necklace and brooch, the former set with garnet cabochons on a translucent enameled ground; the latter with translucent enamels and pearls. *c. 1900*

Pendant: 1½ in (4 cm) long; Brooch: 1½ in (4 cm) wide

$1,800–2,200 (each)   VDB

European Jewelry

European Arts and Crafts jewelry was both dramatic and stylish. Led by René Lalique, French designers including Georges Fouquet and Eugène Feuillatre revived the Renaissance art of enameling and used semiprecious stones and unconventional materials— horn and ivory, for example—for their handcrafted, nature-inspired jewelry designs in gold and silver. Other European artists—such as Josef Hoffmann, Joseph Maria Olbrich, and Richard Riemerschmid—created restrained, geometric styles that remained in tune with jewelry items produced by contemporary British and American Arts and Crafts designers. Danish Skonvirke designers, including Kay Bojesen and Bernard Hertz, produced handcrafted silver jewelry with simple, natural motifs.

Danish silver pendant-brooch by Kay Bojesen, designed in the Skonvirke (Danish Arts and Crafts) style. Its scrolling leaf-and-berry motif openwork frame is set with a large central amber cabochon, two clusters of cornelian cabochons, and four cornelian drops. *c. 1915*

4 in (10 cm) long

$3,000–4,000   **VDB**

Rare Wiener Werkstätte brooch designed by Josef Hoffmann. Its square silver frame has a beaded perimeter enclosing two vertical panels with stylized and gilded potted plants, and three panels of diverse, polychrome, round and oval semiprecious stone cabochons. *1910*

2 in (5 cm) long

$20,000–30,000   **DOR**

Wiener Werkstätte brooch designed by Josef Hoffmann. Its convex, elongated oval body is made of gold-washed silver, and features at its center a large, proportionately elongated, oval lapis lazuli cabochon. Marked on the reverse with "WW" and a "Diana" head stamp. *c. 1910*

2¼ in (5.75 cm) long

$2,000–3,000   **DOR**

Danish Skonvirke pendant-brooch by Bernard Hertz. Its silver frame is embossed with leaf motifs and set with two oval green paste cabochons. *1920s*

$200–300   **L&T**

Oval silver medallion by Bertold Löffler for the Wiener Werkstätte. It is embossed with a seated putto holding a small bird and flanked by stylized, scrolling bellflower tendrils. *1904*

2 in (5 cm) long

$1,200–1,800   **DOR**

Unsigned European dragon pendant
cast in 15-carat gold. It is suspended on
a paperclip chain from a flowerhead pin. The
dragon grips a pearl in its jaws, and its tail
morphs into the scrolling, leafy bough
on which it sits. The pendant terminates
in a pearl drop. *c. 1890*

1¾ in (4.5 cm) long

$500–700   **RG**

German pendant necklace with a large oval
chrysoprase, a mother-of-pearl cabochon,
and a baroque pearl drop, set in cast-silver
scrolling leaves and flowers. *c. 1905*

Pendant: 2½ in (6.25 cm) long

$300–500   **RG**

German pendant necklace with an eye-
shaped pendant cast in silver, suspended
from a silver-link chain, and set with a pearl
and a large rose quartz cabochon. *c. 1905*

Pendant: 2½ in (6.25 cm) long

$600–900   **RG**

German leaf-shaped locket by Meyle
& Mayer. Its silver frame is composed of
sinuous flower, stem, and leaf forms, and is
set with a blue *plique-à-jour* enamel. *c. 1900*

2 in (5 cm) long

$2,000–3,000   **VDB**

Unsigned German pendant necklace
featuring a silver pendant composed of
stylized scrolling leaves and set with a
green onyx stone. *c. 1905*

Pendant: 1¼ in (3.5 cm) long

$180–220   **RG**

German oval pendant-brooch cast in silver
with a jardinière of fruits, flowers, and leaves,
including three sapphire-blue glass highlights.
Set within a bead-and-reel border. *c. 1910*

2 in (5 cm) long

$600–900   **RG**

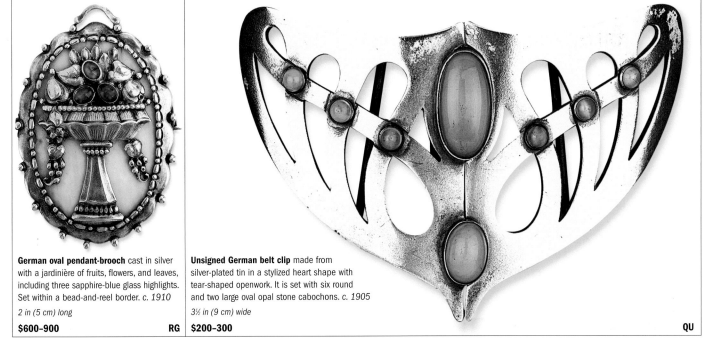

Unsigned German belt clip made from
silver-plated tin in a stylized heart shape with
tear-shaped openwork. It is set with six round
and two large oval opal stone cabochons. *c. 1905*

3½ in (9 cm) wide

$200–300   **QU**

Silver and Metalware

In the Victorian era, the advent of mass production had brought the value of metalware objects to an all-time low. However, the rejection of industrial methods and the reaffirmation of the role of the artist-craftsman in the production process were to elevate Arts and Crafts metalwork to the realm of fine art. With great skill and imagination, craftsmen also made an enduring and viable statement of values by striving to adapt form to function.

The artistic unity demanded by the Arts and Crafts philosophy as stated by the leaders of the movement, William Morris and John Ruskin, resulted in the creation of designs that embraced not only the most obvious architectural features of a building, but also the smallest, seemingly inconsequential household objects within, forging a marriage between the decorative and the utilitarian.

The metalware created by Arts and Crafts designers also underscored the artists' loyalty to the tradition of the medieval guild system. Metalworkers, goldsmiths, silversmiths, and pewterers worked together to create everyday household objects with aesthetic appeal and fine workmanship, while at the same time keeping an eye on function.

In keeping with Arts and Crafts wisdom, since the primary purpose of vases, candlesticks, boxes, and tablewares—such as bowls, trays, and jugs—was a practical one, design was to be subordinate to function. Florid filigree patterns, for example, had no place in the decoration of kitchen utensils, which demanded a simplicity of design that would be appropriate to their frequent and efficient use.

With that in mind, Arts and Crafts designers ennobled their wares with an artistic integrity and a high quality of craftsmanship in the production process, just as their owners—rich or poor—were ennobled by the purity and aestheticism embodied in their use. Mass-produced wares cheapened this ideal and had to be excluded—even from the kitchen.

Detail of a Cotswold School brass fender (*see p.176*) embossed and pierced with a frieze of opposed red squirrels eating acorns; supported by brackets with decorative screws. *c. 1910. 48½ in (123 cm) wide* **$4,000–6,000 L&T**

BEAUTY AND FUNCTION

While innovative in design, Arts and Crafts metalware objects also looked to stylistic motifs that originated in the medieval or Tudor past. The taste for superficial excess beloved by the Victorians gave way to a much cleaner, linear interpretation of traditional decorative schemes that were often inspired by nature and that emphasized the abstract and geometric over the literal and flamboyant, curvilinear style favored by French Art Nouveau.

The handcrafting of household wares by dedicated artisans ensured a quality of production that met the highest standards—both artistically and in terms of function. Like their medieval forebears, these artisans were organized into guilds, which upheld the standards and integrity of their production and contributed to furthering the Arts and Crafts ideal. Among the workshops that championed Morris's principles were C. R. Ashbee's Guild of Handicraft and the Artificers' Guild, founded in 1901 by Nelson Dawson. They created functional domestic metalware with a hand-hammered finish and plain, honest decoration that comprised visible structural details, such as nailheads and rivets. Other small pioneering workshops flourished across Great Britain, from the Cotswolds to Cornwall and from Keswick to Glasgow.

ECCLESIASTICAL COMMISSIONS

Several firms garnered a substantial proportion of their business from the Church, traditionally a large consumer of silverware. This fitted well with the Arts and Crafts aesthetic, since the Church tended to share the atavistic bent of the movement. Crosses, bowls, chalices, and candlesticks with a distinctly medieval, sacerdotal aspect were produced by the Goldsmith's & Silversmith's Co., the Birmingham Guild of Handicraft, and others. Similar items found their way into the department stores—the humble designs favored by the clergy needed little, if any, adjustment for the palate of the general consumer, especially at the height of the Arts and Crafts movement. The plain surfaces and simple forms had no extraneous ornament to detract from the hand-hammered texture that was such a distinctive feature of guild-made silver.

Although many Arts and Crafts workshops looked down on machine production, not all designers pledged to the fundamental theories established by Morris, who absolutely rejected the use of machinery for the creative process. For example, Christopher Dresser—who was ahead of his time in the design of metalware—successfully balanced the Morris ideal with the practical advantages of machinery. This trend was even more pronounced on the continent,

Liberty & Co. English pewter clock designed by Archibald Knox. The circular dial is enameled with exposed copper numerals, set into an upright rectangular case, and embellished with stylized ivy and berries. *c. 1905. 8¼ in (21 cm) high* **$12,000–18,000 MACK**

KEY POINTS

Arts and Crafts metalware is often distinctly ecclesiastical in form, with large spot-hammered surfaces and simple sweeping shapes. In the instances where decoration was used, it was often quintessentially English, like Knox's stylized brambles, or else Celtic—a trend championed by Liberty—in inspiration. Plain metalware was occasionally adorned with enamel. Different metals, especially copper and silver, were often combined within the same piece.

Silver bookmark by Edith and Nelson Dawson, of dagger shape with a pierced flap for attachment to the page. The top of barbed quatrefoil shape is centered with a plaque enameled with a red ladybug design. *1905. 4¾ in (12 cm) long* **$600–900 VDB**

Liberty & Co. English pewter preserve pot and spoon designed by Archibald Knox, cast in low relief with a stylized interwoven bramble motif. The domed cover is similarly decorated and has a loop handle. The spoon is decorated with stems and has an open loop top. *c. 1905. 5¾ in (14.5 cm) high* **$1,800–2,200 WW**

Craftsmen in the Guild of Handicraft metalwork shop at Essex House, before their move to the studio in Chipping Campden in 1902.

at the Wiener Werkstätte in Austria, the Deutscher Werkbund, and at large commercial factories such as the highly successful W.M.F.

BY HAND AND MACHINE

In the United States, the renowned Louis Comfort Tiffany, along with other visionary artisans, including Gustav Stickley, who subscribed to the Morris ideal of the medieval craftsman, openly designed metalwork for machine production but did not face the stigma associated with industrial methods. Many artisans working in the Arts and Crafts style in both Europe and the United States—including Elbert Hubbard at the Roycrofters Copper Shop—remained true to Morris's ideals and were convinced that authentic effects such as planishing could be achieved only by hand.

Not to be outdone by the success of the elegant, graceful handcrafted metalwares created at Ashbee's Guild of Handicraft and the Birmingham Guild, commercial retailers Liberty & Co. launched its highly popular machine-made Tudric and Cymric lines of decorative household objects made of silver as well as more affordable pewter. Many Liberty items were designed by the prolific and imaginative Archibald Knox, Jessie M. King, and Arthur Gaskin, among others.

Kayserzinn pewter five-light candelabrum (one of a pair), designed by Hugo Leven, with a central sconce flanked by four others supported on organic looped stems above a broad column rising from a domed base with further organic strapwork. *c. 1900. 19½ in (49.5 cm) high*
$7,000–10,000 (the pair) TO

Goldsmith's & Silversmith's Co. Ltd. silver bowl with a deep hemispherical vessel supported on three curved and fluted stems above a domed circular base. With overall spot-hammered texturing and London hallmarks. *1918.* **$300–500 B**

Large hammered copper tray by the Kalo Shop, with stones and two applied strap handles. The broad flat bottom has a raised border with five bezel-set cornelian cabochons on each handle. Stone-set holloware pieces are unusual and especially rare on copper items. *c. 1910. 14¾ in (37.5 cm) wide* **$6,000–9,000 CHI**

Guild of Handicraft

Inspired by the writings of John Ruskin, in particular that "Fine art is that in which the hand, the head, and the heart of man go together," the Guild of Handicraft was an experiment in reviving the medieval guild system.

Charles Robert Ashbee (*see below*) founded the Guild of Handicraft in 1888 as a reaction against the mass-produced goods on the Victorian market. He eschewed the use of machinery and actively sought apprentices to school in the techniques of handcrafting. Originally concerned with carpentry, the Guild was successful in both recruitment and the marketplace, eventually allowing construction of a forge for metalwork on its premises in east London. Silver lent itself particularly well to the atavistic, anti-industrial stance adopted by Ashbee and his acolytes, and the Guild's simple designs proved popular with the public.

In 1902, the Guild moved to Chipping Campden, where there was space enough for workshops, schools, and accommodations in an idyllic pastoral setting. However, even as the experiment moved closer to Ashbee's vision of a rural Arcadia, sales began to dwindle: the Guild recorded a loss in 1905 and was liquidated in 1908.

While it was active, the Guild of Handicraft established a reputation that spread around the world, and the distinctive hand-hammered finishes of its celebrated silverware were much imitated. Many of the handcrafted metalwork pieces produced by the Guild are small, high-quality silver items such as plates, bowls, boxes, vases, and glass vessels contained within silver mounts. Ashbee's work in particular can be distinguished by elegant forms incorporating flowing wirework, with semiprecious stones and enamel inclusions.

Above: Round silver box with a drop-in cover that features a plaque depicting a sailing galleon in colored enamels; marks for London. *1901. 2½ in (6.5 cm) high* **$7,000–10,000 VDB**

CHARLES ROBERT ASHBEE

One of the most creative and innovative champions of the British Arts and Crafts movement was the architect, designer, and writer Charles Robert Ashbee (1863–1942). Exhibiting his work throughout England and abroad, he gave a nod to contemporary taste while celebrating his deep-seated admiration of traditional medieval forms, techniques, and materials. Heavily influenced by William Morris and John Ruskin, Ashbee created simple, distinctive designs for his School and Guild of Handicraft, including tea services, vases set with stone cabochons, and silver bowls that looked to the Middle Ages for inspiration. Although he encouraged the ideal of the self-taught artist-craftsman, Ashbee eventually acknowledged—with some reluctance—the economic advantages afforded by the machine and the methods of industrial production.

Silver-and-enamel chalice designed by C. R. Ashbee, embellished around the foot with dolphins. The image is reflected in colored enamels on the domed cover, where three more dolphins support an amethyst ball. *c. 1900 18 in (46 cm) high* **$30,000–50,000 VDB**

CHARLES ROBERT ASHBEE

Square tapering silver inkwell with riveted corner supports. The hinged cover is set with a foil-backed blue-enamel boss; marks for London. *1906*

2½ in (6.5 cm) high

$1,800–2,200　　　　　　　　　　　　　**WW**

Deep circular silver bowl applied with sinuous wirework twin-loop handles punctuated with turquoise cabochons; marks for London. *1906*

4¼ in (10.5 cm) wide

$5,000–7,000　　　　　　　　　　　　　**VDB**

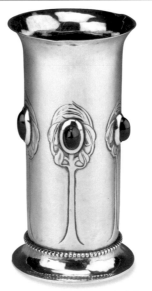

Silver butter dish with pierced sides revealing the glass liner; the wirework loop handle is set with mother-of-pearl. The liner is a replacement. *1900*

7¾ in (20 cm) long

$5,000–8,000　　　　　　　　　　　　　**VDB**

Cylindrical silver vase designed by C. R. Ashbee. The sides are embossed with stylized bushes centered with garnet cabochons, with a beaded band near the base. *c. 1900*

7 in (18 cm) high

$5,000–8,000　　　　　　　　　　　　　**VDB**

Waisted cylindrical silver vase designed by C. R. Ashbee. It is embellished around the base with highly stylized interwoven stems and berries. *c. 1900*

7 in (18 cm) high

$5,000–8,000　　　　　　　　　　　　　**VDB**

A CLOSER LOOK

Rectangular silver box supported on four button feet. It features a hinged cover with a raised center incorporating an enameled plaque depicting in naturalistic colors a landscape at sunset, by Fleetwood Charles Varley of London. *1904*

6½ in (16.5 cm) high　**$5,000–7,000**　**VDB**

Plaque's underside is counter-enameled to prevent cracking

Handcrafted planishing marks

Varley came from a respected family of watercolor artists. Although these enamels are fired in a kiln, with all the attendant risks of destruction, they retain the subtle nuances of color one would expect from a watercolor.

KEY FEATURES

Copper, silver, and brass were the materials preferred by the Artificers' Guild for the production of domestic metalware.

Simple, modest lines are a feature of the Guild's wares, which included vases, boxes, trays, bowls, goblets, lamps, and wall sconces.

Animal motifs and floral and foliage patterns are typical decorative embellishments.

Individual designers remained anonymous and the Guild's metalware pieces are stamped with a London maker's mark.

Artificers' Guild

Among the many guilds founded to promote the principles of the Arts and Crafts movement, the Artificers' Guild produced handwrought metalware that celebrated the dedication to craftsmanship fostered by William Morris and his followers.

Founded in 1901 by Nelson Dawson (1859–1941) from his workshop in west London, the Artificers' Guild focused on the production of jewelry and metalwork based on the aesthetic principles devised by Arts and Crafts pioneer William Morris (*see pp.72–73*). The Guild embraced the design ethic that formed the cornerstone of the Arts and Crafts philosophy, emphasizing the importance of handcraftsmanship and paying tribute to the simple, straightforward designs and decorative motifs that looked to the past for inspiration.

Dawson's association with the Guild proved to be brief, and in 1903 he sold the company to Montague Fordham, a former director of the Birmingham Guild of Handicraft (*see p.168*). Fordham owned a popular gallery in London's Maddox Street, where he displayed works created by an array of talented designers, including Henry

Wilson (1864–1934) and John Paul Cooper (1869–1933), and he was eager to bring the Artificers' Guild into the fold. The Guild's focus on jewelry and metalwork proved extremely popular when on show at the Fordham Gallery. Domestic metalware—vases, boxes, bowls, trays, goblets, and wall sconces, among other designs—rendered mainly in copper, silver, and brass were created along simple lines that were often embellished with decorative patterns highlighted by animal, flower, and foliage motifs.

The company chose to have individual designers remain anonymous and, as a result, the metalware produced by the Artificers' Guild was usually stamped with a London maker's mark. The Guild proved to be a commercially successful enterprise, and it remained in operation until 1942.

Above: Lobed globular copper box featuring a silver cover with a finial in the shape of a bat with outspread wings. Maker's mark for Spencer and hallmark for London. *1931. 4¾ in (12 cm) high* **$700–1,000 DN**

EDWARD SPENCER

After founder Nelson Dawson sold the Artificers' Guild to Montague Fordham in 1903, the talented Edward Spencer (1872–1938) was appointed chief designer. He created a style that looked to the work of John Paul Cooper for ideas and was renowned for his use of precious materials such as ivory. Spencer's imaginative combinations of metal and enamels—a technique originally introduced by Dawson and his wife Edith—was also recognized. In 1909, Edward Spencer and his brother Walter published a history of wrought-iron work that was sumptuously illustrated with examples made by the Artificers' Guild.

Trumpet-shaped plated brass vase by Edward Spencer, with horizontal ribs in relief edged with ropework banding. It is decorated with simple florets and foliage near the base; numbered "216." *c. 1925. 6¾ in (17.5 cm) high* **$600–900 DN**

Copper wall sconce attributed to Edward Spencer. The back plate is embossed and pierced with stylized foliage, florets, and buds. The drip-pan contains two wavy-edged cylindrical sconces. *c. 1910. 10½ in (27 cm) high* **$1,800–2,200 DN**

Set of four silver goblets attributed to Edward Spencer, each with a deep bowl embossed with a band of fish amid aquatic foliage. Each goblet is supported on a spreading faceted foot. Hallmarks for London. *1923*

3½ in (9 cm) wide

$5,000–8,000 (the set)　　　　　　　　　**VDB**

Circular silver box by Edward Spencer, with wirework rim and domed drop-in cover. An arched pedestal supports a lion finial. With maker's mark and hallmark for London. *1928*

4 in (10 cm) wide

$1,000–1,500　　　　　　　　　　　**DN**

Rectangular copper tray the design of which is attributed to Edward Spencer. It has a raised edge with silvered border and silvered handles decorated with foliage and vines. *c. 1910*

21½ in (55 cm) long

$400–600　　　　　　　　　　　　**DN**

Fluted brass bowl attributed to the Artificers' Guild and Edward Spencer. It is internally decorated with radiating flutes and centered with a relief medallion of a sickle and mistletoe. *c. 1910*

6¼ in (16 cm) wide

$400–600　　　　　　　　　　　　**DN**

Silver Scorpio napkin ring with a relief medallion featuring a scorpion flanked by beading and two coral studs; with marks for London. The design is attributed to Edward Spencer. *1915*

1¾ in (4.5 cm) wide

$180–220　　　　　　　　　　　　**DN**

Silver goblet by Edward Spencer, with four dolphins flanking the fluted stem above a knop with shell decoration, on a spreading foot with four fish medallions. Hallmarked. *1926*

6 in (15 cm) high

$2,000–3,000　　　　　　　　　　**TEL**

Duchess of Sutherland's Cripples' Guild

Established by the Duchess of Sutherland around 1900, this was one of several "cripples' guilds" set up by private philanthropists in Great Britain. Typical pieces include copper or silver-plated jars, jugs, goblets, boxes, tureens, or inkwells, often simple in design with embossed or applied decoration. Designers who worked at the Guild include eminent ceramicist Bernard Moore (1850–1935) and metalworker Francis Arthur Edwards. Most pieces are stamped "D.S.C.G."

Copper goblet with a deep bowl, twin bobbinlike handles, and spreading circular foot. It is applied with silvered winged cherubs, swags, and other classical motifs; stamped "D.S.C.G." *c. 1920*

7½ in (19 cm) high

$600–900　　　　　　　　　　　　**DN**

KEY FEATURES

Silver, pewter, and copper were typically used for Liberty's domestic and decorative wares.

Decorative motifs inspired by ancient Celtic ornament—such as Celtic knots and swirling interlaced tendrils called entrelacs, animal and figural symbols, and flowerheads and stylized leaves— are frequently used.

Machine-made pieces in silver typically have been lightly hammered to create the impression of a textured, handcrafted surface.

Cabochons of mother-of-pearl, shell, turquoise, lapis lazuli, agate, or other semiprecious stones are favored decoration for Cymric ware, along with panels of peacock blue and green enameling.

Liberty & Co.

In the mid-1890s, metalwork was added to the fabrics, furniture, and jewelry sold at Liberty & Co. in London, sealing the store's reputation as the innovative leader of the commercial Arts and Crafts style.

At the beginning of the 20th century, the trendsetting retail emporium founded by Arthur Lasenby Liberty (1843–1917) in 1875 on London's Regent Street was widely celebrated for its distinctive collection of highly original silver- and pewterware. One of the company's most successful ventures was the launch in 1899 of its range of handmade Cymric gold- and silverware.

In keeping with the Arts and Crafts philosophy that looked to the past for inspiration, Cymric ware depended heavily on the designs and patterns found in ancient Celtic art. The team of designers who developed the Cymric range included Archibald Knox, Jessie M. King, Oliver Baker, and Rex Silver. The range featured silver mantel clocks, boxes, inkwells, picture frames, tankards, bowls, jewelry, candlesticks, salt cellars, spoons, and cigarette cases.

Although mass-produced by machine, Cymric silverware was finely hammered and left unpolished to create a handcrafted appearance. Typical decoration featured stylized leaves, flowerheads, and swirling interlaced tendrils known as entrelacs, embellished with enamels in rich, vivid shades of bluish green or highlighted with cabochons of semiprecious stones.

A NEW RANGE

Buoyed by the success of its Cymric range, in 1902 Liberty introduced a more affordable second line of metalware, which it called Tudric. It was made in a pewter material that contained a high percentage of silver; this was fairly easy to mold and, once polished, took on the

Above: Tudric pewter twin-handled ice bucket designed by Archibald Knox, embellished with stylized tendrils and foliage, numbered "0706." *c. 1905. 7½ in (19 cm) high* **$4,000–6,000 STY**

ARCHIBALD KNOX

The prolific and imaginative Arts and Crafts designer Archibald Knox (1864–1933) joined Liberty & Co. in 1895. Born on the Isle of Man, Knox looked to ancient Celtic ornament as the main inspiration for his distinctive and designs. He adapted the simple geometric foliate patterns found in Celtic book illustrations and on gravestones and used them to embellish a variety of domestic metalware including inkwells, tea sets, vases, and a range of jewelry. His complex and delicate Celtic designs for Liberty's celebrated Cymric and Tudric ranges echoed the sinuous, organic Art Nouveau style and were widely admired and imitated.

Silver clock designed by Archibald Knox, embellished with stylized leaves and tendrils flanking the blue-and-green enameled circular dial. *c. 1905 7¾ in (20 cm) high* **$15,000–20,000 GDG**

ARCHIBALD KNOX

CYMRIC AND TUDRIC DESIGNS

Liberty's Cymric silverware was heavily influenced by patterns and techniques of ancient Celtic origin, such as hammering marks left on the metal without burnishing or polishing, sinuous animal and figural motifs, curvilinear ornament, and decoration with enamels or semiprecious stones. Mass-produced by die-stamping and then hammered to create a handcrafted effect, Cymric silver was created by a team of talented metalwork designers, most notably Archibald Knox (*see below left*). The Tudric line of pewterware boasted imaginative designs and decoration of enamel cabochons and semiprecious stones, complementing the more expensive Cymric range.

Left: Tudric pewter clock by Archibald Knox, with stylized leaves and tendrils extending to the base and flanking two enameled bosses and a partially enameled dial. *c. 1900* *8 in (20.5 cm) high* **$5,000–8,000 TO**

Right: Cymric silver vase with geometric Celtic knots picked out with colored enamels. The same motifs are reflected on the spreading foot. *c. 1905. 9½ in (24 cm) high* **$15,000–20,000 VDB**

INSPIRATIONS

Bearing in mind John Ruskin's exhortations for a return to simple forms based on purpose, honest materials, and quality craftsmanship, commercial Arts and Crafts metalwork found inspiration in the sinuous, flowing lines and motifs in nature. These included the insects, flower blossoms, and lush foliage of Art Nouveau, the simplicity, asymmetry, and nature-inspired designs of Japanese art, and the complex, curvilinear patterns of ancient Celtic ornament.

CELTIC INFLUENCE

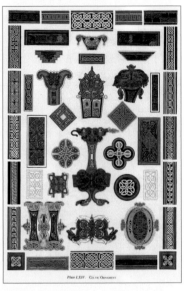

Ancient Celtic ornament played a key role in Arts and Crafts metalwork decoration. Craftsmen enthusiastically took up the Celtic fondness for metalwork wrought with great skill and decorated in a manner similar to manuscripts, with close complex patterns of interlaced ribbons, entangled curvilinear ornament, abstract geometric designs, and stylized animals and figures.

---

luminous, shiny character of silver. The Tudric range of clocks, bowls, flower vases, tea caddies, card and cigar boxes, and chalices for domestic use was less expensive but no less imaginative than the Cymric line, with its own vocabulary of unique, specially created designs, decorated with colorful enamel cabochons and semiprecious stones.

PROMOTING THE LIBERTY NAME

Both the Cymric and Tudric ranges of metalware were made in collaboration with Birmingham silversmiths William H. Haseler & Co., while other Liberty silverware was produced jointly with William Hutton & Sons of Sheffield. The hardware for Liberty's furniture line was fashioned from either pewter or hammered brass and frequently embellished with enamel cabochons. Determined to promote its own name, Liberty's refused to credit the many artist-craftsmen in its employ who were largely responsible for its popular wares, and it registered its own mark in 1894.

Tudric pewter slop bowl that is part of a tea set designed by Archibald Knox. It has a broad tapering cylindrical shape with a loop handle and is embellished in shallow relief with sinuous Celtic knots and stylized honesty plants. Numbered "0231." *c. 1905* *6¼ in (16 cm) wide* **$500–700 WW**

Tudric pewter clock designed by Archibald Knox. The arched case is embellished in relief with foliage flanking a blue enameled dial. *c. 1905*

12½ in (32 cm) high

$12,000–18,000 GDG

Pewter cased clock designed by Archibald Knox. The front is of cruciform shape, embossed with Roman numerals and punctuated with abalone studs. *c. 1905*

14½ in (37 cm) high

$50,000–70,000 GDG

Tudric pewter cigar box the edges of which are embossed with Celtic knots and roundels; the hinged cover is set with a colored enameled plaque showing a wooded landscape. *c. 1905*

12¼ in (31 cm) long

$2,000–3,000 VDB

Tudric pewter clock with a copper and blue-enamel face sporting Roman numerals. *c. 1910*

6½ in (16.5 cm) high

$1,800–2,200 TDG

Cymric silver clock with overhanging and slightly domed rectangular top. The front has buttresslike supports flanking the simple enameled dial. Marks for Birmingham. *c. 1905*

8¾ in (22 cm) high

$2,000–3,000 VDB

Enameled silver coaster designed by Archibald Knox, with two parallel bands of interwoven tendrils picked out with blue-and-green enameling. Marks for Haseler and Birmingham. *1905*

3½ in (9 cm) wide

$2,000–3,000 VDB

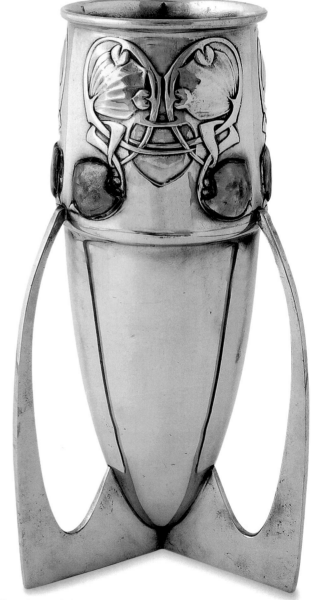

Tudric pewter vase designed by Archibald Knox. It is of bullet shape with three looped bracket feet, embellished with tendrils, leaves, and six enameled plaques. *c. 1905*

11½ in (29 cm) high

$2,000–3,000 TO

Tudric pewter bowl probably designed by Oliver Baker. The rounded shallow vessel is supported on four sinuous legs with trefoil feet; model number "067." *c. 1905*

11 in (28 cm) wide

$700–1,000 WW

A CLOSER LOOK

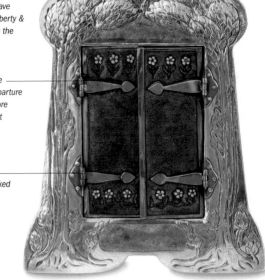

Exquisitely detailed frame would have appealed to Liberty & Co. clientele in the early 1900s

Door's fairy-tale quality is a departure from Knox's more typical abstract Celtic motifs

Borders and hinges are picked out in copper

Unusual enameled silver photograph frame attributed to Archibald Knox. The top has a canopy of foliage above trunks that form the sides of the frame. The red enameled doors are punctuated with blue floral motifs; with blue enameled panels above and below. *c. 1905*

6¼ in (16 cm) high **$20,000–30,000** GDG

Tudric pewter circular dish with a broad everted rim with seven relief foliate motifs set with heart-shaped plaques of abalone shell. Stamped "Tudric" and "0113." *c. 1905*

13 in (33 cm) wide

$600–900 DN

Tudric pewter bowl with twin handles, a pierced foliate rim, and a shaded blue-and-green enameled center. *c. 1905*

11½ in (29 cm) wide

$300–500 TO

Copper-framed rectangular wall mirror probably retailed through Liberty & Co. It is embossed with two flowering blooms set with Ruskin blue-glazed circular plaques. *c. 1900*

25½ in (64.5 cm) long

$3,000–5,000 PUR

Copper-framed wall mirror probably retailed through Liberty & Co. It is embossed with stylized floral decoration punctuated with six Ruskin turquoise-glazed roundels. *c. 1900*

19 in (48 cm) long

$1,200–1,800 PUR

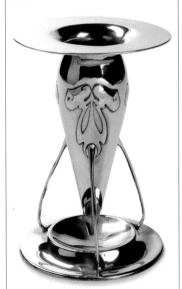

Cymric silver vase attributed to Archibald Knox, with a broad rim embossed with stylized foliage. It is supported on curved stems above a dished circular base. *1903*

5½ in (14 cm) high

$4,000–6,000 L&T

Tudric pewter flower-form vase attributed to Archibald Knox. It has a circular spreading foot, twin sinuous handles, and enameled plaques. Stamped. *c. 1905*

9¾ in (25 cm) high

$1,200–1,500 DRA

Silver tea caddy by Archibald Knox, of broad tapering cylindrical shape. The plain surface is embellished with blue-and-green enameled Celtic knots. Marks for Birmingham. *1906*

3¼ in (8 cm) high

$3,000–5,000 VDB

English pewter square biscuit barrel designed by Archibald Knox, embellished with stylized plant forms and squared foliage. Stamped mark "0237." *c. 1905*

4¾ in (12 cm) high

$1,800–2,200 L&T

KEY FEATURES

Silver and copper were the most frequently used metals at the Birmingham Guild of Handicraft.

Plain, simple lines and a minimum of decoration characterize the Guild's domestic wares, including lamps, boxes, bowls, tea caddies, and spoons.

Decorative details, when used, include flower patterns, Celtic-inspired motifs, or sparingly applied cabochon stones.

Individual artists are rarely acknowledged, with pieces hallmarked with the stamp of the Birmingham Guild of Handicraft.

Birmingham Guild

Inspired by the writings and lectures of the Arts and Crafts trailblazer William Morris, the architect Arthur Dixon brought together a team of craftsmen to found the Birmingham Guild of Handicraft.

THE BIRMINGHAM GUILD LTD
ENGLAND

A thriving center of the silver industry in Great Britain, the city of Birmingham was home to a number of workshops that served the major retailers of London and Manchester. Arthur Dixon's Birmingham Guild was established in 1890 in the spirit of William Morris (*see pp.22–23*). It was guided by the Arts and Crafts principles of good-quality handcraftsmanship, but always with an eye on profit.

The Guild forged close ties with the local schools, including the renowned Birmingham Art School, where Edward Taylor taught pupils such as A. E. Jones (*see p.170*) and future jewelry designer Arthur Gaskin (*see p.141*) the value of mastering a variety of metalworking skills.

The handmade metalware produced by Guild craftsmen typically embraced design principles based on simple lines with a lack of decorative embellishment, save the occasional Celtic-inspired pattern, flower motifs, or cabochon stones, although by the turn of the century, free-flowing lines characteristic of Art Nouveau were favored.

The work of individual artists within the Guild remained largely anonymous, with most pieces hallmarked with the Birmingham Guild stamp.

Due to financial pressures, the Birmingham Guild merged with E. & R. Gittins in 1905.

Above: Birmingham Guild mark found on the underside of a circular copper tray with simple handles. *c. 1920. Tray: 8¼ in (21 cm) wide* **$120-180 HBK**

Silver presentation casket with a flat, hinged lid. It is of rectangular shape tapering toward the base, embellished with a band of Celtic inspiration, otherwise plain. Inscribed with a dedication and marks for Birmingham. *1902*
5½ in (14 cm) long
$4,000-6,000 VDB

Silver morse (fastening for a cape) with a central stylized floral plaque flanked by two fleur-de-lys motifs; marks for Birmingham. *1900*
6½ in (16.5 cm) wide
$300-400 DN

Silver tea caddy of plain hemispherical shape on a spreading circular base. It has a flat drop-in cover with a simple finial and a matching caddy spoon; marks for Birmingham. *1903*
2½ in (6.5 cm) high
$800-1,200 VDB

Keswick School

Based in Cumberland, the Keswick School of Industrial Art promoted the principles of Arts and Crafts design with a range of useful and decorative domestic wares that evoked the tradition of handcraftsmanship.

Established in Cumberland in 1884 by Canon and Mrs. Rawnsley, the Keswick School of Industrial Art initially operated as an evening school. Its faculty included Harold Stabler (1872–1945), who had apprenticed at the Kendal School of Art for seven years before joining Keswick, and metalworker and jeweler Herbert J. Maryon. Both were employed full time as directors and designers.

The Keswick School specialized in the production of simply designed hand-hammered wares made of copper and brass in the Arts and Crafts style and decorated with floral and animal motifs. Stabler's metalwork, however, often tended to be more elaborate and was frequently embellished with painted enamel panels.

Pieces produced by the Keswick School were usually inscribed with a KSIA mark, and while most individual designers were forced to remain anonymous, occasionally their scratched names or initials were also included.

Keswick's domestic metalware retailed through the Home Arts & Industries Association. By 1898, the burgeoning success of the institute saw the expansion to include daytime classes.

The school underwent many changes to remain in business and closed down in 1984.

Above: Copper flagon by W. H. Mawson, inscribed "More Friends And Less Needs Of Them." *c. 1900. 8¼ in (21 cm) high*
$500–700 L&T

KEY FEATURES

Copper or brass were the favored metals for decorative and useful domestic wares.

Designs tended to be modest and restrained, with hand-hammered decoration featuring motifs of plants, flowers, birds, animals, and fantastic creatures such as dragons.

Decorative embellishments—such as brightly colored, elaborately painted panels—sometimes appear on Harold Stabler's wares.

The KSIA diamond-shaped mark appears on most Keswick pieces.

Embossed brass wall pocket by W. H. Mawson, decorated on the curved front panel with a stylized flower and foliage, and pierced at the back for hanging. *c. 1900*
8¼ in (21 cm) long
$300–400   **HBK**

Circular brass plate with slightly curved rim, embossed in relief with a pair of winged dragons confronting each other in flight; with stamped maker's mark. *c. 1900*
8½ in (21.5 cm) wide
$100–150   **L&T**

Rare copper rosewater dish designed by Robert Hilton and executed by Matthew Armstrong. It has a central rose boss and is embellished on the rim with oak leaves and acorns interspersed with hounds chasing stags. *c. 1910*
18½ in (47 cm) wide
$3,000–5,000   **TDG**

KEY FEATURES

An important influence on the early work of A. E. Jones was the Birmingham Guild of Handicraft.

A distinctly ecclesiastical feel is inherent in many of Jones's secular designs.

The influence of the Liberty style can be seen in Jones's work from around 1905.

Silver is sometimes mixed with attractively patinated copper.

Tablewares often have floral friezes picked out in relief, especially around the shoulders.

Ruskin stone inserts and plaques are often found on Jones's work.

Silver bowls and chalices are often mounted on turned wooden bases.

A. E. Jones

Albert Edward Jones produced well-worked silverware with simple designs, stamped with the mark of St. Dunstan, the medieval archbishop who had encouraged priests to teach their parishioners handicrafts as well as the Scriptures.

A. E. Jones (1879–1954) was raised in Birmingham, England, where his father moved from Worcestershire to establish a branch of the family blacksmithing business. After training and working as an apprentice, he briefly joined the Birmingham Guild of Handicraft (*see p.168*) before setting up his own workshop in the city's jewelry quarter.

Jones's work shows the Guild's influence, with its emphasis on simple, traditional forms that showcase the properties of the metal. While he was developing his own style, Jones was commissioned to manufacture pieces for respected designers such as W. T. Blackband and Arthur and Georgina Gaskin (*see p.141*).

Although Jones's business was a strictly commercial concern—he was not in the luxurious position of having wealthy patrons or subsidies—he allied himself firmly with the Arts and Crafts tradition. He made his own tools and used a copper patination process developed by F. W. Salthouse, who worked with Jones from around 1905. It was around this time that he began to use the mark of St. Dunstan hammering a silver bowl, which he acquired from the firm of Jesson Birkett. On Jones's death, the firm passed into the hands of his son, Major Crisp Jones.

Above: Copper-and-silver tobacco jar with a spreading foot, floral motifs, an embossed domed cover, and a simple finial. With marks for Birmingham. *1910. 5¾ in (14.5 cm) high* **$3,000–4,000 VDB**

Silver bowl of compressed globular shape embossed around the neck with stylized roses and foliage. It is supported on four extended feet. Marks for Birmingham. *1906 6¾ in (17 cm) wide*
$4,000–6,000 VDB

Compressed globular bowl embossed with foliage and roses; on four stems with a root-like detail on the base. *1901 8½ in (21.5 cm) wide*
$7,000–10,000 VDB

Deep silver bowl on a broad stem and circular foot, embossed with foliage and banding, and applied with Ruskin pottery plaques. *c. 1905 7 in (18 cm) high*
$4,000–6,000 VDB

Cylindrical sugar caster with twin handles and a pierced domed top, applied with tiny stems and Ruskin pottery studs. *1905 5 in (12.5 cm) high*
$1,000–1,500 VDB

Ramsden & Carr

One of the leading metalsmiths at the turn of the 20th century, Omar Ramsden teamed up with silver designer Alwyn Carr to produce a distinctive range of decorative handmade silver and metalware.

KEY FEATURES

The shapes and decorations of Ramsden & Carr's silver and metalware are influenced by several historic styles, including Celtic and Elizabethan.

Colored enamels or semiprecious stones such as moonstone or chalcedony cabochons embellish the silverware.

Intricate embossed and repoussé designs are often decorated with floral or foliate motifs.

Metalworker, silversmith, and artist craftsman Omar Ramsden (1873–1939) specialized in individually designed presentation silverware. In 1898, with Alwyn Charles Ellison Carr (1872–1940), he established a small workshop in London that produced decorative handmade pieces of silver, as well as vases, bowls, boxes, and tea urns in base metals. All these items exhibited the influence of the Arts and Crafts movement, and many incorporated Art Nouveau motifs.

After the partnership was dissolved in 1919, Carr continued to design silver and wrought iron. Ramsden registered his own mark and remained at the London studio, taking on commissions for ecclesiastical, civic, and domestic metalware. His

high-quality silver, metalwork, and jewelry designs reinterpreted a host of historic styles, including Celtic, Elizabethan, and Queen Anne.

Rejecting machine-made decoration, Ramsden relied on hand-hammered finishes and hand techniques such as chasing, repoussé, and pierced work, and some wares were embellished with colored enamels or hard stones. Ramsden's designs usually bear the engraved or stamped Latin inscription "Omar Ramsden me fecit" ("Omar Ramsden made me").

Above: Silver box embossed with foliage and wave forms. The domed cover has a multilooped finial and an enameled plaque. Marks for London. *1901. 4¼ in (11 cm) high* **$3,000–5,000 VDB**

Silver-and-enamel trefoil-shaped bowl with three twin-branch wirework handles, each applied with an enameled heart motif. Signed. *1902*
4¾ in (12 cm) high
$7,000–10,000   **DN**

Silver shield-shaped tea urn with scrolling handles and a domed cover, supported on a stand with six lion's-paw feet and incorporating a burner. *c. 1910*
12½ in (32 cm) high
$5,000–8,000   **VDB**

Cylindrical silver vase flaring at the neck and base, supported on multiple sinuous feet. The central applied band of interwoven stems is punctuated with green-stained chalcedony cabochons. Maker's marks and marks for London. *1913*
11 in (28 cm) high
$8,000–12,000   **VDB**

KEY FEATURES

Locally mined copper was used for most Newlyn vessels. Occasionally, brass was also used.

Vases, jugs, candlesticks, trays, and tea caddies were among the most popular designs, as well as smaller, more personal items such as inkwells and pin trays.

Pieces are hand-hammered with motifs that echo the sea and the fishing industry, such as shells, the wide-eyed octopus, and fish embellished with realistic scale patterns.

Vessels are usually marked with a "Newlyn" stamp on the base.

Newlyn

In the small Cornish village of Newlyn, the Arts and Crafts style flourished when a group of talented artists dedicated to the craft industry established a thriving community that looked to the sea for inspiration.

The unstable nature of the fishing business—where good weather and a plentiful supply of fish are key to survival—led the small village of Newlyn, in Cornwall, to establish a cottage industry of handicrafts that would provide additional revenue in times of hardship. With the financial backing of the Liberal politician T. B. Bolitho and the support of the band of artists who had settled in the village, the craft industry became an organized enterprise.

Copper mined around the area gave rise to a thriving copperworking industry that shared the ideals of Arts and Crafts pioneer William Morris (*see pp.72–73*). In 1890, painter John D. MacKenzie established the Newlyn Industrial Class, a school that taught a variety of craft techniques, including repoussé copper and enameling.

When the talented metalworker John Pearson (*see p.179*) was invited to demonstrate his copper work in 1892, his designs based on mythical beasts and sea creatures provided fresh inspiration for artists who had always turned to the sea for motifs.

Vases, candlesticks, tea caddies, and jugs were typically hand-hammered with fish patterns and stamped "Newlyn" on the base.

Newlyn ceased production in 1939 with the outbreak of World War II.

Above: Large copper bowl with deep rounded sides embossed with a frieze of fish and aquatic foliage; stamped "Newlyn." *c. 1900* *11½ in (29 cm) wide* **$1,000–1,500 WW**

Copper rose bowl with hemispherical top and base united by a cylindrical stem with floral panels. It is embossed with fruit, foliage, and flowers against a hammer-textured background, with a pierced top for flower arranging. *c. 1900* *15¾ in (40 cm) wide* **$3,000–5,000** **GDG**

Twin-handled copper vase of tapering cylindrical shape, embossed with fish swimming amid aquatic foliage. *c. 1900* *15¼ in (38.5 cm) wide* **$300–500** **L&T**

W. A. S. Benson

Arts and Crafts metalwork owes a debt to architect and designer William A. S. Benson, who balanced the design principles championed by William Morris with the practical advantages afforded by the machine.

In 1880, encouraged by William Morris (*see pp.72–73*), British architect, designer, and leading Arts and Crafts metalworker William Arthur Smith Benson (1854–1924) established a commercial workshop in London for producing turned metalwork. By 1882, the company had grown substantially and included a foundry as well as a showroom in Kensington.

Working primarily in brass and copper, Benson created metalwork that was widely exhibited to great acclaim. His electric lamps, and also his bowls, teapots, kettles, trays, candlesticks, and chandeliers, proved enormously popular when retailed at the prestigious L'Art Nouveau shop of Siegfried Bing in Paris in 1896.

Like Morris, Benson championed good design and unified interior decoration. He provided most of the lighting for Morris's interiors, as well as that sold through Morris & Co.

In contrast to his contemporaries at Keswick (*see p.169*) and Newlyn (*see opposite*), Benson embraced the machine for his domestic wares, and his machine-made parts have much in common with the angular designs of Christopher Dresser (*see p.177*). After Morris's death in 1896, Benson succeeded him as director of Morris & Co.

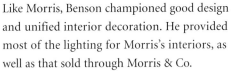

Above: Plated teapot of compressed form supported on a spreading foot; with a loop handle and faceted spout. *c. 1900.* 8 in (20.5 cm) high **$300–500 TDG**

see pp.72–73; see p.169; see opposite; see p.177

KEY FEATURES

Benson's lighting fixtures included chandeliers, candlesticks, lamps, and lanterns, in both wall-mounted and free-standing versions. They were designed for electricity, gas, or flame.

Brass and copper are the favored materials for Benson's domestic wares, which included teapots, bowls, trays, and kettles.

Flower blossoms, buds, and foliage are typical decorative motifs.

A brass, copper, and steel kettle stand with a circular top cast featuring branches raised above baluster columns on a circular base. *c. 1890* 7½ in (19 cm) wide

$400–600 L&T

Copper-and-brass candlestick with branches on a foliate support and circular drip-pans; counterbalanced by a fluted bud-shaped weight. *c. 1900* 12½ in (32 cm) long

$3,000–5,000 DN

Brass-and-copper bowl with curved radiating petals and fluted detail, on four leaf-shaped feet with a curved foliate handle. *c. 1900* 6 in (15 cm) high

$400–600 DN

Circular copper tray with a lobed rim. It is embossed with radiating bands decorated with alternating florets and foliate stems. *c. 1900* 19 in (48 cm) wide

$700–1,000 L&T

Brass table lamp of simple form; the almost circular base has a notch to facilitate wall-hanging. The opalescent glass shade is by Powell. *c. 1900* 11½ in (29 cm) high **$1,200–1,800 MW**

KEY FEATURES

Entrelac designs, crosses, and knotwork, as well as Viking and medieval themes, are among the motifs used, based on Scotland's Celtic and Pictish art.

Metalwork is typically hammered, pierced, and embellished with repoussé or embossed decoration.

Natural imagery, such as stylized, entwined foliage and tendrils, opposed birds or fish, thistles, and poppy-heads, is used.

Enameling and semiprecious stones or roundels are often used to decorate pieces.

Mirrors, spoons, plates, chargers, jardinières, and coal boxes are the most common pieces, often in brass, pewter, or silver.

Scottish School

Scottish metalworkers were prolific during the Arts and Crafts period, with leading designers producing a distinctive Celtic style that was to become known as the "Scottish School."

Influenced by Archibald Knox (*see p.164*) and Liberty's Celtic revival, as well as the heraldic designs of C. R. Mackintosh (*see pp.30–31*), Scottish metalworkers such as Phoebe Traquair (1852–1936) and Alexander Ritchie (1856–1941) developed a new style often using Celtic, Viking, and medieval motifs. Traquair, although born and trained in Dublin, moved to Edinburgh, where she worked mainly as a metalworker, enamelist, and mural decorator. An exceptional colorist, she also executed decorations for buildings and furniture by Sir Robert Lorimer (*see p.34*).

On the west coast of Scotland, inspired by the magnificent Celtic and Viking carvings on Iona and the surrounding islands, Ritchie produced metalwork often with repoussé foliate or knotwork designs adapted from ancient local stone carvings. Many Scottish metalworkers were exploring these ancient themes during this period, including designers such as Marion Henderson Wilson and Margaret Gilmour, and pieces are available at every price point. Glasgow School is similar in style but often more geometric in design and produced by the "Glasgow Four" (*see p.30*) or students of the Glasgow School of Art (*see opposite*).

Above: Brass jardinière of broad-rimmed square section, embossed with stylized floral panels and applied with mottled turquoise roundels. *c. 1900. 9 in (23 cm) wide* **$700–1,000 L&T**

Circular copper wall plaque embossed in the center with the profile head of a girl. The broad rim is embossed with interwoven tendrils and applied with enameled bosses. *c. 1900 16 in (40.5 cm) wide*

$1,000–1,500   **L&T**

Copper mantel clock with single-train movement by Marion Henderson Wilson, of shaped and tapering outline, embossed with a galleon carrying an angel. The dial is embossed with "Time Flies" and birds in flight. Signed with "MHW" monogram. *c. 1900 16¼ in (41 cm) high*

$5,000–8,000   **L&T**

Brass candle sconce in the manner of Margaret Gilmour, embossed with a highly stylized dragonfly against a stippled ground, with a nozzle and a drip tray below. *c. 1900 14 in (35 cm) high*

$400–600   **L&T**

Glasgow School

At the center of the Arts and Crafts movement in Scotland, the cutting-edge Glasgow School of Art planted the seeds for an artistic revolution that was to become known throughout the world as the "Glasgow Style."

Under the progressive director Francis Newbery, the Glasgow School of Art moved beyond its traditional role of formal instruction by introducing studios where artist-craftsmen provided a "technical artistic education" in a range of commercial crafts, including stained glass, bookbinding, ceramics, woodcarving, and metalwork. An admirer of William Morris (*see pp.22–23*), Newbery arranged exhibitions and inspired his students to be creative and to learn as much as they could from the development of the Arts and Crafts style in England and Europe.

A key group of talented architects and designers associated with the Glasgow School—Charles Rennie Mackintosh (*see pp.30–31*), Herbert MacNair, and Margaret and Frances MacDonald, collectively known as "The Glasgow Four"—together created the highly original vision that became world-famous as the Glasgow Style.

A decidedly Scottish and sometimes rather modest interpretation of the Art Nouveau taste that depended heavily on Celtic ornament, the Glasgow Style exerted a powerful influence on the trailblazing architects of industrial design, especially in Germany and Austria.

Above: Pair of brass wall sconces attributed to Agnes Bankier Harvey, each embossed with the profile heads of Art Nouveau maidens and flanked by tendrils and poppy seed-pods. *c. 1900* 11¾ in (30 cm) high **$1,800–2,200 L&T**

Rectangular beveled wall mirror in the manner of C. R. Mackintosh. The frame is faced with pewter and embossed with rose balls rising from highly stylized foliate stems, the blooms picked out with mauve enamels. *c. 1905*

30¼ in (77 cm) wide

$20,000–30,000 **GDG**

Enameled devotional triptych by De Courcy Lewthwaite Dewar, depicting Kentigern flanked by two attending angels, enclosed within a steel frame showing the arms of Glasgow, inscribed "Let Glasgow Flourish" and studded with moonstones. Signed on enamel "D.C.L.D." *1906*

13 in (33 cm) high

$10,000–15,000 **L&T**

British Silver and Metalware

In Great Britain, the artists who led the renaissance in metalwork skills and techniques—Charles Robert Ashbee, Albert Edward Jones, Archibald Knox, and Gilbert Leigh Marks—championed the ideal of the artist-craftsman. Silversmiths such as John Paul Cooper, John Pearson, and Charles Edwards rejected industrial methods in favor of handcraftsmanship, embellishing their wares with semiprecious stones, colorful enamels, or mother-of-pearl. Eventually, as economic necessity dictated the need to reach a wider market, a number of designers accepted commissions from retailers and manufacturers to create Arts and Crafts silverware designs.

Commemorative silver bowl of quaich form, by Alwyn Carr. The twin handles embellished with Tudor roses centered with green chalcedony cabochons; with a spoon of similar design. *c. 1925*

Bowl: 8¼ in (21 cm) wide

$3,000–5,000 VDB

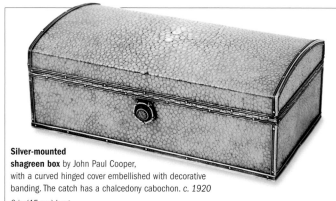

Silver-mounted shagreen box by John Paul Cooper, with a curved hinged cover embellished with decorative banding. The catch has a chalcedony cabochon. *c. 1920*

6 in (15 cm) long

$7,000–10,000 VDB

Cotswold School brass fender embossed and pierced with squirrels flanking oak leaves and acorns, in the manner of Gimson or Llewellyn-Roberts of the Birmingham Guild Ltd. *c. 1900*

48½ in (123 cm) wide

$4,000–6,000 L&T

Silver wine-bottle coaster by William Hutton & Sons Ltd., of cylindrical shape with twin angular handles. It is embossed and pierced with a band of stylized floral buds. *1904*

6½ in (16.5 cm) high

$1,000–1,500 JBS

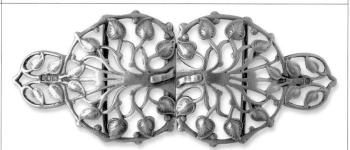

Silver two-piece buckle of shaped outline, enclosing an openwork design of simplified foliage and stems. With maker's mark for Charles Edwards of London. *1900*

5¾ in (14.5 cm) wide

$200–300 DN

Silver centerpiece designed by Kate Harris for William Hutton & Sons Ltd. It is of oval shape with twin loop handles, figural and floral decoration, and a green glass liner. *1899*

19¾ in (50 cm) high

$5,000–8,000 VDB

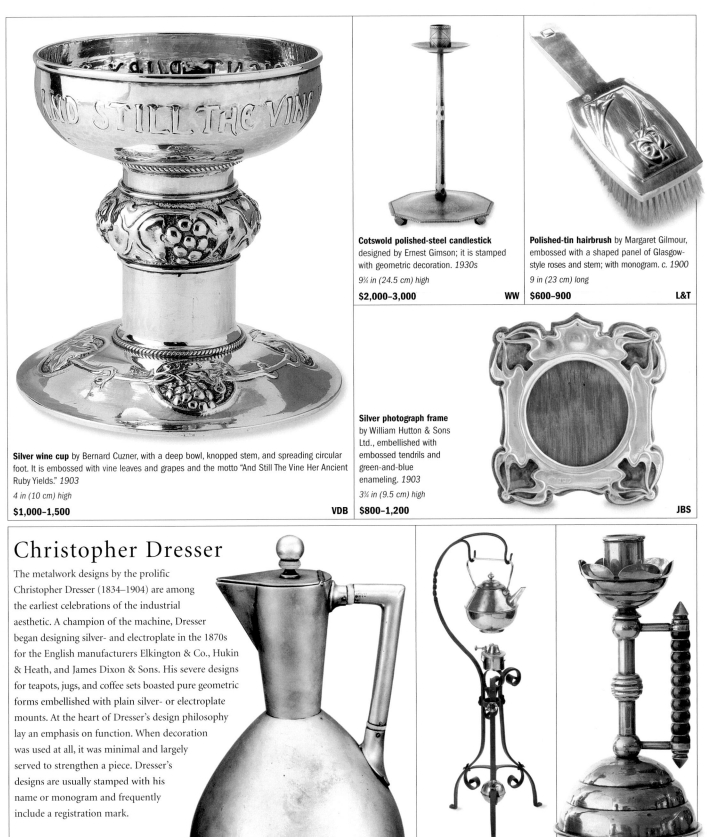

Silver wine cup by Bernard Cuzner, with a deep bowl, knopped stem, and spreading circular foot. It is embossed with vine leaves and grapes and the motto "And Still The Vine Her Ancient Ruby Yields." *1903*

4 in (10 cm) high

$1,000–1,500   **VDB**

Cotswold polished-steel candlestick designed by Ernest Gimson; it is stamped with geometric decoration. *1930s*

9¾ in (24.5 cm) high

$2,000–3,000   **WW**

Polished-tin hairbrush by Margaret Gilmour, embossed with a shaped panel of Glasgow-style roses and stem; with monogram. *c. 1900*

9 in (23 cm) long

$600–900   **L&T**

Silver photograph frame by William Hutton & Sons Ltd., embellished with embossed tendrils and green-and-blue enameling. *1903*

3¾ in (9.5 cm) high

$800–1,200   **JBS**

Christopher Dresser

The metalwork designs by the prolific Christopher Dresser (1834–1904) are among the earliest celebrations of the industrial aesthetic. A champion of the machine, Dresser began designing silver- and electroplate in the 1870s for the English manufacturers Elkington & Co., Hukin & Heath, and James Dixon & Sons. His severe designs for teapots, jugs, and coffee sets boasted pure geometric forms embellished with plain silver- or electroplate mounts. At the heart of Dresser's design philosophy lay an emphasis on function. When decoration was used at all, it was minimal and largely served to strengthen a piece. Dresser's designs are usually stamped with his name or monogram and frequently include a registration mark.

Christopher Dresser silver-plated wine jug designed for James Dixon & Sons. This shape is shown in Dresser's account book for 1881. *c. 1890*

8½ in (21.5 cm) high

$20,000–30,000   **DN**

Copper-and-brass kettle attributed to Christopher Dresser for Benham & Froud, supported on a cast-iron stand incorporating a burner. *c. 1880*

33½ in (85 cm) high

$400–600   **WW**

Copper-and-brass candlestick (one of a pair) attributed to Benham & Froud and Dresser, with a knopped stem and ebonized handle. *c. 1890*

7½ in (19 cm) high

$500–700 (the pair)   **TDG**

Copper and wrought-iron plant holder of tulip shape embossed with hearts and lilies of the valley, supported on an iron stem with leaves, three of which form the feet. *c. 1900*

16¼ in (41 cm) high

$500–700 DN

Circular silver centerpiece designed by Kate Harris for Goldsmith's & Silversmith's Co. It has short twin handles and a replacement glass liner. The sides are pierced with stylized tendrils and foliage. It is supported on button feet. *1901*

8 in (20.5 cm) wide

$2,000–3,000 VDB

A CLOSER LOOK

Silver vase by Gilbert Leigh Marks, of slender baluster form, heavily embossed and chased with dog roses against a hammer-textured ground. The thorny foliate branches extend upward from the base, where four sinuous roots support the vessel. Signed "Gilbert Marks" and dated. *1899. 12½ in (32 cm) high*

$20,000–30,000 VDB

Essence of the plant is wonderfully captured with skillful embossing and chasing

Roots act as feet, and were cast and applied separately

This typical engraved signature is usually accompanied by a date some time after that of the initial hallmark, allowing for the time taken to emboss the vase.

Silver dish by Gilbert Leigh Marks, with a curved extended rim embossed and chased with flowers and foliage against a textured ground. *1900*

17¾ in (45 cm) wide

$20,000–30,000 VDB

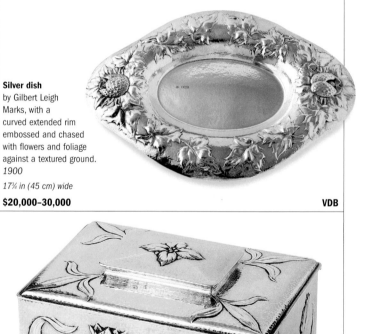

Silver rectangular casket on splayed feet by Gilbert Leigh Marks. The sides are embossed with tulips, the hinged cover with foliage and a floret. Signed and dated. *1898*

5 in (13 cm) wide

$8,000–12,000 VDB

Silver rose bowl by Harold E. Landon, of compressed form on a spreading foot, with finely engraved foliate motifs punctuated with amethyst and moonstone cabochons. The drop-in cover has pierced foliate apertures and a central amethyst-set finial. *1919*

10 in (25.5 cm) wide

$15,000–20,000   VDB

Silver bowl attributed to Latino Movio, embossed and chased with fruiting branches. Supported on four curved legs. *c. 1900*

7 in (18 cm) wide

$3,000–4,000   VDB

Iron-and-copper firescreen embossed with an elliptical panel centered with an enamel roundel. *c. 1900*

27½ in (70 cm) high

$800–1,200   L&T

Tudric pewter clock by Liberty & Co. The dial has a copper-colored chapter ring and a blue-and-green enameled center. *c. 1910*

7¾ in (20 cm) high

$4,000–6,000   WW

Silver-plated mantel clock of squared bullet shape with riveted banding, resting on a wooden base. *1909*

14¼ in (36 cm) high

$1,800–2,200   PUR

Hammered copper tray of rounded rectangular form, with a raised rim, hammered with stylized leaves and a Tudor-rose motif. *c. 1900*

21½ in (54.5 cm) wide

$300–500   WW

John Pearson

A highly skilled copper craftsman, John Pearson was one of the founder members of the Guild of Handicraft in 1888 and one of the first metalwork instructors. He taught his repoussé copperworking techniques at Newlyn Industrial Class from 1892 to 1899, before opening his own workshop to produce for Liberty & Co. His celebrated achievements included the repoussé work exhibited by the Guild at the 1888 Arts and Crafts Exhibition. Pearson possibly acquired his taste for motifs such as birds, fish, galleons, and fantastic grotesque creatures while working at William de Morgan's London tileworks.

John Pearson large circular copper charger embossed on the everted rim with birds amid stylized foliage. This motif is repeated in the sunken center. Signed "J. Pearson" and dated. *1896*

24¾ in (63 cm) wide

$3,000–5,000   WW

John Pearson copper planter with a short neck, embossed with three galleons above stylized waves. Signed and dated. *1894*

12 in (30.5 cm) wide

$5,000–7,000   VDB

John Pearson copper deed box with a peacock on the cover and de Morgan–style birds on the sides. Signed and dated. *1898*

9¾ in (25 cm) wide

$1,000–1,500   VDB

KEY FEATURES

Conical shades of pressed mica panels and hollow, vase-shaped bases are typical features of van Erp's lamps and hanging fixtures.

Copper details such as a simple band of structural rivets or strapwork decorate domestic wares and lighting fixtures.

Clean, architectural shapes and lustrous patinas in shades of red, amber, gold, and brown are hallmarks of van Erp's metalware.

Most lamps are stamped with the hammered outline of a windmill over the name Dirk van Erp, with some variations.

Dirk van Erp

Dutch immigrant Dirk van Erp brought light to the American Arts and Crafts movement with his range of original hand-hammered metal lamps covered with distinctive, richly colored patinas.

Having arrived in San Francisco in 1885, the influential, highly skilled coppersmith Dirk van Erp (1860–1933) initially took up metalworking as a hobby. His early pieces were vases and other decorative holloware, some crudely hammered out of brass artillery shell cases found in the naval shipyard where he worked.

By 1908, the hobby had turned into a business. After opening The Copper Shop in nearby Oakland, van Erp returned to San Francisco, where he forged an alliance with Canadian interior designer Eleanor D'Arcy Gaw (1868–1944). Although their partnership lasted only a year, Gaw's training with C. R. Ashbee's Guild of Handicraft (*see pp.160–61*) in England brought important experience to the enterprise that left a lasting impression on van Erp and heavily influenced his work.

He built the business into a thriving concern that was widely celebrated for handwrought copper vases, bowls, desk sets, and other domestic wares, as well as for the production of electric table lamps and lighting accessories with translucent shades made of pressed mica.

The Arts and Crafts metalwork produced in van Erp's workshop was superbly executed with meticulously hand-hammered decorative surfaces, exposed riveting, and a minimum of embellishments. Although he shared with his British counterparts an aversion to machinery, he accepted its practical advantages and used machine sheet metal for the base of his wares.

A series of successful experiments for creating a variety of colorful surface patinas is another example of van Erp's mastery of metalwork techniques. Authentic copies of van Erp's wares tend to be of inferior quality and are stamped with modern marks.

Above: Detail from the base of a hand-hammered copper vase showing maker's windmill mark and "Dirk van Erp San Francisco." *c. 1910*

ORIGINAL PATINA

Dirk van Erp's superb technical skill and his mastery of metalwork techniques prompted a series of successful experiments for creating a variety of different patinas. A hallmark of van Erp's metalwares, these patinas lend a distinctive protective and decorative surface to his hand-hammered copper vessels, vases, and table lamps. Disparate materials, including driftwood, oak chips, and even brick dust, were added in the firings to produce a broad palette of warm, natural colors—deep, earthy brown tones; rich, sumptuous golds; and mottled red hues—that create a soft, atmospheric lighting effect when coupled with a mica shade.

Hand-hammered copper table lamp featuring a conical shade with four mica panels within copper bands. The shade rests on arms riveted to the shoulders of the textured globular base. *c. 1910. 17¼ in (44 cm) high* **$20,000–30,000 GDG**

Rare, early hand-hammered copper bulbous jug with a hinged domed cover ending in a riveted loop finial. The jug has an ear-shaped handle, leaded interior, and original patina. *c. 1910. 11¾ in (30 cm) high* **$4,000–6,000 DRA**

Rare, early table lamp with a hammered-copper trumpet base. The flaring conical shade has a vented cap, three mica panels secured by narrow copper strips, three original sockets with acorn pulls, and a closed-box mark. *c. 1910*

21½ in (55 cm) high

$20,000–30,000　　　　　　　　　　　　**DRA**

Exceptional early table lamp with large hammered-copper milk-can base with riveted arms supporting a conical shade. The shade has original mica panels held by copper banding, sockets with ball chains, and an open-box windmill mark. *c. 1910*

24 in (61 cm) high

$120,000–150,000　　　　　　　　　　**DRA**

Hammered-copper table lamp the conical shade of which has four mica panels banded by narrow copper strips supported on riveted arms above a broad ovoid base. With two original sockets, open-box mark, and new patination. *c. 1915*

18 in (45.7 cm) high

$12,000–18,000　　　　　　　　　　　**DRA**

Hammered-copper shallow circular bowl with rounded sides and incurving rim, exhibiting hammered texturing and reddish-brown patina. With open-box mark. *c. 1915*

8½ in (22 cm) wide

$600–900　　　　　　　　　　　　　　**DRA**

Hammered-copper table lamp with a large drum shade pierced with quatrefoils over mica panels, above a riveted trumpet base. With open-box windmill mark. *c. 1920*

19 in (48.5 cm) wide

$12,000–18,000　　　　　　　　　　**DRA**

Rare warty hammered-copper bulbous vase with a brass collar fastened with rivets. The vase is applied with two ring handles. With original patina and open-box mark. *c. 1910*

9 in (23 cm) high

$3,000–5,000　　　　　　　　　　　　**DRA**

Hand-hammered copper vase of broad baluster shape with a slightly raised neck rim and flaring at the base. It shows a slightly planished surface, indicating hand-raising, and exhibits a rich reddish-amber patination. With windmill mark on the base. *c. 1910*

7½ in (19 cm) high

$12,000–18,000　　　　　　　　　　**GDG**

KEY FEATURES

Bronze was the favored material for Tiffany Studios metalware, which was frequently embellished with glass or colorful enamels.

Silver pieces were gently hammered to dull the shiny surface of the silver.

Small useful items in bronze are most typical—desk accessories, boxes, bowls, bookends, picture frames, candlesticks and candelabra, and vases.

Holloware pieces of silver are rare but are usually the most important, especially those that feature finely tooled designs.

Most wares are inscribed with an impressed "Tiffany Studios New York" mark.

Tiffany Studios

Following in the footsteps of his father, Louis Comfort Tiffany established the Tiffany Studios, which aimed to make a distinctive and affordable range of Arts and Crafts glass, silver, and metalware.

The son of Charles Lewis Tiffany (1812–1902), whose New York-based firm Tiffany & Co. was acclaimed throughout the world for its silverware and jewelry, Louis Comfort Tiffany (1848–1943) traveled extensively in Europe and trained as a painter and glassmaker before setting up his own decorating business in 1879. Louis Comfort Tiffany & Associates specialized in the famous Tiffany leaded-glass lamps and stained-glass windows, as well as silver and metalware accessories.

When his father died in 1902, Louis became artistic director of Tiffany & Co., which was then renowned for its Victorian silver, and in the same year renamed his business Tiffany Studios. His workshops produced a variety of affordable Arts and Crafts metalwork, including the bases and fixtures for lamps, a range of desk accessories—inkwells, pen trays, stamp boxes, and stationery racks—as well as small desk lamps, boxes, bowls, clocks, bookends, picture frames, candlesticks and candelabra, jugs, and vases.

Metalwork produced at the Tiffany Studios mainly centered on bronze, which was frequently married with glass. A favorite design featured pierced-vine and glass-trellis decoration with exposed colored marbles beneath. The most collectible pieces have a gilt or gold-doré finish. Enameled copper vases and bowls are also highly collectible. These are often sculpted in the shape of flowers or foliage with vivid enamel colors.

Silver production at the Studios was rare and limited to special commissions. These pieces were delicately hammered to give the mirrorlike surface of the silver a handcrafted, matt appearance. The Tiffany Studios closed in 1938.

Above: Bronze ashtray from the Zodiac series. It is of rounded rectangular shape and cast with scrolling bands and a Leo motif. *c. 1905. 4¾ in (12 cm) wide* **$200–300 CW**

Bronze eight-light table candelabrum of treelike organic form, on a molded circular foot. The branches support globular sconces and the central handle conceals a snuffer. Signed "L. C. Tiffany Studios, New York." *c. 1900 15 in (38 cm) high* **$20,000–30,000 MACK**

PATTERNS AND MOTIFS

Like their contemporaries in Great Britain, American metalwork designers working in the Arts and Crafts style looked to a wide variety of influences to inform the decoration of their wares. At the Tiffany Studios, useful and decorative domestic objects cast in bronze were embellished with distinctive shallow-relief patterns that evoked ancient Egyptian art, stylized American Indian motifs, and a series of symbols based on the signs of the zodiac. Other popular themes looked to nature for inspiration, including lush fruit, flowers, scrolling vines and foliate branches, and insects such as the dragonfly.

Large gilt-bronze Venetian square inkwell with canted corners and a hinged lid. Centered on a square tray, it is cast with foliate and geometric banding and scrollwork roundels. Stamped. *c. 1905. 9½ in (24 cm) wide* **$2,000–3,000 DRA**

Stationery rack with three shaped dividers in gilt bronze pierced with a trellis-and-foliage pattern revealing honey-colored marbled-glass panels. Stamped. *c. 1900*

10 in (25 cm) wide

$800–1,200   **L&T**

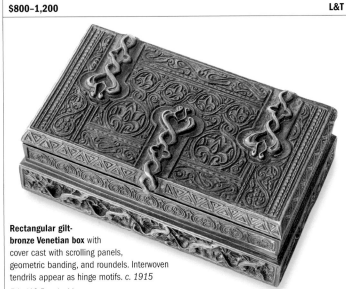

Rectangular gilt-bronze Venetian box with cover cast with scrolling panels, geometric banding, and roundels. Interwoven tendrils appear as hinge motifs. *c. 1915*

5 in (12.5 cm) wide

$1,000–1,500   **TDG**

A pair of enameled gilt-bronze Zodiac bookends cast with astrological motifs alternating with scrolling roundels and picked out with colored enameling. Stamped. *1901*

6 in (15 cm) high

$2,000–3,000   **JDJ**

Patinated-bronze inkwell with turtleback glass panels around the broad cylindrical revolving body. The three wells have iridescent panels on the lids. Marked. *c. 1900*

7 in (17.5 cm) wide

$50,000–70,000   **MACK**

Bronze ceiling-light fixture with six lights suspended from heavy chains alternating with bronze balls, also hanging. Original verdigris patination. *c. 1900*

17¾ in (45 cm) wide

$25,000–30,000   **DRA**

Rare bronze combined inkwell-and-pen tray cast with fluid organic linear motifs, having remnant of Favrile glass liner. With original patination and stamped "Tiffany Studios New York, 10034." *c. 1900*

11½ in (29 cm) wide

$3,000–5,000   **DRA**

Gilt-bronze Zodiac inkwell of tapering hexagonal shape with a hinged lid, decorated with signs of the zodiac and scrollwork. With removable clear glass liner. *c. 1910*

6¾ in (17 cm) wide

$500–700   **JDJ**

Bronze circular ashtray decorated around the everted rim with stylized flowers and foliage in colored enamels. The central handle has intertwined tendrils. *c. 1900*

4¼ in (11 cm) wide

$300–500   **CW**

Rare gilt-bronze Zodiac Rolodex with sloping front embellished with cosmic signs. A knob on the side advances the paper roll within. Stamped. *c. 1910*

4½ in (11.5 cm) long

$2,000–3,000   **JDJ**

Bronze Grapevine photograph frame with rounded corners and brown, green, and red patination. The pierced design reveals green slag glass beneath. Marked. *c. 1905*

7¼ in (18.5 cm) high

$2,000–3,000   **JDJ**

KEY FEATURES

Bronze is the material of choice for wares made by the Heintz Art Metal Shop, such as vases, bowls, lamps, candlesticks, and desk accessories.

The technique of silver overlay is a decorative hallmark of metalware produced in the Heintz workshops.

Typical silver-overlay designs include flowers, plants, birds, and geometric patterns.

A range of colored patinas— brown, green, red, and gray among the preferred hues— is another feature.

The impressed mark "HAMS" in diamond over "Sterling in bronze" was used after 1912.

Heintz Art Metal Shop

The family jewelry firm of Heintz Brothers of Buffalo, New York, joined the pantheon of American Arts and Crafts designers when it moved into the business of producing quality, highly decorative metalware.

The Arts and Crafts Co. in Buffalo was already producing an undistinguished array of copper and bronze vases, bowls, and other small items when Otto Heintz purchased it in 1903. He renamed it the Heintz Art Metal Shop, and under his stewardship the company broadened its range to include bronze desk sets, covered boxes, candlesticks, and lamps.

A distinctive feature of Heintz Art Metal wares was the preference for bronze over copper as the material of choice. Unlike other contemporary Arts and Crafts studios such as the Roycrofters (*see pp.190–91*), Heintz craftsmen eschewed traditional hand-hammering methods, choosing instead to "spin" the pieces. This was achieved by pressing flat sheets of bronze against a spinning form mounted on a lathe, or by cutting them out using shears and then shaping them with minimal hand-hammering.

Decoration and texture came in the form of a covering of sterling silver overlays applied to the surface without using solder, and a range of richly colored patinas. Over the years the Heintz Art Metal Shop experimented with a variety of unusual patinas. Among the most popular were a deep, dark green shade called Verde; an iridescent red one known as Royal; Bronze (a light brown hue); and French Gray, which gave an effect similar to silver-plating. The company closed in 1930.

Above: Unusual rectangular bronze humidor with a curved top overlaid with a stylized foliate motif in silver. It is raised on ball feet and marked "HAMS 4106." *c. 1920. 5½ in (14 cm) wide* **$700–1,000 DRA**

STERLING ON BRONZE

A hallmark of the metalware produced by the Heintz Art Metal Shop was the technique of using silver overlay for decorative effect. A special heating process patented by Otto Heintz in 1912 allowed the silver overlay to be attached to the bronze. The overlay patterns were designed to complement the shape of the piece, from a robust table lamp to a slender candlestick or a delicate flower vase. The silver-overlay decoration was made in a variety of forms, including Art Nouveau designs, plants and flowers, branching foliage, birds, and geometric shapes.

Bronze baluster vase with a gently flared neck rim, decorated with a silver appliqué of flowers resembling full-blown poppies with twisting stems and leaves. With maker's marks. *c. 1920 11 in (28 cm) high* **$1,000–1,800 HBK**

Sterling-on-bronze boudoir lamp with waterlily overlay on the base. The shade, which is missing its silk lining, has a cut-out waterlily motif with fine verdigris patination. With foil label. *c. 1920 9½ in (24 cm) high* **$2,500–3,000 DRA**

Brass-washed and etched sterling-on-bronze boudoir lamp featuring a bulbous base overlaid with a poppy. The conical mica-lined shade is pierced with three panels of poppies. With replaced mica, unmarked. *c. 1920*

10¼ in (26 cm) high

$1,200–1,800 DRA

Sterling-on-bronze vase with flared cylindrical neck, the bright polished ground overlaid with a jonquil. With stamped maker's mark. *c. 1920*

6½ in (16.5 cm) high

$120–180 DRA

Sterling-on-bronze humidor of broad cylindrical shape with press-on cover, overlaid on one edge with "FGA"; base stamped. *c. 1920*

5 in (12.5 cm) high

$120–180 DRA

Sterling-on-bronze pyramid-shaped chamberstick with circular drip-pan, strap handle, and original patina. Stamped. *c. 1910*

4 in (10 cm) high

$700–1,000 DRA

Sterling-on-bronze cylindrical vase with gently flared neck and a floral overlay against a verdigris-patinated surface. Die-stamped. *c. 1920*

7½ in (19 cm) high

$300–500 DRA

Sterling-on-bronze cylindrical vase with rolled rim, overlaid with a design of cattails on original verdigris-patinated surface. Stamped. *c. 1920*

6 in (15 cm) high

$500–800 DRA

Sterling-on-bronze cylindrical bud vase with a sparse overlay of a floral spray on original patinated surface. Die-stamped "HAMS." *c. 1920*

6 in (15 cm) high

$500–700 DRA

Sterling-on-bronze trophy cup of flared cylindrical shape with spreading foot. It is applied with twin angular handles and overlaid with interwoven trailing vines from the neck. Stamped on base, repainted finish. *c. 1925*

11¼ in (28.5 cm) high

$200–300 DRA

Sterling-on-bronze rectangular humidor overlaid on the hinged cover with stylized floral swags, repeated on the sides, against a dark patinated surface. It is cedar-lined and stamped "HAMS" with patent. *c. 1920*

10 in (25.5 cm) long

$300–400 DRA

Kalo Shop

In addition to jewelry, the highly successful Kalo Shop in Chicago originally produced a range of handwrought copperware that included bowls, trays, and desk accessories. Early success led to the rapid expansion of the enterprise, and handmade silverwork was soon added to the company's repertoire. A prolific source of handmade tableware, the Kalo Shop specialized in sterling silver bowls, candlesticks, tea and sugar sets, pitchers, and flatware in the prevailing Arts and Crafts style, with plain, paneled, and fluted shapes typically featuring a hand-hammered textured surface that was occasionally embellished with decorative chased designs.

Lightly hammered silver bowl with twin D-shaped handles, hourglass shaped lobes to the sides, a ring foot, and with an interlaced "GH" monogram. *1905–14*
10 in (25.5 cm) wide

$5,000–8,000   CHI

The presence of the words "Hand Wrought at the Kalo Shop" indicates manufacture after 1914; the words "Hand Beaten" signify manufacture 1905–14.

Pair of sterling silver candlesticks with broad-flanged, tulip-shaped sockets rising from slender club-shaped stems on broad, stepped circular feet. *1920–25*
14 in (35.5 cm) high

$15,000–20,000   CHI

Copper letter-holder
made in a truncated pyramid shape, with a large repoussé stylized tulip, stem, and leaf design, and retaining its original dark patina. The base is engraved with the monogram "HHF," and bears the mark "Hand Beaten at Kalo Shops Park Ridge Ills." *c. 1910*
5½ in (14 cm) wide

$3,000–5,000   CHI

Large 5811 silver bowl featuring a footed body with five scalloped lobes with applied wire rims. The 5811 design (made 1915–70) was produced in at least three sizes. *1940s*
10½ in (26.5 cm) wide

$1,800–2,200   CHI

Sterling silver water pitcher with a squat, ovoid body, gracefully arched spout, applied wire rim, and a large, hollow D-loop handle. Signed "Sterling Hand Beaten at Kalo Shops Park Ridge Ills. 7978." *c. 1910*

8¾ in (22.25 cm) wide

$4,000–6,000
CHI

Prior to the 18th century, interlaced initials, or monograms, were the preserve of aristocrats. By the late 1800s, however, they had become popular denotations of ownership among most sections of society on both sides of the Atlantic.

Hexagonal sterling silver water pitcher tapering to an applied wire rim with a raised V-shaped spout, and with a square-section, C-profile hollow handle. Signed "Sterling Hand Wrought at the Kalo Shops Chicago." *1912–15*

7¼ in (18.5 cm) high

$5,000–8,000
CHI

Sterling silver pitcher with an applied interlaced "ML" monogram. Part of a matching six-piece tea and coffee set, it has an angular, C-shaped handle and a fluted and corseted body, the latter tapering to a circular base and flaring to an applied wire rim with a curvaceous U-shaped spout. *c. 1915*

8¾ in (22 cm) high

$3,000–5,000 (pitcher only)
CHI

Sterling silver bud vase of elongated trumpet form, with a slightly flared applied wire rim and a lightly hammered surface. *c. 1915*

6¾ in (17 cm) high

$3,000–5,000
CHI

KEY FEATURES

Simple, elegant shapes with few decorative details characterize Jarvie candlesticks and other domestic wares—including bowls, trays, vases, jugs, bookends, lanterns and wall sconces, inkwells, and smoking sets.

Copper, brass, and bronze are the favored Jarvie materials, although occasionally silver or silvered brass were also used.

A striking antique green finish was achieved on some pieces cast in bronze by treating them with acids.

Wares are usually marked with the name "Jarvie" in script, and sometimes inscribed with "Made by the Jarvie Shop."

Jarvie Shop

In the best Arts and Crafts tradition, the cultivated American designer Robert Riddle Jarvie carved a niche in the market for a range of metalware that evoked the art of the past with a stylish twist.

Many small, independent metalware workshops in Great Britain and the United States responded to the fashion for handcrafted domestic wares by developing niche markets that were frequently linked to the transition from oil-burning lamps to electric lighting. One of these was the Jarvie Shop, established in Chicago in 1904 by Robert Riddle Jarvie (1865–1941), who specialized in the production of slender candlesticks cast in copper, brass, bronze, and occasionally silver.

From a hobby grew a thriving business, with designs for candlesticks and other useful wares— such as bowls, vases, trays, and bookends—rendered in simple, elegant shapes, with a minimum of decorative detail.

Jarvie gave a nod to the past with a line of silver tea sets in the colonial style of Paul Revere, by treating bronze-cast pieces with acids to create an antique green patina, and by naming his range of designs for candlesticks after Greek letters of the alphabet: Alpha, Beta, Lambda, and Iota. Jarvie retailed his popular candlesticks at the Kalo Shop (*see pp.186–87*), and he also took on commissions for large trophies and commemorative cups. The Jarvie Shop closed in 1917.

Above: Sterling silver sauce bowl of teardrop shape with an elongated angular handle and an integral oval undertray. *c. 1917* *8½ in (21.5 cm) long* **$2,000–3,000 CHI**

Pair of Alpha brush-polished candlesticks whose thin, circular bases, elongated stems, and flowerhead-like sockets reflect Jarvie's typically elegant, fluid form. *1904–17* *11½ in (29.25 cm) high* **$500–800 (the pair)** **DRA**

Handwrought silver chalice trophy with a lightly hammered surface embellished, on the bowl, with chased, stylized organic decoration by George Grant Elmslie. *1915* *7¾ in (19.5 cm) high* **$10,000–15,000** **ARK**

Pair of Lambda candlesticks in brush-polished copper. Their *demi-oeuf* sockets (one missing its original bobeche) taper to short stems flared and pinched into broad, round bases. *1904–17* *6½ in (16.5 cm) high* **$1,000–1,500 (the pair)** **DRA**

Four-piece smoking set made of hammered and brush-polished copper, comprising a humidor with a riveted cover, a matchbook holder, a cigarette container, and a rectangular tray. *1904–20* *Tray: 15¾ in (40 cm) wide* **$3,000–4,000** **DRA**

Gustav Stickley

Arts and Crafts ideals were loosely interpreted in the United States, but Gustav Stickley stood apart from his contemporaries by insisting on creating high-quality, handcrafted metalware.

Disillusioned with the stamped hardware available, the celebrated Arts and Crafts practitioner Gustav Stickley (1858–1942) established a metalworking studio at his Craftsman Workshops in Eastwood, New York. With an eye to producing simple, high-quality strap hinges, key escutcheons, and handles for his furniture, he set up a smithy to forge them, along with useful domestic wares (table lamps, bowls, candlesticks, trays, door plates, and desk sets), coal scuttles and other fireplace furniture, and small decorative items, such as covered boxes, vases, and wall chargers. Eventually the shop expanded to include the production of larger architectural features such as balustrades and fireplace hoods.

Stickley worked mainly in copper, wrought iron, and brass, and his relatively small output of handcrafted designs was of exceptional quality. Wares conspicuously boast the planishing marks of the metalsmith's hammer and a lustrous dark patina, occasionally rivet and strap patterns, and repoussé decoration of plain stylized flower motifs that betray the influence of English metalware. The studio closed in 1916.

Above: Rare log-holder made by the Craftsman workshops of Gustav Stickley. Its riveted wrought-iron straps display a fine, dark iron patina. *c. 1910. 28¾ in (73 cm) wide* **$10,000–15,000 GDG**

KEY FEATURES

Obvious hammer marks, rivet and strap patterns, repoussé stylized flower designs, and a dark, lustrous patina are all features of Stickley metal wares.

Copper and brass are the materials of choice for furniture metalware such as key escutcheons, hinges, and door handles, as well as for domestic wares—trays, lamps, desk sets, candlesticks, vases, and bowls.

Large wrought-iron fireplace furniture, such as firedogs and coal scuttles, features hammered surfaces and a dark silvery patina.

Wares are marked with the impressed carpenter's compass surrounding the motto "Als Ik Kan."

Hammered-copper Islamic-style coffee pot by the Stickley Bros. It has a domed, hinged lid, whiplash handle, squat body, and a snakelike spout. *1904–15*
15 in (38 cm) high
$400–600   **DRA**

Rare Stickley Bros. vase in hammered copper with a conical body tapering to a bulbous cupped rim and joined by two slender, looped handles. *1904–15*
14¼ in (36.25 cm) high
$800–1,200   **G5**

Fireplace companion set made in wrought iron by the Craftsman workshops of Gustav Stickley, and comprising a footed stand, poker, tongs, and shovel, all with unusual budlike handles. *c. 1910*
29½ in (75 cm) high
$20,000–30,000   **GDG**

Roycrofters

In 1903, the Roycrofters Copper Shop was established at Elbert Hubbard's artistic community in East Aurora, New York. The Shop specialized in hand-hammered decorative and useful wares in copper, brass, and metal wash. In 1908, production expanded with the arrival of Karl Kipp, who had earlier worked in the bookbinding workshop. He adapted favorite bookbinding techniques, such as stitched border patterns, for decorative copperwork on items ranging from bookends to lanterns. Popular items sold at the Shop or through its catalogs included vases, bowls, bookends, ice buckets, candlesticks, and table lamps, along with the celebrated American Beauty vase.

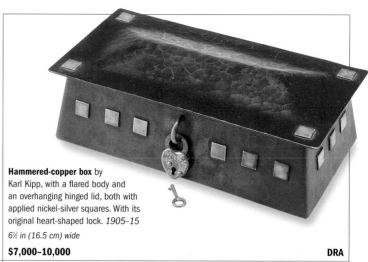

Hammered-copper box by Karl Kipp, with a flared body and an overhanging hinged lid, both with applied nickel-silver squares. With its original heart-shaped lock. *1905–15*

6½ in (16.5 cm) wide

$7,000–10,000　　　　　　　　**DRA**

Pair of hammered-copper ovoid bookends on rectangular bases, with convex oval center panels set in etched and roped borders. *1905–15*

5 in (12.75 cm) high

$120–180　　　　　　　　**DRA**

Pair of Princess candlesticks in brass-washed, hammered copper; with pyramid bases and split stems. *1905–15*

7½ in (19 cm) high

$800–1,200　　　　　　**DRA**

Pair of hammered-copper candlesticks with spindlelike stems topped and tailed with bead forms; on circular bases. *1905–15*

8 in (20.25 cm) high

$500–700　　　　　　**DRA**

Hammered-copper bowl of bulbous, circular form with a folded, pinched, and gently undulating rim, and a very desirable chocolate patina. *1905–15*

4½ in (10.75 cm) wide

$600–900　　　　　　**G5**

Hammered copper-based table lamp (one of a pair). The shade is riveted with acanthus leaf straps and has original mica panels. *c. 1910*

14 in (35.5 cm) high

$8,000–12,000 (the pair)　　**DRA**

Small ovoid hammered-copper bud vase with a closed-in rim. With its original patina and the orb-and-cross mark. *1905–15*

4½ in (11.5 cm) high

$500–700　　　　　　**DRA**

Up to around 1915, the Roycrofters mark was an "R" within an orb and a cross; thereafter, the word "Roycroft" was added.

Hammered-copper plate chemically treated to instantly produce a patina that would normally take several decades of air exposure to develop. *1905–15*

8 in (20.25 cm) wide

$300–400　　　　　　**G5**

A CLOSER LOOK

Copper table lamp with a helmet-shaped shade topped with a ball finial. It is secured to the base with two curved copper straps. The base is topped with a candlestick-like socket for the light bulb, and has a slim stem, with two annular knops, that flares into a spreading, circular foot. Its on/off switch is controlled by a beaded copper pull. As candle power gave way to electricity during the first decade of the 20th century, table lamps such as this became an increasingly important product for metalware manufacturers. *c. 1910* *20½ in (52 cm) high* **$4,000–6,000 G5**

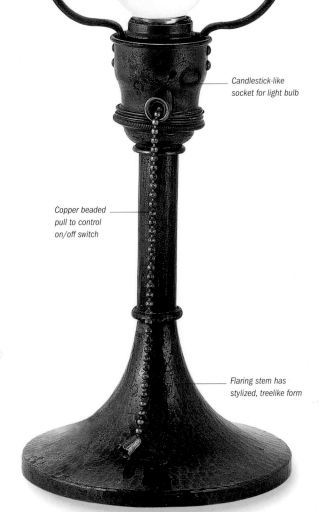

Candlestick-like socket for light bulb

Copper beaded pull to control on/off switch

Flaring stem has stylized, treelike form

Hammered-copper cylindrical vase that is also brass-washed. Around its upper body, it has a decorative verdigris band embellished at intervals with quatrefoil motifs. *c. 1910*

4¾ in (12 cm) high

$500–700   **DRA**

Cylindrical bud vase by Karl Kipp, with four buttressed handles and four silver squares below the rim. It has a hammered, patinated, and lacquered faux-woodgrain finish. *1910–15*

8 in (20.5 cm) high

$5,000–7,000   **DRA**

Dark-patinated copper American Beauty vase with a footed, squat ovoid body rising, via an annular knop, to an elongated, trumpetlike neck and rim. *1905–10*

21 in (53 cm) high

$3,000–5,000   **GDG**

Wall-hung hammered-copper planter by Karl Kipp. It has an L-shaped bracket with looped and scrolled stylized flowerhead and leaves, and a pot with an undulating rim. *1910–15*

12½ in (31.75 cm) high

$500–800   **G5**

American Silver and Metalware

Like their British counterparts, metal craftsmen in the United States embraced the ideals promoted by the Arts and Crafts movement, rejecting machine-made, mass-produced wares in favor of quality, handcrafted household objects that were both decorative and practical. By the early 1900s, metalsmiths such as Dirk van Erp and Karl Kipp, and companies including the Heintz Art Metal Shop, the Kalo Shop of Chicago, Roycroft, and Arthur Stone in Boston employed highly skilled craftsmen to create lines of hand-hammered vases, bowls, bookends, desk sets, and lighting fixtures in copper, silver, pewter, and brass in the Arts and Crafts style.

Coffee pot with waste and sugar bowls with ivory insulators and finials. From a five-piece sterling silver tea and coffee set by the Randahl Shop of Park Ridge, Illinois. *1920s*

9¾ in (24.75 cm) high

$4,000–6,000 (the set) CHI

Sterling silver bowl by Heinrich Eicher with a ribbed body and foot, an applied wire rim, a pair of curved strap handles, and an "S" monogram. *c. 1920*

7½ in (19 cm) wide

$800–1,200 CHI

Sterling silver chocolate pot from a five-piece set by Lebolt & Co., with a melon-ribbed body, a loop handle, and ivory insulators. *c. 1925*

12 in (30.5 cm) high

$2,000–3,000 (pot only) CHI

Sterling silver water pitcher by the Marshall Field Craft Shop. With a floral and foliate band and an interlaced "SV" monogram. *c. 1925*

7¾ in (19.5 cm) high

$2,000–3,000 ARK

Sterling silver underplate from a three-piece sauce set (*see also right*), by Mary C. Knight. The rim is decorated with a blue champlevé band of grapes and vines. *c. 1905*

6 in (15.25 cm) wide

$4,000–6,000 (the set) CHI

Sterling silver bowl and spoon from a three-piece sauce set (*see also left*) by Mary C. Knight. The champlevé decoration is augmented with repoussé work at the bottom of the bowl. *c. 1905*

Bowl: 4½ in (11.5 cm) wide

$4,000–6,000 (the set) CHI

Rare sterling silver bowl by John Pontus Petterson. Its handwrought sides flare out from a circular foot tooled around its circumference with American Indian motifs. *c. 1920*

6 in (15.25 cm) wide

$1,000–1,500   **DRA**

Sterling silver footed bowl by Porter Blanchard. Its hammered sides flare up from a spreading circular foot and are flanked by a pair of elongated, D-loop handles. *c. 1925*

14 in (35.5 cm) wide

$1,200–1,800   **DRA**

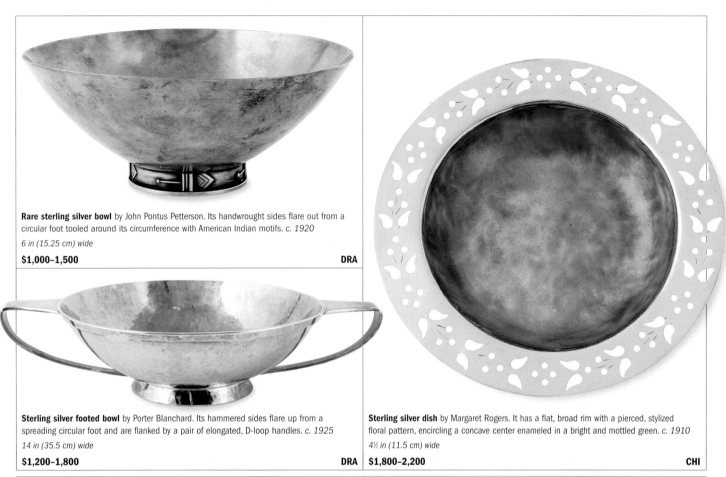

Sterling silver dish by Margaret Rogers. It has a flat, broad rim with a pierced, stylized floral pattern, encircling a concave center enameled in a bright and mottled green. *c. 1910*

4½ in (11.5 cm) wide

$1,800–2,200   **CHI**

Arthur Stone

Trained as a silversmith in England, Arthur Stone (1847–1938) moved to the United States in 1884. After working for several silver manufacturers, he opened a studio in 1901 in Gardner, Massachusetts, where he produced a range of commercially successful silverware—tea sets, bowls, tankards, boxes, trays, and vases—with decorative chasing, piercing, fluting, and repoussé techniques. A highly skilled craftsman, Stone used his own elegant designs to create finely crafted, prize-winning silverware embracing Celtic, Gothic, Moorish, and Renaissance influences that also reflected his passion for decorative motifs such as berries, flowers, and scrolling foliage.

Arthur Stone rare sterling silver pillbox with a slightly domed oval top chased with a band of 20 small floral motifs between four applied 14-carat gold floral motifs. *c. 1920*

2¼ in (5.5 cm) wide

$4,000–6,000   **ARK**

A hammer joined with the word "Stone," as above, denotes made 1906–37. The hammer joined with just the letter "S" indicates made 1901–05.

Arthur Stone sterling silver footed bowl the sides of which curve up from a spreading circular foot and terminate in an applied wire rim. They are chased around the lower circumference with stylized plant motifs.

9½ in (24 cm) wide

$3,000–5,000   **ARK**

Copper cigarette box with an oval polychrome enamel plaque depicting a sailing ship. It was made by Gertrude Twitchell of Boston. *c. 1920*

5 in (12.5 cm) wide

$2,000–3,000   **ARK**

The Carence Crafters shopmark comprised their name, home city, and a pair of interlaced "C"s within a square.

Rectangular brass tray by Carence Crafters. Its raised edges border a black-patinated center with an acid-etched pattern of leaves, stems, and clusters of berries. *Early 20th century*

9 in (23 cm) long

$800–1,200   **CHI**

Unsigned three-piece fireplace set comprising a firescreen with a cut-and-applied Japanese-style marsh scene, and a pair of andirons with brass ball finials. *c. 1920*

Screen: 41 in (104 cm) wide

$1,200–1,800   **FRE**

Round copper bowl with cover by Rebecca Cauman of Boston. The center of the cover has a small, raised copper ring encircling a carved agate rooster finial; the colors of the latter echo the orange enameled interior. The surface of the bowl displays a fine, lustrous patina. *1920s*

6 in (15.25 cm) high

$2,000–2,500   **CHI**

Heavy-gauge copper vase by Falick Novick of Chicago. Its bulbous ovoid body is lined with tin and flanked by a pair of angular strap handles. It tapers to a cylindrical collar with an applied wire rim. *c. 1915*

9¼ in (23.5 cm) high

$5,000–7,000   **CHI**

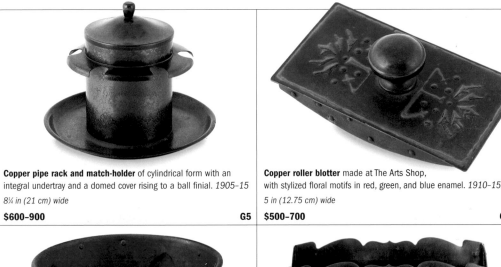

Copper pipe rack and match-holder of cylindrical form with an integral undertray and a domed cover rising to a ball finial. *1905–15*
8¼ in (21 cm) wide
$600–900 — G5

Copper roller blotter made at The Arts Shop, with stylized floral motifs in red, green, and blue enamel. *1910–15*
5 in (12.75 cm) wide
$500–700 — G5

Hammered copper-and-brass fernery by the Onondaga Metal Shops, with arrowhead motifs in relief and riveted curlicue legs. *1901–06*
12 in (30.5 cm) wide
$500–700 — DRA

Copper letter rack by The Arts Shop, with serpentine-top dividers, curlicue feet, and floral and foliate enameling. *1907–15*
8¼ in (21 cm) wide
$1,200–1,800 — G5

Hammered-copper candlestick (one of a pair) by the Benedict Art Studio, with applied leaf forms on the base. *1907–15*
10 in (25.5 cm) high
$500–700 (the pair) — DRA

OLD MISSION KOPPER KRAFT

In the early 1920s, German immigrant Hans W. Jauchen (d. 1970) established Old Mission Kopper Kraft in San Jose, California, in collaboration with Italian Fred T. Brosi (d. 1935). The pair had worked together on a number of metalworking ventures before setting up the company, and they remained in partnership for some time after it closed in 1925. During its brief tenure, Old Mission Kopper Kraft produced and sold a range of copper table lamps with paneled mica shades that owed much to the designs of San Francisco's most celebrated coppersmith, Dirk van Erp. The company sought to produce quality lamps that were constructed from the same materials but could be made for a fraction of the cost. While at first glance Old Mission Kopper Kraft table lamps bear a striking resemblance to those made by van Erp, they were not handcrafted, but manufactured using molds, die-presses, and machines, and then assembled by hand. Lamps were stamped with "Old Mission Kopper Kraft" and marked with the outline of a mission.

Semitranslucent mica panels

Riveted hammered-copper frame

Mica is also known as "isinglass"

Foliate motifs cover the stem

Hammered-copper boudoir lamp by Old Mission Kopper Kraft. Its bulbous base sits on a spreading circular foot, and supports a riveted conical shade with three mica panels. *1922–25. 12 in (30.5 cm) high* **$4,000–6,000 DRA**

Hammered-copper table lamp by Old Mission Kopper Kraft. Rising from a spreading and stepped circular foot, its stem is trailed with foliate motifs and supports a shade with three mica panels and a domed lid rising to a ball finial. *1922–25. 12½ in (31.75 cm) high* **$3,000–5,000 G5**

Fine-quality domestic tableware, kitchen utensils, and cutlery were mainly rendered in silver plate and continental pewter, with the metals occasionally combined with glass.

Richly decorated household wares include punch bowls, wine coolers, fruit stands, cake baskets, candlesticks, mirrors, and clocks.

Geometric Jugendstil patterns and nature-inspired designs, such as flowers, foliage, animals, and birds, are favorite decorative motifs.

A maker's mark is always impressed on W.M.F. pieces, but it tends to be so small that a magnifying glass is needed to read it.

W.M.F.

From the late 19th century until World War I, the German factory W.M.F. enthusiastically accepted the advantages offered by the machine, producing a handsome and stylish range of domestic metalware.

One of the most prolific and lucrative producers of commercial metalware in Germany began life as the Wurttemberg Electroplate Co., established in 1853 by Daniel Straub in Geislingen. Following the alliance of several companies, in 1880 the firm was renamed the Württembergische Metallwaren Fabrik, or W.M.F. The early years began with a mere 16 workers, but by 1914, the team included more than 6,000 employees, working in factories based in Germany, Poland, and Austria, and in showrooms in London, Paris, Hamburg, and Berlin.

The Wurttemberg region had a manufacturing history dating back to the 15th century, and it was the birthplace of a lucrative metalworking industry. W.M.F. made full use of the craftsmen on its doorstep—modelers, engravers, draftsmen,

chasers, turners, and brass-founders—and they contributed to the company's success. W.M.F. triumphed on the international stage, growing from a modest enterprise into one of the world's leading producers of quality tableware, kitchen utensils, and cutlery made of continental pewter—an electroplated metal alloy—and silver plate.

Art, technical proficiency, and commerce came together at W.M.F. Under director Albert Mayer, the company turned out a profusion of useful domestic wares—from cake baskets, bonbon dishes, biscuit barrels, toast racks, jugs, vases, and lamps, to candlesticks, tea and coffee pots, visiting-card and pin trays, mirrors, picture frames, and clocks. Decoration tended to favor the Tudric and Cymric interlace patterns popularized by Liberty & Co. (*see pp.164–67*) or the geometric designs of the Jugendstil.

Above: Silver-plated tea caddy of casketlike form, with a hinged lid and sides decorated with stylized leaf and flower strapwork. *c. 1905* *5½ in (14 cm) wide* **$400–600 TO**

GEOMETRIC DESIGNS

Although W.M.F.'s domestic metalware paid tribute to the prevailing fashion for curvaceous shapes coupled with decorative motifs inspired by nature, it also recognized the popular demand for forward-looking, modern designs for useful and decorative objects for the home. Vases, picture frames, jugs, bowls, and candlesticks in pewter and silver plate were rendered in the dramatic geometric and abstract interpretation of the natural world that was favored for decorative metalware by the Wiener Werkstätte and the German Jugendstil designers.

Pair of pewter candlesticks with Eiffel Tower–like bases rising via slender, square-section, waisted stems to arrowhead tops. They are pierced with stylized foliate motifs and support single sconces with circular drip-pans. *c. 1900. 10¾ in (27.5 cm) high* **$2,000–3,000 STY**

Silver-plated picture frame of trapezium-like form, with a pair of stylized and partly pierced fleur-de-lys motifs and a pair of heart-shaped studs on horizontal ribbing, all under a carved, openwork arch. *c. 1905* *12¼ in (31 cm) high* **$1,800–2,200 STY**

Silver-plated centerpiece comprising a twin-handled openwork frame with stylized fruit, flower, and foliage decoration, and an original clear glass liner. *c. 1900*

12¼ in (31 cm) long

$700–1,000 STY

Oval pewter centerpiece with a pair of small, angular, openwork handles and stylized bud, seed, and foliage decoration. Complete with original clear glass liner. *c. 1905*

11¾ in (30 cm) wide

$500–700 TO

Silver-plated chalice with an inverted bell-shaped bowl above a ribbed stem with fruit and foliage decoration. It flares into a circular spreading foot. *c. 1910*

$300–500 TDG

Unusual pewter vase with dragon and foliage decoration. It tapers via a paneled stem to a circular foot, which is joined to the body with four stylized plant-form straps. *c. 1900*

12½ in (32 cm) high

$300–500 WW

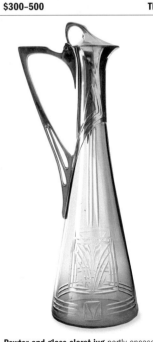

Large pewter vase of classical urnlike form, cast with twin, stylized foliate handles and griffin-among-foliage decoration. It retains its original green glass liner. *c. 1900*

15¼ in (39 cm) high

$600–900 WW

Pewter siphon stand with a partly pierced floral and foliate strapwork on the body and a stepped, circular base. The two handles are of stylized whiplash foliate form. *c. 1905*

8½ in (21.5 cm) high

$400–600 TO

Pewter-and-glass claret jug partly encased in a pewter sleeve with a whiplash foliate handle and a stylized flowerhead and stem hinged lid. *c. 1905*

17 in (43 cm) high

$1,200–1,800 TO

Wiener Werkstätte and Austrian Metalware

In Austria, the celebrated workshops of the highly influential Wiener Werkstätte, led by cofounders Josef Hoffmann and Koloman Moser, gave impetus to the Arts and Crafts movement. They employed highly accomplished silversmiths, who worked with talented designers to produce a broad range of distinctive metalwork. The majority of wares in silver, copper, and pewter boasting clean lines and geometric shapes were produced by the Wiener Werkstätte using mechanical processes. However, a number of widely admired designs created by artisans such as Peter Behrens and Joseph Maria Olbrich were faithful to the Arts and Crafts spirit and handcrafted to order.

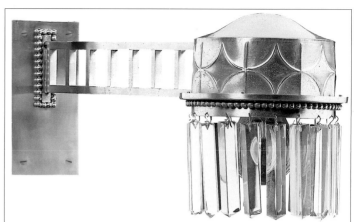

Wagner School wall lamp in nickel-plated brass. Its hinged ladder arm terminates in an octagonal shade with a repeat-lozenge pattern and beading and glass prism drops. *c. 1905*
19¼ in (49 cm) long
$5,000–8,000 DOR

Tin butter dish and cover designed by Joseph Maria Olbrich and made by Eduard Hueck, with embossed floral motifs and its original green glass liner. *c. 1900*
8 in (20 cm) wide
$2,000–3,000 QU

Five-piece coffee/tea set designed by Karl Hagenauer. The coffee- and teapots, covered sugar bowl, creamer, and tray are of copper and brass, with wooden handles and finials. *1920s*
Coffee pot: 6½ in (16.5 cm) high
$1,200–1,800 DRA

Nickel-silver breadbasket by the W.M.F. with an earthenware plate base. The blue underglaze and black overglaze geometric-pattern design is in the style of Olbrich. *1910*
10 in (25.5 cm) wide
$300–500 QU

Wiener Werkstätte silver beaker and bowl (latter not shown) designed by Koloman Moser, with a repeat, stylized flowerhead pattern around its circumference. *c. 1905*
4¼ in (11 cm) high
$8,000–12,000 (beaker and bowl) WKA

Wiener Werkstätte Alpaka box by Koloman Moser, embossed with rhombus and trellis patterns, edged with pearl beading, and topped with a rose quartz finial. *1909–10*
7 in (18 cm) high
$8,000–12,000 DOR

Viennese metal-and-glass vase with a footed, openwork frame and twin pierced handles in silver-plated brass, enclosing a smoky-gray, cylindrical glass body. *c. 1900*

8 in (20 cm) high

$300–500 VZ

Hot-water kettle with a tripod stand and heater, designed by Peter Behrens in silver- and nickel-plated brass. It has a wooden handle and a black wooden knob on its lid. *1910*

13½ in (34 cm) high

$300–500 VZ

Hammered-brass water kettle designed by Peter Behrens, of domed octagonal form with two rows of beading. It has a canework handle and a black wooden knob on its lid. *c. 1910*

7½ in (19 cm) high

$500–700 QU

Josef Hoffmann

In the first decade of the 20th century, the distinctive, highly original "basket" designs created by Josef Hoffmann for the Wiener Werkstätte evoked the pure lines and abstract geometric forms that celebrated the Arts and Crafts ideal. Fashioned in severe, elongated shapes, a range of silver, white-lacquered metal, and painted metal wares—vases, table clocks, candlesticks, and desk stands—was produced, employing the pierced fretwork and checkerboard patterns of traditional handmade wickerwork baskets for decorative effect. The smooth, shiny surfaces characteristic of popular metalware were ultimately transformed by Hoffmann and his followers as they embraced the new fashion for planished, faceted surfaces that acknowledged the prevailing appetite for handcrafted decorative objects.

Josef Hoffmann silver-plated brass basket for the Wiener Werkstätte. Of pierced-fretwork design, it has its original glass liner. *c. 1905*

6 in (15.25 cm) high

$1,800–2,200 QU

Josef Hoffmann silver flower basket for the Wiener Werkstätte, with demi-anvil ears and a punched geometric motif. *c. 1905*

7¾ in (19.5 cm) high

$10,000–15,000 WKA

Josef Hoffmann pair of bottle tops for the Wiener Werkstätte, with cork plugs and hammered silver-plated brass heads. *c. 1910*

2 in (5 cm) long

$700–1,000 (the pair) QU

Josef Hoffmann silver basket for the Wiener Werkstätte, with twin handles and 23 moonstone cabochons. *1905*

6¾ in (17 cm) wide

$20,000–30,000 WKA

Josef Hoffmann white metal flower vase for the Wiener Werkstätte. It is of rectilinear form with a loop handle and of pierced fretwork, basketlike design. It is without its original glass liner. *c. 1905*

9½ in (24 cm) high

$3,000–5,000 L&T

German and European Metalware

In the late 1800s, the metal workshops of the Wiener Werkstätte and the Austrian Secessionist movement favored sharp, geometric shapes and abstract decorative motifs, as did the avant-garde artists' colonies in Darmstadt and Munich, which were the pioneering centers of silver- and metalwork in the German Jugendstil style. Designers such as Bruno Paul, Joseph Heinrichs, and Henry van de Velde brought a formal, abstract view of the natural world to decorative wares, sharing with the Arts and Crafts movement in both Great Britain and the United States a taste for clean lines, simplicity, and restraint.

Hammered-copper samovar by Joseph Heinrichs, with wooden handles and finial and horizontal bands of sterling silver. *c. 1900*

13½ in (34 cm) high

$200–300　　　　　　　　**DRA**

Lidded brass bowl of cylindrical form designed by Bruno Paul and made by the United Manufacturers for Art of Munich. *1904*

8¼ in (21 cm) high

$2,000–3,000　　　　　　**QU**

Silver jardinière by Friedrich Felger, with a serpentine rim undulating into a pair of volute handles and with openwork decoration on the sides. It is inset with gilded brass and raised on an oval foot. *c. 1905*

13¾ in (35 cm) wide

$3,000–4,000　　　　　　　　　　　　　　　　　**VZ**

Brass table lamp by A. H. Eichberg, featuring a stylized-blossom shade above a plant-form stem and a domed rosette foot. *c. 1900*

25½ in (65 cm) high

$1,000–1,800　　**VZ**

Pewter-and-glass decanter by Friedrich Adler. Its glass body is set in a footed pewter mount with a beaklike lid and spout. *1904*

9 in (23 cm) high

$700–1,000　　**QU**

Pewter decanter by Albin Müller, of waisted form with a beaklike spout and lid. With embossed stylized plant-form motifs. *c. 1900*

15¾ in (40 cm) high

$1,800–2,200　　**TO**

Pewter decanter by Albin Müller. Its body tapers to a beaklike spout and hinged lid; embossed with peacock feathers. *1903-04*

14 in (35.5 cm) high

$1,000–1,500　　**QU**

Gobletlike silver vase with a tapering stem on a pedestal foot. It is decorated in relief with bands of heart and leaf motifs. *c. 1905*

10¼ in (26 cm) high

$2,000–3,000   CALD

Brass ceiling lamp by Richard Riemerschmid, with openwork plant-form imagery and shades (two missing) of bellflower-like form. *c. 1910*

25½ in (65 cm) long

$8,000–12,000   QU

Pewter candelabrum (one of a pair) by Albert Reinneman, with a stylized plant-form foot, a split stem, and curved interlaced arms. *c. 1900*

15½ in (39.5 cm) high

$1,800–2,200 (the pair)   TO

Mantel clock made by Orivit from a design by Albin Müller. Its silvered pewter casing is embellished with plant-form details. *c. 1900*

9¼ in (23.5 cm) high

$3,000–4,000   TGD

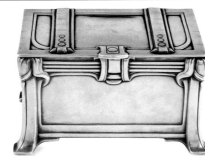

Silver box by Bruckmann & Sons, with stylized leaf-form corners and feet, strapwork moldings on the lid, and a gilded interior. *c. 1905*

6¼ in (16 cm) wide

$1,000–1,500   FIS

Henry van de Velde inkwell with a large, domed silver-plated cap on a clear-glass, ovoid body with a cube-shaped well. *c. 1905*

6½ in (16.5 cm) wide

$1,800–2,200   VZ

Kayserzinn

Founded in 1885 by Engelbert Kayser (1840–1911) at Krefeld-Bochaum, near Dusseldorf, Germany, Kayser & Son specialized in the mass production of pewter tableware, as well as vases, lamps, and ashtrays. Many talented artists, including Jean Garnier and Hugo Leven, worked for the company. Kayser & Son was awarded gold medals at the Paris World Exhibition in 1900, the First Exhibition of Modern Art in Turin two years later, and the 1904 St. Louis Universal Exhibition. The firm went into decline after 1904, although production continued until 1925. Pieces were typically curvilinear in design, featuring foliate decoration. The mark "Kayserzinn" was used, with a number above and below, or encircled in a frame.

Kayserzinn pewter liquor set designed by Hugo Laven, comprising an oval tray, six cups, and a decanter. The body, spout, and lid of the latter are in the shape of a goose. *c. 1905*

Tray: 14 in (35.5 cm) wide

$700–1,000   TO

Kayserzinn pewter bonbonnière with a slightly bulbous and footed circular body, twin loop handles, and a cover molded as a stylized leaf form rising to a bud finial. *c. 1900*

6 in (15 cm) wide

$800–1,200   CALD

Kayserzinn pewter candlesticks with lily-pad drip-pan bases. The tapering stems have leaf and split-pod decoration overflowing with fruits and seeds under the rim and at the base. *c. 1900*

10 in (25.5 cm) high

$800–1,200 (the pair)   TO

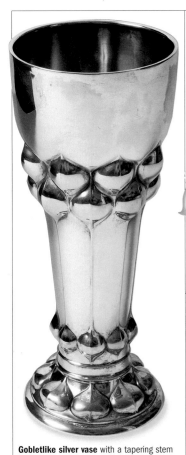

201

Glass and Lamps

A distinctive dimension of the Arts and Crafts movement was the revival of the Gothic art of stained glass, where design mingled with sumptuous colors to create dramatic luminous effects. This taste for colorful decorative glass found a voice in the creation of both stained-glass windows and panels and domestic glassware and electric-lighting fixtures in a range of rich, vibrant hues.

It was the Arts and Crafts pioneer William Morris who was largely responsible for stimulating renewed interest in the ancient art of stained glass for the decoration of both churches and domestic dwellings. Morris's legendary enthusiasm for the 14th-century tradition of creating jewel-like stained-glass windows as a means to celebrate the architecture and to enhance and unite the interior space was shared by his fellow collaborators at The Firm, including Walter Crane and Edward Burne-Jones. A prize-winning effort at London's 1862 International Exhibition resulted in a host of commissions for church windows, many of which were designed by Morris and Burne-Jones themselves, Dante Gabriel Rossetti, and William de Morgan.

Glass also played a pivotal role as the material of choice for useful domestic objects—all kinds of tableware, vases, and desk accessories. Another aspect of the modern interior that was addressed by Arts and Crafts designers was lighting. The gloom of Victorian rooms punctuated by gas lighting was challenged by Thomas Edison's invention of the electric light bulb, which led to a dramatic change in the way functional and decorative lighting fixtures were conceived. In the United States, Louis Comfort Tiffany experimented widely and produced more than 5,000 new types of glass. He is probably best known for his leaded-glass lamps, as well as his stunning range of finishes and inventive shapes.

Detail of a floor-lamp shade (*see p.205*) by the Tiffany Studios, with a geometric pattern of leaded green, pink, and white glass. *c. 1905*
80 in (203 cm) high **$70,000–100,000 VZ**

DECORATIVE STAINED GLASS

Bold, vibrant colors, free-flowing lead and painted lines, Gothic lettering, and naturalistic shapes were typical of William Morris's stained glass, which remains one of his greatest contributions to the Arts and Crafts style. Painters and designers such as those working at C. R. Ashbee's Guild of Handicraft and the Century Guild, as well as celebrated independents (such as Charles Rennie Mackintosh and E. A. Taylor in Glasgow), established studios dedicated to stained-glass production. The United States also took up the baton for medieval-style stained glass and carried the spirit of Morris forward, particularly in the work of John La Farge in Boston and in the striking leaded-glass window designs by Louis Comfort Tiffany, whose creations featured exotic birds, flowers, and landscapes in bright, luscious hues.

Architects such as Philip Webb, M. H. Baillie Scott, and C. R. Mackintosh were especially fond of using stained glass as a pivotal part of their integrated design schemes for enhancing the interior of the home. Designed with great care and attention to detail, jewel-like panels of decorative glass featured not only on doors and windows, but as art glass "pictures" to be hung on a wall, screens, overmantles, skylights, lighting fixtures, or as small compartments incorporated into the design of furniture. These imaginative ways of applying decorative stained glass to complement and lift the interior of a room were influential throughout Europe, and are notably reflected in the designs created by Josef Hoffmann and Koloman Moser for the Wiener Werkstätte in Austria.

INNOVATIVE GLASSMAKING

In Great Britain, craftsmen experimented with techniques and forms to create decorative glass boasting colorful and dramatic visual effects. Mass-produced, affordable domestic glassware based on the work of Arts and Crafts designers and architects was turned out by the Sowerby family in Gateshead, while at the opposite end of the spectrum, James Powell & Sons in Whitefriars carried the torch for Morris's ideal of the artist-craftsman, producing handcrafted glass vessels.

Another innovator in the design of glass was the multitalented and prolific designer Christopher Dresser, who raised glassware to new heights. Embracing the machine, Dresser forged a link between Morris's Arts and Crafts ideals and the path to Modernism, creating for the Glasgow firm of James Couper & Sons the spectacular range of Clutha glass—twisted opaque green glass vases marked with golden streaks—which was sold through Liberty & Co.

In the United States, Louis Comfort Tiffany moved the art of glassmaking in new directions, creating simple, graceful vases, bowls, and other decorative wares in his groundbreaking technique known as "Favrile."

Handel & Co. table lamp with an amber-tinted glass domed shade painted with a frieze of red and green flowers and leaves against a chipped-glass surface. The lamp is supported on a patinated-metal base. *c. 1910. 20½ in (52 cm) high* **$3,000–4,000 G5**

KEY POINTS

Leaded-glass windows, both ecclesiastical and secular, were often intricate and always colorful. They drew themes from the Scriptures, folklore, and the natural world, mixing Arts and Crafts motifs such as Glasgow roses with devotional scenes. Leaded lampshades more often featured geometric and floral patterns, although some had complex reverse-painted shades allowing more subtle compositions. The most complex examples mimic foliage in their form as well as their decoration.

Detail of a leaded-glass window in the Glasgow School style. The central image is of a yellow-winged butterfly above a stylized tulip and leaves and geometric banding. This is flanked by rose-balls, leaves, and stems in colors against a ground of textured frosted glass. *c. 1900. 34 in (86.5 cm) high* **$300–500 FRE**

Pot-metal stained-glass panel designed by Edward Burne-Jones and Sir Edward Coley, and made by Morris & Co. It is one of the "King René's Honeymoon" series, entitled *Painting*. The series featured in the library window of the artist Myles Birket Foster's house in Whitley. *1863. 25½ in (64.5 cm) high* **NPA V&A**

GLASS LIGHTING

Intended to complement the light, clean interiors designed by the Arts and Crafts luminaries in Great Britain, table, floor, ceiling, and wall lamps were now being created with an eye on the integrated whole. The most typical lighting fixtures featured a clean-lined frame rendered in wood or metal that was inset with stained or etched glass and embellished with plain geometric or floral patterns. The harshness of electric lamps was tempered by the revolutionary designs of W. A. S. Benson, whose shades made of copper, steel, or brass and using opaque glass deflected the light downward, creating a soft, subtle ambience.

Across Europe, designers such as Emile Gallé and Daum Frères produced sinuous, sumptuous glass lamps in the Art Nouveau style, while Richard Riemerschmid at the Dresden and Munich Werkstätten and Josef Hoffmann and Otto Prutscher at the Wiener Werkstätte created plain modern designs in geometric and architectural forms that were manufactured by celebrated Bohemian companies such as the Loetz glassworks.

The United States was quick to respond to the revolution in lighting. Louis Comfort Tiffany had forged his reputation making stained-glass windows, tiles, and door panels designed to bring light and warmth into a dim, wood-paneled room. After he purchased his own glass furnace, the Tiffany Studios began to produce lampshades made from leaded stained glass that quickly became icons of the Arts and Crafts style. Tiffany experimented with various chemical techniques to create exciting new effects, textures, and unusual surface finishes for lamps that were widely celebrated and enjoyed international acclaim. His groundbreaking endeavors in the realm of glass lighting were imitated by several of his former employees, who established factories that produced similar, affordable versions of the original, colorful and elaborately wrought lampshades made from Tiffany glass. Among such companies were the Quezal Art Glass & Decorating Co. and the Steuben Glass Works.

Tiffany Studios floor lamp with a large domed geometric shade with green, pink, and white glass segments leaded together, on a patinated-bronze column incorporating an oil reservoir. The circular foot has scrolling decoration. *c. 1905. 80 in (203 cm) high* **$80,000–120,000 VZ**

Glass ceiling fixture attributed to Duffner & Kimberly. It is of globular shape, formed by six curved panels of frosted glass marbled in shaded green and purple, leaded together, and held in a bronzed metal frame with foliate decoration suspended from a multi-arm mount. *c. 1900. 22 in (55.5 cm) high* **$1,200–1,800 JDJ**

Large stained- and leaded-glass window depicting a young woman with a naturalistically painted face. She wears a red dress with swirling scarves and dances holding a tambourine above her head. Flowers stained on both sides of the glass give a three-dimensional effect. *c. 1900. 37½ in (95.5 cm) high* **$10,000–15,000 JDJ**

KEY FEATURES

Being handmade, every Tiffany lamp is unique.

Nature plays an important role in Tiffany's designs, with vases in flower shapes or embellished with floral decoration, and lamps featuring leaded-glass shades formed as flower blooms, or embellished with insects or foliage.

Most Tiffany glass vessels are marked, usually with the initials "LCT." Sometimes "Favrile" is written in script.

Tiffany Studios

At the Tiffany Studios, Louis Comfort Tiffany created a dazzling range of glass vases and tablewares in opulent colors. However, he is best remembered for his exquisite, handmade lamps with leaded-glass shades.

Louis Comfort Tiffany was expected to take over Tiffany & Co., the luxury-goods business established by his father Charles. He, however, aspired to a career as an artist. Although Tiffany trained as a painter, it was the study of glass with Venetian glassblower Andrea Baldini that would bring him international acclaim. Having established Louis Comfort Tiffany & Associated Artists in 1878, Tiffany experimented with several glassmaking techniques, and two years later he patented his unique type of iridescent glass, called "Favrile," meaning "handcrafted" in German.

Tiffany's free-blown glass vases were produced in hundreds of shapes in a broad range of bright colors, often in imaginative combinations and sometimes with blown-in floral decoration. Some vases were so difficult to craft, they took up to four months to produce.

But it was for the dazzling array of handmade lamps with leaded-glass shades that the Tiffany Studios, established in 1900, were most widely celebrated. The lamps also represented the most commercially successful area of production. These exquisite confections could be strikingly simple—a geometric pattern rendered in a single hue, for example—or extraordinarily complex, with intricate arrangements of flower blossoms, leaves, and branches in sumptuous jewel-like colors. Some lamps were created as a whole, while others were made with separate stands.

Above: Wall sconce with three rounded rectangular paneled shades of rich amber glass, each centered with a lime green iridescent turtleback tile. *c. 1905. 6¼ in (16 cm) high* **$3,000–5,000 JDJ**

Unusual table lamp with a domed shade composed of geometric panels of marbled green glass and a band of diamond-shaped turtlebacks. The urn-shaped bronze base is set with further turtleback plaques and held between three arms rising from a spreading circular foot. *c. 1905. 20¾ in (53 cm) high* **$60,000–90,000 GDG**

LEADED LAMPS

Since visiting Byzantine churches in his youth, Louis Comfort Tiffany had been fascinated by stained glass and, in particular, the effects of daylight on colored glass. By introducing a range of lamps in 1899, he was able to experiment with decorative glass and artificial light while bringing his work to a wider domestic audience. The first leaded shades to be introduced included Nautilus, Dragonfly, and Wisteria; by 1906, over 125 different types were on sale. Shades tended to be hemispherical in shape and designs ranged from simple geometrical patterns to complex depictions of flowers, foliage, and insects. The lamps were handmade by laying stained glass on wooden molds.

LOUIS COMFORT TIFFANY

Leaded-glass conical-shaped hanging shade decorated with nasturtiums and a trellis in naturalistic colors. With the original bronze beaded rim and mounts for suspension. *c. 1905*

28 in (71 cm) wide

$100,000–150,000　　　　　　　　　　　　　　**JDJ**

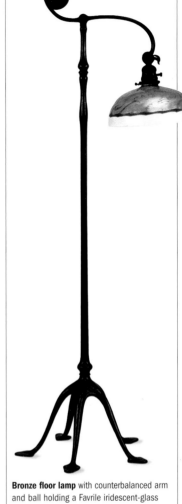

Evergreen table lamp featuring a trumpet-shaped base with verdigris patination. The green Arabian Favrile shade has yellow spots and silver-colored prunts. *c. 1905*

15¾ in (40 cm) high

$5,000–7,000　　　　　　**DRA**

Oil candle lamp with a gold luster-glass candlestick base and a ruffled shade. The oil lantern has a corked white-glass stem. Marked on the base and shade. *c. 1900*

12 in (30.5 cm) high

$2,000–3,000　　　　　　**DRA**

Tall standard lamp with a domed leaded shade featuring a geometric top on a band of peonies and foliage in natural colors. With a decorated bronze base. *c. 1905*

75½ in (192 cm) high

$300,000–400,000　　　　**GDG**

Bronze floor lamp with counterbalanced arm and ball holding a Favrile iridescent-glass shade. On a slender stem with five curved spreading feet. Marked and stamped. *c. 1905*

51¼ in (130 cm) high

$10,000–15,000　　　　　**DRA**

Leaded-glass Acorn table lamp featuring a domed shade decorated with a slender band of stylized acorns on a brick-pattern yellow ground, above a simple bronze base. *c. 1905*

32 in (81 cm) high

$30,000–50,000　　　　　**GDG**

Lily Pond table lamp with leaded conical shade decorated with overlapping lily pads graduating in size. Supported on a twist-trunk bronze base above a circular foot. *c. 1905*

26¾ in (68 cm) high

$150,000–200,000　　　　**GDG**

Leaded-glass Poinsettia table lamp with a shade featuring a red floral band amid pale green foliage, on a bud-embellished bronze base. Signed. *c. 1905*

26 in (66 cm) high

$60,000–90,000　　　　　**JDJ**

Leaded-glass Crocus table lamp with a shade decorated with blossoms and foliage, above a broad bronze base. Originally made for paraffin, now electrified. Signed. *c. 1910*

23 in (58.5 cm) high

$30,000–50,000　　　　　**QU**

KEY FEATURES

Natural landscapes, woodland scenes, flowers and vines, and colorful exotic birds inspired the designs for shades and bases.

Stunning three-dimensional effects were achieved by combining exterior and reverse-painting on a single lampshade.

Molded lamp bases were designed to match the motif of the shade, such as classical urns, tree trunks, or Chinese vases.

Handel lampshades are usually marked with the name of the firm, along with a style number and often the artist's surname.

Handel Co.

Based in Connecticut, the Handel Co. was renowned throughout the whole United States for its range of high-quality, finely crafted glass lamps made in the Arts and Crafts style.

Philip Julius Handel hailed from the town of Meridien, Connecticut, which was one of the most important centers for glassmaking in the United States. In 1885 he joined in a partnership with Adolph Eydam to establish the Eydam & Handel Co. At this early stage, the company's primary focus was the decoration of opal glassware, such as lampshades and vases, for which they purchased blanks.

When the collaboration with Eydam came to an end, in 1892, the firm was renamed the

Handel Co. and incorporated in 1903. In addition to producing a range of decorative glassware, the company also made lamps, a product line that ensured its burgeoning success, especially with the rapid spread of domestic electricity across North America.

Handel produced a broad range of exquisitely crafted table, floor, and hanging lamps with shades that were leaded or reverse-painted and typically decorated with landscapes, seascapes, or floral patterns, and occasionally Greek ruins and Venetian or tropical scenes.

The company was also celebrated for the creation of an enamel-decorated, textured glass with a unique frosted-ice finish dubbed Teroma, as well as for a range of art glass known as Handel Ware.

Above: Teroma covered jar of broad cylindrical shape. It is painted in muted colors with birds flying in a bamboo thicket. *c. 1910 7½ in (19 cm) high* **$2,000–3,000 DRA**

REVERSE-PAINTING

One of the Handel Co.'s most popular techniques for decorating lamps was reverse-painting, which created dramatic effects when the lamp was lit. The company's famous reverse-painted Teroma lampshades were created from clear blown-glass blanks. The frosted, lightly textured finish of the shade was painted with a design taken from watercolor drawings, sometimes requiring the hand of several artists as well as undergoing several firings. The most spectacular lampshades were those that were painted on the exterior as well as on the reverse, a technique that produced unusual three-dimensional results.

Twin-light table lamp with a mixed-metal slender baluster base with riveted strapwork. Two slender arms support hexagonal bell-shaped shades with brick-pattern overlay leading in bronze against yellowish glass. *1900–15. 21½ in (55 cm) high* **$5,000–8,000 G5**

Reverse-painted table lamp with a conical shade in naturalistic colors showing tall trees in a wooded landscape. The plain bronze base of slender baluster shape has a spreading circular foot. *1900–15 23½ in (60 cm) high* **$10,000–15,000 G5**

Hanging ceiling light featuring four flared cylindrical glass shades, painted in colors with geometric motifs. The shades are held in hammered-copper mounts suspended from a circular copper band. The whole light hangs from the ceiling by heavy chains. *1900–15*

26 in (66 cm) high

$7,000–10,000 G5

Boudoir lamp with a hemispherical glass shade painted in colors with diamond and linear decoration. The shade is attached to an articulated curved arm rising from a plain solid base.
1900–15

13¾ in (35 cm) high

$3,000–4,000 G5

Piano lamp with cylindrical glass shade overlaid with a brick pattern. The shade, with a lyre and open-wreath motif, is supported on a bronze-patinated adjustable metal base. *c. 1910*

12 in (30 cm) high

$1,200–1,800 DRA

Desk lamp with a shaped shade painted in naturalistic colors with a band of red flowers within bunches of bright green leaves connected by tendrils. The slender baluster stem is in bronzed metal.
c. 1910

14¼ in (36 cm) high

$3,000–4,000 G5

Reverse-painted table lamp with a hemispherical chipped-glass shade painted with an autumnal landscape and stamped "Handel Lamps Patent." The bronzed base is embossed with trees. *c. 1910*

23½ in (59.5 cm) high

$5,000–8,000 DRA

Table lamp featuring a domed shade with curved panels of honey-colored marbled glass showing through metal mounts embellished with an openwork design of oak leaves. Slender stem and circular foot.
1900–15

13¾ in (35 cm) high

$5,000–8,000 G5

American Glass Lamps

The advent of electricity gave the Arts and Crafts movement in the United States the chance to revolutionize the design of lighting fixtures. Glass lamps remained both functional and decorative, with the illumination enhancing the ornamental motifs outlined on the shades. Tiffany & Co. became an icon of Arts and Crafts interiors with its celebrated leaded stained-glass lampshades, which softened the harshness of electric lighting while spreading color around a darkened room. Duffner & Kimberly, Wilkinson, and Pairpoint produced similar lines of extravagant lampshades made of colorful, iridescent glass.

Leaded-glass ceiling lamp attributed to Duffner & Kimberly, with a border of pink flowers on a brown-and-tan geometric background. Suspended from three chains. *c. 1910*

21¾ in (55.5 cm) wide

$12,000–18,000 JDJ

Leaded-glass table lamp by Wilkinson with a conical shade of pink and green geometric panels, above a bronzed classical base with rams' heads decoration. *c. 1910*

23½ in (60 cm) high

$3,000–4,000 DRA

Leaded-glass table lamp by Wilkinson. It features a domed shade with pink tulips and green foliage against a geometric ground. On a bronze base with a quatrelobe foot. *c. 1910*

25¼ in (64 cm) high

$3,000–5,000 FRE

Roman leaded-glass table lamp by Duffner & Kimberly with a domed shade with grapes and vines. On a bronze-patinated stand with four paw feet on a quatrelobe base. *c. 1910*

21 in (53.5 cm) high

$8,000–12,000 JDJ

Leaded-glass table lamp by Duffner & Kimberly. It has a domed shade of geometric panels, on a fluted and lobed bronze base. With a replacement cap and finial. *c. 1910*

22½ in (57.5 cm) high

$3,000–4,000 DRA

Reverse-painted Florence table lamp by Pairpoint, with a stylized floral design on a turquoise blue background; the obverse is highlighted with gold. Signed. *c. 1910*

19½ in (49.5 cm) high

$3,000–5,000 JDJ

Reverse-painted table lamp by Pairpoint, with a domed shade depicting clipper ships. It is raised on a base with three stylized dolphin supports. Signed. *c. 1910*

20½ in (52 cm) high

$3,000–5,000 POOK

Table lamp by Pairpoint with a mushroom-shaped chipped-glass shade stenciled with colored geometric blossoms, on a circular bronzed twin-handled base. Shade marked "Patented April 19, 1923."

12 in (30 cm) high

$1,800–2,200 DRA

Brass-patinated and hammered-metal chandelier with five cylindrical fixtures lined in caramel slag glass and hanging by short chains from a ring frame. *c. 1900*

29½ in (75 cm) high

$1,800–2,200 **DRA**

Table lamp by Bradley & Hubbard with a domed shade painted with stylized poppies and leaves, on a strapped and hammered base with the original bronze patina. *c. 1910*

25¼ in (64 cm) high

$5,000–7,000 **DRA**

Leaded-glass table lamp featuring a domed shade with geometrically arranged green and amber slag-glass panels, on a brass stem with a spreading stepped base. *c. 1920*

18 in (45.5 cm) high

$400–700 **DRA**

Waterlily table lamp by Elizabeth Burton. The brass-patinated coiled tube base forms a stem terminating with open leaves and three abalone shell shades. *c. 1910*

16¾ in (42.5 cm) high

$2,000–3,000 **DRA**

Reverse-painted table lamp with a shade painted with three bull elk grazing. Supported on metal tree trunks flanked by a moose on an onyx base. Signed. *c. 1900*

23½ in (59.5 cm) high

$5,000–7,000 **JDJ**

Oak, copper, and glass table lamp with a plain pyramid-shaped shade inset with honey-colored glass panels. It is supported on a tapering square-section column applied with copper strapwork above a square foot with rounded edges. *c. 1900*

19¾ in (50 cm) high

$1,000–1,800 **G5**

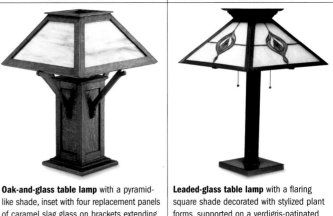

Oak-and-glass table lamp with a pyramid-like shade, inset with four replacement panels of caramel slag glass on brackets extending from a square-section base. *c. 1900*

21¾ in (55 cm) high

$700–1,000 **DRA**

Leaded-glass table lamp with a flaring square shade decorated with stylized plant forms, supported on a verdigris-patinated metal square-section base. *c. 1910*

23½ in (60 cm) high

$1,800–2,200 **DRA**

British and European Glass and Lamps

Among the leading Arts and Crafts makers of glass in Europe were Josef Hoffmann and Otto Prutscher of the Wiener Werkstätte, Richard Riemerschmid, and the artisans of Bohemia. All produced domestic glassware and light fixtures in geometric, architectural forms. By contrast, the French artist-craftsman Emile Gallé created sinuous glass confections that looked to nature for inspiration. In Britain, W. A. S. Benson created a range of original lamps, while companies such as Liberty & Co., Powell & Whitefriars, Webb & Sons, and Stevens & Williams produced ornamental glassware in rich, glowing colors with a variety of decorative effects.

Brass-and-copper hall lantern with lattice-molded cylindrical glass shade within a mount. The steep conical top is embellished with scrolling strip banding. *c. 1900*

33 in (84 cm) high

$1,200–1,800   L&T

Gothic leaded-glass hall light with panes of amber and white frosted glass beneath a tall conical top with foliate motifs and fluted vents. *c. 1900*

27¼ in (69 cm) high

$400–600   DN

English oval glass window (one of a pair) painted in naturalistic colors with the profile of a medieval maiden holding a rose and standing in a landscape with stylized fruiting trees and clouds in the distance. Framed. *c. 1900*

29 in (73.5 cm) wide

$200–300 (the pair)   FRE

English vaseline glass vase of trumpet shape, decorated internally in yellow opalescence with stylized irises. It is supported on a circular foot. *c. 1900*

10 in (25 cm) high

$300–500   MW

English clear-glass water jug (one of a pair) by John Grinsell & Sons, London. It is of broad ovoid shape, applied with glass tears and with a silver collar. *1901*

7 in (18 cm) high

$1,000–1,800 (the pair)   WW

Liberty & Co. pewter and Clutha-glass bowl by Archibald Knox. The mount is pierced and embellished with simple leaf forms, on three flange legs above a slightly domed circular base. The bubble-suffused pale green glass has milky streaks and aventurine inclusions. *c. 1905*

6½ in (16.5 cm) high

$3,000–5,000   DN

Copper-and-glass hanging lantern with a broad cylindrical shade with slag-glass panels. The domed top has vents and strapwork and the original reddish brown patina. *c. 1900*

14¾ in (37.5 cm) high

$3,000–4,000   **DRA**

Tapering cylindrical green glass vase (one of a pair) applied with a geometric copper mount. It is pierced to reveal the glass beneath and set with green glass cabochons. *c. 1900*

7¼ in (18.5 cm) high

$800–1,200 (the pair)   **DN**

Loetz golden iridescent glass vase designed by Karl Kellerman, held within a bronze frame by handles embellished with stylized foliate motifs; raised on four feet. *c. 1900*

10 in (25.5 cm) high

$5,000–7,000   **TO**

Bohemian iridescent glass ewer probably by Pallme Koenig. The webbed decoration on the body is reflected on the collar, which has a hinged lid and an angular handle. *c. 1900*

10¾ in (27.5 cm) high

$1,000–1,500   **DRA**

W.M.F. plated claret jug with pale green glass held within a mount embellished with the profiles of young maidens amid flowers and tendrils. With a replacement stopper. *c. 1900*

10½ in (27 cm) high

$220–280   **L&T**

Austrian table lamp with domed iridescent glass shade supported by a mahogany, iridescent glass, and bronze stem and base embellished with Glasgow roses. *c. 1900*

27 in (68.5 cm) high

$8,000–12,000   **DRA**

Bohemian iridescent glass vase of tapering ovoid form with dimpled sides, a flared trefoil neck, and pale blue swirling decoration against a deep greenish blue. *c. 1900*

9 in (23 cm) high

$200–300   **JDJ**

Stained-Glass Panels

In the 19th century, under the influence of William Morris, the Arts and Crafts movement in Great Britain was largely responsible for rekindling interest in the Gothic art of stained glass. The Gothic Revival brought about a renewed enthusiasm for stained-glass windows in churches as well as in domestic settings. As proven by Morris and his fellow practitioners Edward Burne-Jones, Walter Crane, and Charles Rennie Mackintosh, the practice of using colorful stained-glass windows and panels—frequently boasting medieval themes—as decoration came to define the character of the typical Arts and Crafts home. In the United States, the interest in this Gothic art could be observed in the work of John La Farge, who invented a type of glass he dubbed "American opalescent art glass," which inspired the technical experiments of his competitor, and ultimately more celebrated successor, Louis Comfort Tiffany.

Leaded polychrome glass window with a central foliate heart-shaped motif enclosing flowers resembling bluebells and flanked by stylized thistles, against a plain background. Probably English or Scottish. *c. 1900*

38½ in (97.5 cm) wide

$300–500   **FRE**

Leaded-glass panel showing in bright colors the figure of a dark-haired wood nymph cradling a basket and resting by a stream with a rustic cottage in the background. *c. 1930*

36 in (91.5 cm) high

$30,000–50,000   **PUR**

Leaded-glass panel painted in soft naturalistic colors depicting a maiden in voluminous medieval garb standing in a meadow of daisies and collecting some of the blooms in her robes. Flanked by an extract from a poem believed to be by Dante Gabriel Rossetti. *c. 1870*

10½ in (26.5 cm) high

$1,000–1,500   **WW**

MEDIEVAL IMAGERY

Influenced by Pugin and Ruskin's writings, William Morris and Philip Webb traveled in France together in the late 1850s and admired the beauty of stained glass and tapestries in the medieval cathedrals there. Morris & Co.'s output in the 1860s was mainly ecclesiastical stained glass designed by leading artists such as Dante Gabriel Rossetti and Edward Burne-Jones. The medieval imagery of angels, musical minstrels, and saints was highly idealized.

Details from a pair of leaded polychrome glass windows showing a medieval maiden, birds, and the motto: "Gather ye rosebuds while ye may, Old Time is still a-flying." *c. 1920* **33 in (84 cm) long** **$1,800–2,200 (the pair) DRA**

Leaded-glass window showing in naturalistic colors a Dutch peasant girl, with handpainted detail, standing on a path near a windmill in a highly stylized landscape. *c. 1920* *31¾ in (80.5 cm) wide*
$800–1,200 **DRA**

Leaded-glass window with a red Glasgow-style rose within a frame of colored stylized foliage against textured clear and amber panes. Mounted in a new pine frame. *c. 1900* *33½ in (85 cm) wide*
$200–300 **DRA**

Stained-glass panel depicting in bright colors a scene from Lewis Carroll's *Alice in Wonderland*: at the court of the Queen of Hearts, the King, the white rabbit, and a knave dispute ownership of jam tarts. *c. 1930*
36 in (91.5 cm) high
$20,000–30,000 **PUR**

Leaded stained-glass panel inscribed "Literature." The central panel is painted with an allegorical female figure framed within an archway, surrounded by ornate panels of foliage and flowers within floral borders. Unframed. *c. 1895*
110¼ in (280 cm) high
$5,000–8,000 **L&T**

American arched stained-glass window with a George Washington portrait medallion at the center. The border panels of dolphins and a spewing dragon alternate with panels of five-point stars. *c. 1900*
54 in (137 cm) high
$1,800–2,200 **NA**

Books and Graphics

The Arts and Crafts movement was rooted in the desire of its practitioners to generate a meaningful dialogue with the consumers of their work. Through printed media and the graphic arts, they were able to realize this ambition in a more literal fashion than was possible through the decorative arts, expressing themselves almost solely through their use of surface decoration.

The antiquarian instinct typical of the Arts and Crafts movement was demonstrated most strikingly by the private presses established at the turn of the 20th century. In an era where presses were becoming increasingly automated—1884 had seen the introduction of Mergenthaler's Linotype machine—Arts and Crafts printers consciously headed in the opposite direction, taking their lead from the pre-Gutenberg incunabula of the 15th century and even earlier.

Woodcut illustrations, hand-tooled leather bindings, even handmade paper and vellum—all labor-intensive creations—were the weapons wielded in the war against the mass-produced books that dominated the Victorian market. William Morris led the way with his Kelmscott Press. Established in 1891, it rolled until 1907, having passed into the ownership of C. R. Ashbee

on Morris's death. During its life span, the Press produced some truly exceptional works, including the celebrated Kelmscott Chaucer, considered one of the finest books ever created. The type was designed by Morris specifically for this project and is incorporated into the overall design of the pages. Along with the patterned borders, drop capitals, and illustrations, it imparts a rich, layered texture to the book that is almost overwhelming in its intricacy. The decision to publish an edition of Chaucer, the great Middle English poet, is typical of Morris's predilection for his heritage.

Elbert Hubbard, who founded the Roycroft Press in emulation of Morris's great achievement, summed up the philosophy behind the private presses of the era by saying: "One machine can do the work of 50 ordinary men. No machine can do the work of one extraordinary man."

Golden Gate roundel by Edward Burne-Jones from a page in *The Flower Book*. It depicts a central angel holding a glowing fiery globe, attended by a pair of angels at the golden entrance to Heaven. *c. 1905. 6½ in (16.5 cm) wide*
$1,800–2,200 PC

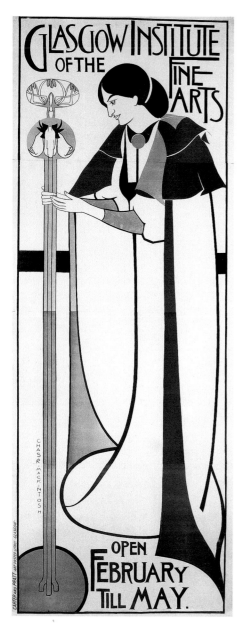

Glasgow Institute of the Fine Arts colored lithographic poster by Charles Rennie Mackintosh. It shows a young woman in a cape standing beside a highly stylized flowering shrub. *1895.* **NPA CHR**

GRAPHIC WORKS IN GREAT BRITAIN

Some Arts and Crafts practitioners became well known for their work with a particular aspect of book design. Among them was Talwin Morris, whose covers featured on many books of the period and were also illustrated in contemporary periodicals. His style was steadfastly architectural, and his lettering characterized by its narrow and angular nature. Edward Burne-Jones produced a series of frontispiece woodcuts that was used by the Kelmscott Press. Typically atavistic, it displays a distinctly medieval flavor that befits the manner of its creation. Burne-Jones's illustrations for *The Flower Book*—a series of 38 pictures that he presented to his wife—show the mark of the Arts and Crafts aesthetic in their mix of the ethereal and the pastoral. With their devotional subject matter, they hark back to the work Burne-Jones carried out in stained glass for William Morris, a lifelong friend since they met while studying for the priesthood at Oxford University.

Burne-Jones was a leading light of the second generation of Pre-Raphaelites, a society whose ideals were very closely aligned with those of Morris and his followers. In particular, their doctrine of painting subjects almost exclusively from classical, medieval, and biblical mythology finds echoes in the pristine creeds that pervaded the Arts and Crafts movement. Another celebrated British artist of the time was Annie French, a watercolorist from the Glasgow School who produced evocative and empyrean tableaux depicting fairies and folkloric themes.

DEVELOPMENTS AND TECHNIQUES

In America, Arthur Wesley Dow took the British Arts and Crafts manifesto and fused it with his own predilection for Japanese art. His seminal textbook on composition was instrumental in the development of the American Arts and Crafts scene, spanning the decorative arts as well as fine art. Dow's Impressionistic landscapes display careful observation and are democratic in their choice of locale: his riverbanks, lakes, hilltops, and clumps of trees are beautiful and anonymous, testament to Dow's belief that the "study of composition of line, mass, and color leads to appreciation of all forms of art and the beauty of nature." As part of his advocacy of Japanese art, Dow championed the technique of woodblock-printing, which was enthusiastically adopted by other American artists working within the Arts and Crafts idiom. Blanche Lazzell, in particular, went on to become a master of white-line printmaking among the Provincetown Printmakers.

Block-printing techniques were also used to make wallpaper. William Morris's output in

Celadine wallpaper block-printed by Morris & Co. Wallpaper produced by block-printing used to be retouched by hand. Often, hand-painting marks and inconsistencies in the pattern can be spotted. *22 in (55 cm) wide* **$550–750 (per repeat) PC**

KEY POINTS

A yearning for more innocent days can be felt in the wholesome and edifying illustrations of the Arts and Crafts period. Medievalism and pastoral themes unite much of the work carried out under the Morrisian banner, with repeating patterns of flowers and greenery providing the backdrop for the entire movement. Revived handicrafts such as block-printing and custom materials such as vellum were the tools used to create these scenes.

Decorative panel painted by B. Moore in the manner of Henry Stacy Marks. It shows a medieval countryman wearing simple robes and a hood, in a rural setting beside blossoming bushes. Against a golden background and mounted in an ebonized Aesthetic-movement sideboard. *1870s 20 in (51 cm) high* **$3,000–5,000 PUR**

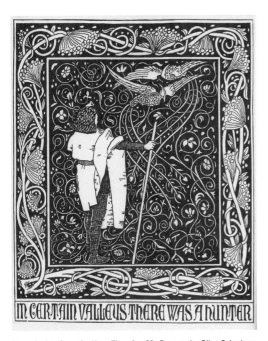

Page design from *So Here Then Are My Dreams* by Olive Schreiner published by the Roycroft Shop. It shows a stylized foliage and floral design and a medieval-style typeface. *1901.* **NPA FML**

has touched up an area of the pattern. Other factors in the high cost of Morris's wallpapers were the organic and mineral pigments that were used instead of cheaper chemical dyes (a sore point, since it later emerged that the green pigment used in some of the papers was laden with arsenic). Jeffrey & Co., whose skilled block-printers won the commission to produce Morris & Co. wallpapers, also carried out work for Walter Crane, whose elaborate designs drew both praise and criticism.

THE ULTIMATE PLATFORM

The graphic arts emerging from the Arts and Crafts movement were championed around the turn of the 20th century by political and literary journals, such as *Harper's* and *Scribners*. They published posters and prints alongside the text on their pages and commissioned cover art from the best contemporary artists. William Bradley and Louis J. Rhead contributed strong images to these periodicals, which made full use of the relatively new process of chromolithography to reproduce their striking artwork. This is just one more instance in which the antiquarian bias inherent within the Arts and Crafts movement found an unlikely ally in modern technology.

Title page of *A Book of Verse* by William Morris. Morris put together this illustrated collection of his poems as a birthday present for Georgiana Burne-Jones. He was responsible for the calligraphy and most of the border decorations, though various friends helped. *1870.* **NPA COR**

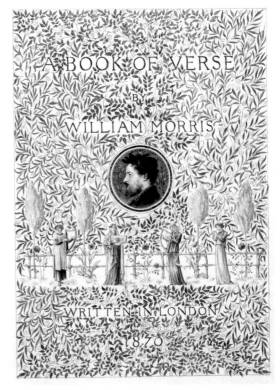

this field was prolific: indeed, despite his immense contributions to so many disciplines, it is his wallpapers that have left the most indelible mark in the popular imagination. He designed many of the patterns himself, along with John Henry Dearle, who continued to devise new ones after Morris's death. William Morris had a talent for rich pattern-making and a predilection for luxurious dense colors such as peacock blue, russet browns, and deep reds. Designs were invariably floral, with large repeated patterns.

Morris & Co. wallpapers were very expensive because the woodblock-printing process was often finished by hand—it is usually possible to discern slight irregularities where the hand of an artist

Franz von Zulow screenprint for the Wiener Werkstätte, produced as a four-layer collage of stenciled images of sunflowers, dahlias, daisies, and roses, with butterflies and other insects amid dense and lush foliage; in bright colors with black edges. *c. 1905. 47¾ in (121 cm) high* **$12,000–18,000 WKA**

Green Gate ink on vellum design for a bookplate, by Jessie M. King. This simplified image could have been for the artist's own use, perhaps as an ex-libris, as her home in Kilmacolm was Green Gate, and she used this motif on ceramics painted by her. *c. 1900. 4¾ in (12 cm) high* **$500–700 L&T**

Books

Influenced by early illuminated manuscripts and the work of the first printers such as William Caxton, William Morris set up the Kelmscott Press in 1891. He wanted each book to be seen as a complete work of art: this meant taking great care with all aspects of production, including the paper, the type, the spacing of the letters, and the position of the printed matter on the page. Leading designers such as Talwin Morris and Walter Crane were inspired by Morris's ideas on book design. Several private presses were set up to perpetuate these aims both in Great Britain and the United States, including Elbert Hubbard's Roycroft Press in East Aurora, New York.

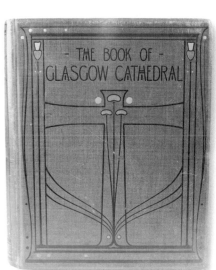

A Talwin Morris–designed bookbinding for *The Book of Glasgow Cathedral*, published by the Morison Brothers of Glasgow. It has stylized plant and linear decoration highlighted with green and gilt. *c. 1890*

$100–150   L&T

The *Magazine of Art* (one of ten volumes of various dates: 1881–84, 1886, 1891, 1895–97). The books came in a variety of bindings with monochrome illustrations. *c. 1890*

$200–300   WW

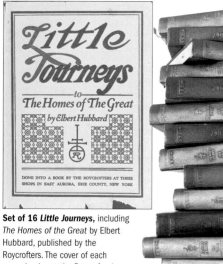

Set of 16 *Little Journeys*, including *The Homes of the Great* by Elbert Hubbard, published by the Roycrofters. The cover of each magazine bears the Roycroft orb mark, adapted from the mark of Cassiodorus, a 14th-century monk scribe. *c. 1895*

8½ in (21.5 cm) high

$300–500 (the set)   G5

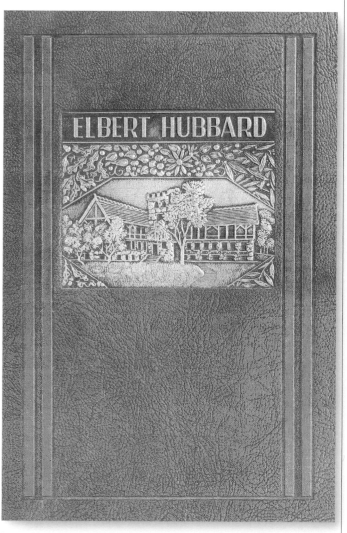

Leather-bound volume of *Little Journeys* (one of a set of 16) by Elbert Hubbard, published by the Roycrofters. The volumes are embossed with a panel showing the Roycroft Inn. Hubbard was a writer and publisher before he began retailing furniture.

8½ in (21.5 cm) high

$20–50 (the volume)   G5

Illustration from period catalog *Craftsman Furnishings for the Home*, published in October 1912. It depicts a stylized flower resembling a daffodil printed with a bold black outline picked out in yellow and orange. *1912*

$200–300 DRA

Period catalog *The Work of L. & J. G. Stickley—Fayetteville, New York*, depicting a comfortable sitting room furnished with items from their workshops as shown in the catalog. *1910–12*

9½ in (24 cm) high

$180–220 G5

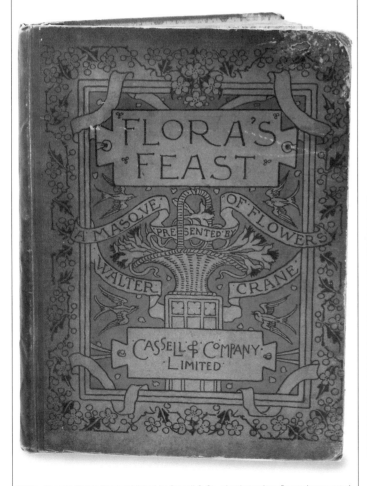

Walter Crane's *Flora's Feast* published by Cassell & Co., showing various flowers incorporated with appropriate figures or animals, such as tigers with tiger lilies. This copy was presented to the celebrated silversmith Omar Ramsden while a pupil at the Sheffield School of Art. *1895*

$400–600 B

PRIVATE PRESSES

Perhaps the most famous of the private presses, the Kelmscott Press was established by William Morris in Hammersmith, London, in 1891. Kelmscott was the culmination of Morris's life as a craftsman in many diverse fields. He set out to prove that the high standards of the past could be repeated—surpassed, even—in the present. The books Morris produced were medieval in design, modeled on the incunabula of the 15th century. Roman "golden" type, for example, was inspired by that of the early Venetian printer Nicolaus Jenson. In the UK, numerous other private presses were established, including Doves Press, the Ashendene Press, and the Eragny Press. More than 50 small presses came into existence in the United States between 1895 and 1910. All reflected Arts and Crafts ideals in their craftsmanship, use of fine handmade materials, and the dense medieval appearance of the type. Editions were often limited, signed, and illustrated with woodcuts or wood engravings.

Details of frontispiece woodcuts designed by Edward Burne-Jones for William Morris's book *A Dream of John Ball*. The frontispiece was handprinted by the Kelmscott Press and is signed by the artist. Burne-Jones and Morris met while they were both students at Oxford University, and they collaborated on many book projects together. *c. 1885*

$4,000–5,000 PC

Illustrations, Paintings, and Prints

Arts and Crafts illustrators and painters such as Edward Burne-Jones, Jessie M. King, and Annie French explored common subjects and themes, including old English myths, Celtic and Christian symbols, and idyllic rural scenes. In the United States, color prints made from handcarved wood blocks were popular during this period. Inspired by Japanese prints, artist Arthur Wesley Dow (1857–1922) revolutionized the technique by eliminating the separate roles of artist, engraver, and printer and doing everything himself. Dow, who was also a prolific lecturer and teacher, influenced a whole generation of American artists.

The Procession of Psyche **illustration** by Edward Burne-Jones on handmade paper. Originally designed for a book by William Morris telling the story of Psyche and Cupid, it was not used at the time. The book was published in the 1970s complete with illustrations. *c. 1900*

6 in (15 cm) wide

NPA   **PC**

The Tree of Knowledge original drawing by T. Herbert McNair created for a bookplate for John Turnbull Knox. It shows the flower-adorned tree with an advisory verse surmounted by two maidens and, above them, a bird with human heads suspended from its wings. *c. 1905*

6¾ in (17 cm) high

NPA   **GDG**

Scattered Starwort **roundel** by Edward Burne-Jones. It depicts in soft pastel colors four angels suspended in the ether, with their robes gathered like aprons from which they cast starwort seeds. Taken from a page in *The Flower Book*. *c. 1905*

6½ in (16.5 cm) wide

$1,800–2,200   **PC**

$7,000–10,000

The Town by the River ink on vellum by Jessie Marion King. It depicts a sleepy idyllic cluster of houses. Signed and inscribed by the artist. *c. 1900*

8 in (20 cm) wide

$8,000–12,000   L&T

Study for a Roundel drawing in ink and pencil by Dagobert Peche. It depicts a chariot drawn by four horses. Initialed and dated by the artist. *1910*

4 in (10 cm) high

$700–1,000   L&T

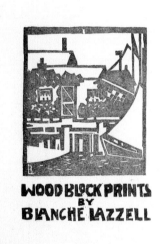

Pen-and-ink drawing by Ethel Isadore Brown, heightened with watercolor, depicting a winter cityscape with a snow-covered tree and a park bench in the foreground. *1904*

6¾ in (17 cm) high

$300–500   DRA

Modern Art by Arthur Wesley Dow. It is a lithographic cover of Bowles and Prang's periodical, depicting a river scene with freehand text; signed by the artist. *c. 1900*

10 in (25.5 cm) high

$700–1,000   DRA

Wood Block Prints by Blanche Lazzell. This block-printed cover of an exhibition catalog depicts a Providence dock scene in black on white paper. *1928*

8 in (20.5 cm) high

$500–700   DRA

A Queen and her Attendants watercolor in vibrant autumnal hues by Annie French. The queen is installed on a rocky throne flanked by swaths of colored flowers, with two female attendants and a further attendant with flame red hair and elaborate jeweled costume standing by a blossoming tree; all are placed against a bright blue cloud-streaked sky. *c. 1900*

19 in (48.5 cm) wide

L&T

Wallpaper and Posters

Simple, stylized wallpaper patterns based on medieval motifs and natural forms were created by William Morris and, later, by his assistant John Henry Dearle, and retailed through Morris & Co. From 1864, Morris's wallpapers were designed for him by Jeffrey & Co., to whom leading artists such as Walter Crane, C. F. A. Voysey, and A. H. Mackmurdo also supplied designs. By the late 1870s, Morris & Co. wallpapers were widely available in the United States. Popular American designs were also provided by L. C. Tiffany, Christian Herter, and Candace Wheeler. The typographical revolution brought about by the private presses also extended to posters and magazines. Leading poster designers of the period were Louis J. Rhead, William H. Bradley, and Edward Penfield.

Section of colored wallpaper frieze designed by Walter Crane. It depicts peacocks amid foliate scrolls and lilies. This piece is from the former residence of Arthur Balfour, British prime minister from 1902 until 1905. *1902–11*

40¼ in (102.5 cm) wide

$4,000–5,000   **DRA**

The Flowering Scroll wallpaper designed by John Henry Dearle for Morris & Co. It has pale red stylized flowers and buds nestling amid scrolling green foliage. *c. 1880*

22 in (56 cm) wide

$500–700 (per repeat)   **PC**

Celadine block-printed wallpaper for Morris & Co., with pale pink blooms sprouting from olive green clusters of leaves reminiscent of the company's tile decoration. *c. 1880*

22 in (56 cm) wide

$500–700 (per repeat)   **PC**

Golden Lily wallpaper designed by John Henry Dearle. Its complex multicolored image of lilies, tulips, and other small florets made it expensive to produce. *c. 1900*

22 in (56 cm) wide

$600–900 (per repeat)   **PC**

Acorn wallpaper by Morris & Co. It is symmetrically printed in golden yellow against pale blue, with acorns and oak leaves amid flowers and foliage. *c. 1880*

22 in (56 cm) wide

$500–700 (per repeat)   **PC**

Original watercolor design for Blackthorn, one of the last wallpapers produced by Morris & Co. Many of these original designs are now in public collections. *1892*

40 in (101.5 cm) wide

$50,000–80,000   **L&T**

Flock of Swans chromolithographic poster by Louis J. Rhead, depicting a group of swans gliding across a pond strewn with waterlilies and with reeds and irises in the foreground. *1897*

60½ in (154 cm) wide

$5,000–7,000   **SWA**

Chromolithographic poster by Edward Penfield for the July edition of *Harper's*, showing two cats curiously investigating a planter, bearing the artist's logo monogram, from which sprouts a bush. *1898*

15 in (38 cm) wide

$1,200–1,800   **SWA**

Scribners for Xmas chromolithographic poster by Louis J. Rhead, depicting an orange-haired woman in a dark blue and black costume bearing an armful of holly gathered in the winter woodland. *1895*

19¾ in (50 cm) high

$1,200–1,800   **SWA**

Edward Penfield poster for the May edition of *Harper's*, showing a young woman in a dark blue outfit and a broad-brimmed hat walking with her pale brown hound. With orange lettering against a tan background. *1897*

18 in (46 cm) high

$800–1,200   **SWA**

***Womens Edition (Buffalo) Courier* chromolithographic poster** by Alice Russell Glenny. One of only two by this artist, it shows the head and shoulders of a young woman, her hair dressed with roses and a wayward-looking ribbon. *1895*

27 in (68.5 cm) high

$2,000–3,000   **SWA**

***The Inland Printer* lithographic cover** by William H. Bradley for the March edition of this periodical. It shows a woman losing her hat in a breeze, flanked by a complex foliate panel. *c. 1900*

11 in (28 cm) high

$300–400   **SWA**

Glossary

Acid-etching In glass decoration, a process in which one or more layers of colored glass are applied to a vessel and a design is blocked out with an acid-resistant material. When dipped in hydrofluoric acid, the untreated areas are removed, leaving the image in relief.

Adzed surface A slightly undulating surface of wood finished with an adze, a type of ax with the blade set at a right angle to the handle.

Aestheticism A short-lived late 19th-century artistic movement advocating "art for art's sake." It overlapped with Arts and Crafts, but the Aesthetic movement's denial of any social or moral value in art differed from the teachings of Ruskin and Morris. In the decorative arts, its most prominent figure was E. W. Godwin, whose Anglo-Japanese and Queen Anne Revival furniture truly typified the Aesthetic style. Other Arts and Crafts figures associated with the movement are C. R. Ashbee, Walter Crane, and Louis Comfort Tiffany.

Appliqué A textile technique in which pieces of fabric are attached to another piece of material of contrasting color or texture.

Art Nouveau A decorative style that emerged around 1890 and lasted until World War I, influenced partly by the Arts and Crafts movement. Art Nouveau pieces are characterized by flowing, free-form imagery based on organic forms.

Aventurine A translucent brown glass given a sparkling appearance by the inclusion of golden or copper flecks of oxidized metal. It can also be used as a glaze.

Baluster One in a series of short posts or pillars, usually circular in section, supporting a rail and forming a balustrade. The name "baluster" is also used to describe similarly shaped vases, drinking-glass stems, and other items.

Bas-relief Low-raised work executed upon, and attached to, a flat surface.

Bentwood In furniture-making, wood that has been bent into curves using steam.

Bevel Generally referring to glass or wood, a bevel is a sloped or slanted edge of a flat surface.

Bezel In jewelry, a bezel setting features a collar of gold or silver hammered around the jewel, which adds height to a flush-style setting.

Bijouterie French term meaning jewelry or trinkets.

Bisque An unglazed porcelain that is fired twice. The first firing happens at a high temperature; after its surface is painted, the item is fired again, this time at a lower temperature.

Blindstamp An embossed mark devoid of any ink that is applied to a work of art on paper to designate its creator.

Blister pearl A raised area of mother-of-pearl cut from the inside of a shell and resembling a blister. The dark-brown underside is sometimes left visible.

Blown glass A method of making glass in which a glassmaker blows through a hollow rod, shaping a gather of molten glass at the other end. The glass can be either free-blown or blown into a mold.

Bobeche A device, often in the form of a ring, that catches the drips from wax candles.

Bolection A molding, usually with an S-shaped section, used to cover the joint between two elements whose surfaces are not level. Often found as a framework around panels.

Brocatelle 1. A woven fabric, usually in silk and wool, with a relief pattern, the background of which has a satinlike appearance. Widely used in 18th-century upholstery. 2. A type of variegated marble used for 18th-century tabletops.

Buttressed handles In pottery, handles in the form of supporting projections on the body of a vessel; typical of the Arts and Crafts period.

Cabochon A smooth, domed gem with no faceting or cutting to its surface. The term is more generally used to denote raised circular or oval decorative ornaments in carving, stonework, and furniture. The Arts and Crafts movement revived cabochon decoration of metalware.

Cameo glass Glass made up of two or more separate colored glass layers. The top layer is wheel-carved or acid-etched to produce a relief image and reveal the different colored glass beneath.

Canted A chamfered or beveled surface, obliquely faced.

Cartouche In furniture, a panel or tablet in the form of a scroll with curled edges, sometimes bearing an inscription, monogram, or coat of arms, and used as part of the decoration.

Casting Creating a product by pouring molten material (silver, bronze, or glass, for example) into a mold.

Celadon A distinctive gray-green or blue-green glaze. The technique imitates nephrite jade and has been used in China, South Korea, and Japan for more than 2,000 years.

Chamfer A furniture surface produced by beveling off a corner.

Champlevé An enameling technique in which the background of an object is hollowed out into individual cavities with thin metal walls, filled with powder enamel, and then fired in a kiln.

Chasing A method of improving the detail on an embossed metal object. The surface is carefully engraved with a chasing tool resembling a small chisel to add texture and pattern without removing any metal.

Chromolithograph A picture printed in tints and colors by repeated impressions from a series of stones prepared by the lithographic process.

Cloisonné A method of enameling in which thin strips of metal are soldered on to the surface of an object to form individual decorative cells. These are filled with powdered enamel and then fired in a kiln.

Clutha glass A cloudy glass developed by James Couper & Sons of Glasgow around 1885. Chemicals added to the glass batch produce air bubbles during the melting process, giving the finished glass an ancient look. Christopher Dresser produced many designs for Clutha glass.

Cold enameling Painting on ceramic, glass, and bronze without firing.

Corbel A bracket or block of stone or wood projecting from a vertical component, used to support a beam or a horizontal feature from below.

Cornice A decorative, molded projection that crowns a piece of furniture, particularly tall cupboards or display cabinets.

Craquelé (or crackle) The deliberate crazing of the glazed surface on ceramics. A black stain is sometimes used to enhance the decorative effect.

Crazing A glaze defect in ceramics caused by different rates of contraction in the body and glaze during firing. The result is a network of fine cracks.

Crewelwork Embroidery work using loosely twisted, worsted yarn in a free-flowing design, usually on a linen-based ground.

Crystalline A glaze suspended with zinc or calcium crystals

created by a slow-cooling kiln, which gives the effect of patches of color.

Cuenca A Spanish tile-making process in which soft, moist tiles are impressed with a design to create raised outlines. After firing, the resulting depressions are glazed.

Cuerda seca A decorative technique for pottery in which pattern outlines are drawn in a mixture of manganese and grease to prevent the different colored glazes from intermingling.

Cymric A silver and jewelry range introduced by the English retailer Liberty & Co. that incorporated Celtic motifs in many of the designs.

Demilune French term for a half-moon shape.

Die-stamping In metalware, a method of forming the body, or part, of a piece. A metal sheet is sandwiched by machine between two shaped steel blocks (also known as dies).

Dovetailing In furniture, the technique of joining two pieces of wood at right angles by means of wedge-shaped tenons and mortises carved out of each piece.

Dowel A small, headless wooden pin used in furniture construction to join two pieces of wood.

Earthenware Low-fired pottery made of a porous clay body that has to be waterproofed by a coating glaze. It has a porosity of more than 5 percent.

Ebonized wood Wood that has been stained black in imitation of ebony.

Electroplate Wares made of metal, usually nickel or copper, that have been coated with another metal, generally silver, by electrolysis.

Embossed Decoration produced by raising a pattern in relief from the body of a piece.

Enamel A colored, opaque composition derived from glass that is fired onto jewelry, metalware, ceramics, and glass as protection and decoration.

Entrelacs Interwoven sinuous tendrils, of Celtic origin, used as ornament. They are often used in jewelry and were revived by the Arts and Crafts designers.

Escutcheon A protective or ornamental plate, sometimes in the shape of a shield.

Etagère A set of shelves, usually free-standing, though sometimes part of another piece of furniture. Known as a "whatnot" in 19th-century England.

Everted An outward-turned or flaring shape. The term is often used to describe the lip of a jug, pitcher, or sauceboat, or the rim of a ceramic or glass vessel.

Faience The French name for tin-glazed earthenware of a buff or pale red color covered with white enamel or glaze, which gives it the appearance of porcelain.

Favrile A type of glass developed by Louis Comfort Tiffany,

patented in 1894. The name comes from the German *fabrile*, meaning "handmade."

Finial A decorative turned or carved ornament surmounting a prominent terminal. Finials frequently appear on furniture and on the covers of silver, glass, or ceramic vessels, where they often double as handles.

Fire-polished A process in which a glass piece is reheated to reduce any imperfections in manufacture. Fire-polishing gives the item a bright finish.

Flambé glaze A copper glaze fired at a high temperature (2,190°F/ 1,200°C), producing a lustrous rich red color with flamelike streaks of purple or blue.

Flange A projecting flat rim, collar, or rib on an object, used to strengthen, as an attachment, or as decoration.

Foliate Shaped like a leaf.

Folk Art A term used by the American Arts and Crafts movement to describe work created by artists who were not formally trained.

Gesso A composition of gypsum (plaster of Paris) and sizing, and sometimes linseed oil and glue, used mainly by sculptors for casts, but also used for the decoration of furniture from the Middle Ages onward.

Glaze A transparent or opaque coating for ceramics. It is a thin layer of glass that strengthens and seals the surface, making it waterproof. Initially applied as a layer of powder, it vitrifies when fired in a kiln.

Gothic The dominant style of European ecclesiastical architecture from the 12th to the 15th centuries. Characterized by richly fashioned, elaborate, and ceremonial designs, it inspired architecture and decorative arts in the 18th and 19th centuries. The Gothic style remained an influence on William Morris and the Aesthetic movement.

Grain of rice In porcelain, a decorative technique in which small perforations, like grains of rice, are made to the body of the vessel. These are then filled in and sealed by a transparent glaze covering the whole piece, and remain faintly visible.

Ground color The surface color of ceramics, onto which painted decoration is applied. The term is also used in textiles to denote the background color.

Guild A medieval association of craftsmen or merchants. The idea was revived by the Arts and Crafts movement in a reaction against mass-production and the social structures of the Industrial Age.

Hammer-textured The effect achieved when metals are shaped by hand using a hammer and deliberately left unfinished, with a textured, rather than a smooth, surface.

Handicraft (or handcraft) A particular skill of making decorative objects by hand, or an object made by such a skill.

The Arts and Crafts movement strongly emphasized the importance of handcraftsmanship.

Incised decoration A pattern scratched into the body of a ceramic or glass vessel with a sharp instrument, such as a metal point, as decoration or to record an inscription, date, or name.

Iridescence A surface effect that creates the appearance of a rainbow of colors caused by differential refraction of light waves, as sometimes observed on an oil spill. It is produced by spraying a mist of metallic salts on the hot ceramic or glass vessel.

Knop The decorative knob on lids and covers, or the cast finial at the end of a spoon handle. A knop is also the decorative bulge on the stem of a drinking glass, goblet, or candlestick, usually halfway up the stem.

Luster Originating in Mesopotamia and Persia in the 8th century, the shiny, iridescent metallic surface known as luster glazing was created by painting onto the face of a ceramic vessel a mixture of gold, silver, or copper pigments made from metallic oxides suspended in oil.

Majolica A ceramic ware created by the English Minton factory and first presented in 1851. It is an elaborately modeled earthenware with thick, colorful glazes. The name derives from the Italian word for tin-glazed earthenware (*maiolica*).

Marbleize A decorative effect in ceramics in which the finished

pieces resemble heavily veined, colored marble. This can be achieved by combining clays of different colors, by covering the surface with slip of different colors, or by coloring the glaze using different metallic oxides.

Marquetry A furniture-decorating technique involving the insertion of preformed pieces of wood exhibiting different grains or colors into a panel or piece of furniture.

Mica A shiny silica mineral that occurs in igneous and metamorphic rocks.

Mission style Simple and functional architecture, furniture, and decorative arts of the US Arts and Crafts period. The term may derive from the designers' belief that furniture had a mission—to be used. It is usually applied to the practical and robust oak furniture made in the United States from the late 1880s to the 1940s.

Morse The metal clasp for fastening a cape across the chest. It is often richly wrought and jeweled.

Mortise In furniture, a hole that is made in the wood to receive a tenon.

Oatmeal A glaze color in ceramics that varies from light cream to mid-brown and is fly-specked or mottled to resemble oatmeal.

Opalescence An effect usually seen in glass that emulates opal. It gives a milky blue appearance by reflected light and an amber tint by transmitted light.

Openwork A decorative technique that has open elements created by piercing or wirework, allowing light to pass through the apertures.

Overlay A glass layer over the main glass body that can be decorated by various techniques—for example, carving, acid-etching, or painting with enamels.

Parquetry A decorative process similar to marquetry, in which woods are inlaid into furniture or floors, often in a geometric pattern.

Pâte-sur-pâte A French term meaning "paste on paste," in which layers of slip are applied to ceramics to produce a subtle relief image, sometimes with a degree of carved detail. Introduced by Sèvres around 1850.

Patina A surface effect usually acquired over time. A manufacturer may sometimes use chemical treatments to give a piece the appearance of age.

Pegged furniture Furniture joined together with pegs or dowels. This method of construction was first used in the 16th century to strengthen mortise-and-tenon joints, and was revived by Arts and Crafts furniture makers.

Planishing Hand-raising a metal object with the use of hammers to create the required shape. The by-product of this technique, if left unpolished, is a pleasing hammer-textured surface.

Plique-à-jour A jewelry technique creating an effect similar to stained glass, in which translucent enamel is held in an unbacked frame, allowing the light to shine through.

Porcelain A translucent ceramic made from china clay, quartz, and feldspar. It was first produced in ancient China, and then, from 1709, in Europe, initially at the Meissen works, in Germany.

Queen Anne The style of architecture and decorative arts, especially silver and furniture, dominant in England during Queen Anne's reign (1702–14) and adopted in the United States c. 1725 with strong regional characteristics. It favored restraint and limited ornament.

Queen Anne Revival A style of architecture and decorative arts popular in the late 19th and early 20th centuries in England, based on the Queen Anne style. The simplicity of Queen Anne furnishings appealed to several designers. Direct reproductions of early 18th-century items were also popular during this period, but their craftsmanship is rarely as fine as that of the originals.

Repoussé A French term for relief embossing on metalware, which is created by hammering the reverse side of the piece.

Reverse-painting Painting an image in reverse on the inner surface of a glass vessel. This technique was popular on Art Nouveau lamps in the United States.

Salt-glaze A thin, glassy coating on stoneware, produced by throwing ordinary salt into the kiln at the end of firing. The combination of salt and steam produces a gas that turns into natrium oxide and hydrochloric acid. Natrium oxide combines with silicic acid to form a glaze.

Sang-de-boeuf French for oxblood, a brilliant red or plum-colored glaze first developed in 17th-century China, derived from copper fired in a reducing atmosphere. It tends to run, leaving a streaky effect with pale greenish areas or pink markings.

Scroddled A pottery technique in which an object or decoration is made of clay scraps of different colors.

Secessionists Now used to indicate Austrian Art Nouveau, the term derives from an avant-garde group that broke away from the Academy of Fine Arts in Vienna. Founded in 1897, the Vienna Secession promoted modern design under the chairmanship of the artist Gustav Klimt. Other members were Josef Hoffmann, Koloman Moser, and Joseph Maria Olbrich.

Sgraffito From the Italian for "little scratch," a term for the technique of scratching a pattern through the overlaid slip of a vessel to reveal the color of the clay underneath.

Slag glass A type of inexpensive opaque colored press-molded glass that incorporates an admixture of slag from local foundries, resulting in a marbled appearance.

Slip A mixture of clay and water that is richer than the body of a piece of ceramic. It is used to smooth surfaces or to add decoration and color. It can also be used as a "glue" to join sections of clay together.

Soufflé A method of applying glaze by insufflation, developed by the Chinese. A 7-in (17.75-cm) tube, traditionally of bamboo, has one of its ends bound with a fine gauze. It is dipped repeatedly into the glaze and blown through from the other end. The term is also used to describe the final effect of this process, where the glaze, generally red or blue, is finely mottled.

Spline-jointed A method used in furniture to join two pieces of wood. The spline, a thin strip or slat of wood or metal, is glued into grooves cut into the pieces being joined. Spline-jointing is typically used to fasten panels together and to strengthen the corners of picture frames.

Sterling silver Metal alloy composed of 92.5 percent silver and 7.5 percent copper. This standard measure was adopted in Great Britain in 1300, and is also used in the United States and Denmark.

Stoneware A watertight ware made with clay and a fusible stone such as feldspar. It also features salt or lead glazes.

Strapwork An ornament reminiscent of leather straps or carved fretwork originating in antique motifs, which can be plain or highly elaborate.

Stretcher A rod or bar extending between two legs of a chair or table.

Sussex Chair A chair first produced in the mid-1860s by Morris & Co. The design was taken from a country-made chair from a Sussex village and then modified. A Sussex Chair is light in appearance, with plain turned legs and struts, and gently shaped arms and back spindles. The seats are of woven rush.

Swag Cloth ornament in the form of a garland, tied and suspended at both ends in a loop.

Tenon In furniture, the tongue of a joint made to fit in the rectangular mortise.

Trillium A three-leaved plant belonging to the lily family, used in carved ornament and other decoration.

Tube-lining A ceramic decoration in which thin trails of slip are applied as outlines to areas of colored glaze.

Tudric A range of pewterware from Liberty & Co., made to complement the silver Cymric range. Each range had its own unique designs.

Turtleback A type of Tiffany lamp incorporating heavy glass lozenges arched like a turtle's back.

Verdigris A green or bluish chemical deposit formed on copper, brass, or bronze surfaces.

Wirework A technique in which small items are crafted out of gold or silver wire shaped into a lattice.

Wrythening Swirled or twisted fluting or ribbing on a glass vessel.

Key to Source Codes

Each Arts and Crafts piece shown in this book has an accompanying letter code that identifies the dealer or auction house that either is selling or has sold it, or the museum or picture agency where the piece or image is held. It should be noted that inclusion in this book in no way constitutes or implies a contract or a binding offer on the part of any contributing dealer or auction house to supply or sell the pieces illustrated, or similar items, at the price stated.

ADE
Art Deco Etc
73 Upper Gloucester Road
Brighton BN1 3LQ, UK
Tel/Fax: 011 44 1273 329 268
Email: johnclark@artdecoetc.co.uk

ARK
Ark Antiques
P.O. Box 3133
New Haven, CT 06515
Tel: (203) 498-8572
Email: info@ark-antiques.com
www.ark-antiques.com

ATL
Antique Textiles and Lighting
34 Belvedere, Landsdowne Road
Bath BA1 5HR, UK
Tel: 011 44 1225 310 795
Fax: 011 44 1225 443 884
Email: johnproops@ukonline.co.uk
www.antiquetextilesandlighting.co.uk

AVW
Circa 1900
Shop 17, Georgian Village
Camden Passage
London N1 8DU, UK
Tel: 011 44 771 370 9211
Email: info@circa1900.org
www.circa1900.org

B
Dreweatt Neate, Tunbridge Wells (formerly Bracketts)
The Auction Hall, The Pantiles
Tunbridge Wells TN2 5QL, UK
Tel: 011 44 1892 544 500
Fax: 011 44 1892 515 191
Email: tunbridgewells@dnfa.com
www.dnfa.com

BMN
Auktionhaus Bergmann
Möhrendorfer Strasse 4
D-91056 Erlangen
Germany
Tel: 011 49 9131 45 06 66
Fax: 011 49 9131 45 02 04
Email: kontakt@auction-bergmann.de
www.auction-bergmann.de

BONM
Bonhams Knowle
The Old House
Station Road, Knowle
Solihull B93 0HT, UK
Tel: 011 44 1564 776 151
Fax: 011 44 1564 778 069
Email: knowle@bonhams.com
www.bonhams.com

BRI
Bridgeman Art Library
Agency

CALD
Calderwood Gallery
1622 Spruce Street
Philadelphia, PA 19103-6736
Tel: (215) 546-5357
Fax: (215) 546-5234
Email: jc@calderwoodgallery.com
www.calderwoodgallery.com

CHEF
Cheffins
The Cambridge Saleroom
Clifton House, 2 Clifton Road
Cambridge CB1 7EA, UK
Tel: 011 44 1223 213 343
Fax: 011 44 1223 271 949
Email: fine.art@cheffins.co.uk
www.cheffins.co.uk

CHI
Chicago Silver
Chicago, IL
Email: chicagosilver@charter.net
www.chicagosilver.com

CHR
Christie's Images Ltd.
Agency

COR
Corbis
Agency

CW
Christine Wildman Collection
Private collection

DN
Dreweatt Neate
Donnington Priory Salerooms
Donnington, Newbury
Berkshire RG14 2JE, UK
Tel: 011 44 1635 553 553
Fax: 011 44 1635 553 599
Email: fineart@dreweatt-neate.co.uk
www.dreweatt-neate.co.uk

DOR
Dorotheum
Palais Dorotheum
Dorotheergasse 17
A-1010 Vienna
Austria
Tel: 011 43 1 515 600
Fax: 011 43 1 515 60443
Email: kundendienst@dorotheum.at
www.dorotheum.com

DP
David Pickup
115 High Street
Burford
Oxfordshire OX18 4RG, UK
Tel: 011 44 1993 822 555

DRA
David Rago Auctions
333 North Main Street
Lambertville, NJ 08530
Tel: (609) 397-9374
Fax: (609) 397-9377
Email: info@ragoarts.com
www.ragoarts.com

FIS
Auktionshaus Dr Fischer
Trappensee-Schlösschen
74074 Heilbronn
Germany
Tel: 011 49 7131 15 55 70
Fax: 011 49 7131 15 55 720
Email: info@auctions-fischer.de
www.auctions-fischer.de

FML
Falvey Memorial Library
Villanova University, Villanova, PA
Agency

FRE
Freeman's
1808 Chestnut Street
Philadelphia, PA 19103
Tel: (215) 563-9275
Fax: (215) 563-8236
Email: info@freemansauction.com
www.freemansauction.com

GDG
Geoffrey Diner Gallery
1730 21st Street NW
Washington, DC 20009
Tel: (202) 483-5005
Email: mgd@dinergallery.com
www.dinergallery.com

G5
Gallery 532
142 Duane Street
New York, NY 10013
Tel: (212) 964-1282
Fax: (212) 571-4691
Email: gallery532@aol.com
www.gallery532.com

GORL
Gorringes, Lewes
15 North Street
Lewes BN7 2PD, UK
Tel: 011 44 1273 472 503
Fax: 011 44 1273 479 559
Email: clientservices@gorringes.co.uk
www.gorringes.co.uk

HBK
Hall-Bakker @ Heritage
Heritage
6 Market Place
Woodstock
Oxon OX20 1TA, UK
Tel: 011 44 1993 811 332
Email: info@hallbakker.co.uk
www.hallbakker.co.uk

HERR
Herr Auctions
W.G. Herr Art & Auction House
Friesenwall 35
D-50672 Cologne, Germany
Tel: 011 49 221 254 548
Email: kunst@herr-auktionen.de
www.herr-auktionen.de

JBS
John Bull Silver
139a New Bond Street
London W1S 2TN, UK
Tel: 011 44 20 7629 1251
Email: elliot@jbsilverware.co.uk
www.jbsilverware.co.uk

JDJ
James D. Julia Inc.
P.O. Box 830
Fairfield, Maine 04937
Tel: (207) 453-7125
Email: jjulia@juliaauctions.com
www.juliaauctions.com

JF
Jill Fenichell
305 East 61st Street
New York, NY 10021
Tel: (212) 980-9346
Email: jfenichell@yahoo.com

JN
John Nicholsons
The Auction Rooms, "Longfield"
Midhurst Road, Fernhurst
Haslemere GU27 3HA, UK
Tel: 011 44 1428 653 727
www.johnnicholsons.com

L&T
Lyon and Turnbull Ltd.
33 Broughton Place
Edinburgh EH1 3RR, UK
Tel: 011 44 131 557 8844
Email: info@lyonandturnbull.com
www.lyonandturnbull.com

LANE
Eileen Lane Antiques
150 Thompson Street
New York, NY 10012
Tel: (212) 475-2988
Email: EileenLaneA@aol.com
www.eileenlaneantiques.com

LG
Legacy
G50/51 Alfie's Antique Market
13–25 Church Street
London NW8 8DT, UK
Tel: 011 44 20 7723 0449
Email: legacy@alfies.clara.net

MACK
Macklowe Gallery
667 Madison Avenue
New York, NY 10021
Tel: (212) 644-6400
Email: email@macklowe
gallery.com
www.macklowegallery.com

MEPL
Mary Evans Picture Library
Agency

MNZ
**Museum of New Zealand
Te Papa Tongarewa**
Agency

MW
Mike Weedon
7 Camden Passage
London N1 8EA, UK
Tel: 011 44 20 7226 5319
Email: info@mikeweedon
antiques.com
www.mikeweedonantiques.com

NA
Northeast Auctions
93 Pleasant Street
Portsmouth, NH 03801
Tel: (603) 433-8400
Email: contact@
northeastauctions.com
www.northeastauctions.com

PC
Private Collection

POOK
Pook & Pook
463 East Lancaster Avenue
Downingtown, PA 19335
Tel: (610) 269-4040
Email: info@pookandpook.com
www.pookandpook.com

PUR
Puritan Values
The Dome, St Edmund's Road
Southwold IP18 6BZ, UK
Tel: 011 44 1502 722 211
Email: sales@puritanvalues.com
www.puritanvalues.co.uk

QU
Quittenbaum
Hohenstaufenstrasse 1
D-80801 Munich
Germany
Tel: 011 49 859 33 00 75 6
Email: info@quittenbaum.de
www.quittenbaum.de

RG
Richard Gibbon
34/34a Islington Green
London N1 8DU, UK
Tel: 011 44 20 7354 2852
Email: neljeweluk@aol.com

RP
Rosie Palmer
26–28 High Street, Otford,
Sevenoaks TN14 5PQ, UK
Tel: 011 44 1959 522 025
www.otfordantiques.co.uk

RUM
Rumours
4 The Mall, Antiques Arcade
359 Upper Street
London N1 0PD, UK
Tel: 011 44 20 7704 6549
Email: rumdec@aol.com

SDR
**John Sollo/David Rago
(joint sales)**
333 North Main Street
Lambertville, NJ 08530
Tel: (609) 397-9374
Email: info@ragoarts.com
www.ragoarts.com

STY
Style Gallery
10 Camden Passage
London N1 8ED, UK
Tel: 011 44 20 7359 7867

SWA
Swann Galleries
104 East 25th Street
New York, NY 10010
Tel: (212) 254-4710
Email: swann@swann
galleries.com
www.swanngalleries.com

TCS
The Country Seat
Huntercombe Manor Barn
Nr Henley on Thames RG9 5RY, UK
Phone: 011 44 1491 641 349
Email: ferry-clegg@
thecountryseat.com
www.thecountryseat.com

TDG
The Design Gallery
5 The Green
Westerham TN16 1AS, UK
Tel: 011 44 1959 561 234
Email: sales@
thedesigngallery.uk.com
www.thedesigngallery.uk.com

TEL
Galerie Telkamp
Maximilianstrasse 6
D-80539 Munich, Germany
Tel: 011 49 89 22 62 83
Fax: 011 49 89 24 21 46 52

TO
Titus Omega
Shop 21, The Mall, Camden
Passage, London N1 0PD, UK
Tel: 011 44 20 7688 1295
Email: info@titusomega.com
www.titusomega.com

V&A
Trustees of the V&A, London
Agency

VDB
Van Den Bosch
Shop 1, Georgian Village
Camden Passage
London N1 8DU, UK
Tel: 011 44 20 7226 4550
Email: info@vandenbosch.co.uk
www.vandenbosch.co.uk

VZ
**Von Zezschwitz Kunst und
Design**
Friedrichstrasse 1a
D-80801 Munich, Germany
Tel: 011 49 89 38 98 930
Email: info@von-zezschwitz.de
www.von-zezschwitz.de

WKA
**Wiener Kunst Auktionen –
Palais Kinsky**
Freyung 4
A-1010 Vienna, Austria
Tel: 011 43 15 32 42 00
Email: office@palais-kinsky.com
www.palais-kinsky.com

WROB
Junnaa & Thomi Wroblewski
Box 39, 78 Marylebone High Street
London W1U 5AP, UK
Tel: 011 44 20 7499 7793
Fax: 011 44 20 7499 7793
Email: echo.base@dial.pipex.com

WW
Woolley & Wallis
51–61 Castle Street
Salisbury SP1 3SU, UK
Tel: 011 44 1722 424 500
Fax: 011 44 1722 424 508
Email: enquiries@
woolleyandwallis.co.uk
www.woolleyandwallis.co.uk

Directory of Other Dealers, Auction Houses, and Museums

UNITED STATES

Berman Gallery
136 N. Second Street
Philadelphia, PA 19106
Tel: (215) 733-0707
Email: ber441@aol.com
www.bermangallery.com

Bonhams & Butterfields
220 San Bruno Avenue
San Francisco, CA 94103
Tel: (415) 861-7500
Fax: (415) 861-8951
Email: Info.US@bonhams.com
www.butterfields.com

Carol Grant Decorative Arts
510 S. Washington
Royal Oak, MI 48067
Tel: (248) 398-411
Fax: (248) 586-1104

Circa 1910 Antiques
7206 Melrose Avenue
Los Angeles, CA 90046
Tel/Fax: (323) 965-1910
Email: west1910@pacbell.net
www.circa1910antiques.com

Craftsman Antiques
Olde Lafayette Village
75 Rt. 15, Bldg. J
Lafayette, NJ 07848
Tel: (973) 383-0212
Email: craftantiq@earthlink.net
www.craftsmanantique.com

Crones Collectibles
P.O. Box 2306
Brewster, MA 02631
Phone: (508) 896-5038
Email: crones@capecod.net
www.cronescollectibles.com

Dalton's Antiques
1931 James St.
Syracuse, NY 13206
Tel: (315) 463-1568
Email: rudd@daltons.com
www.daltons.com

David H. Surgan
328 Flatbush Avenue
P.M.B. 123
Brooklyn, NY 11238
Tel/Fax: (718) 638-3768

Don Treadway Gallery
2029 Madison Road
Cincinnati, OH 45208
Phone: (513) 321-6742
Email: info@treadwaygallery.com
www.treadwaygallery.com

George Reavis
Midland Antiques Market
907 E. Michigan
Indianapolis, IN
Tel: (317) 924-4298

House of Hubbard
541 Fillmore Avenue
East Aurora, NY 14052
Tel: (716) 652-0213

J. Austin Antiques
1100 Cambridge Street
Cambridge, MA 02139
Tel: (617) 234-4444
Email: jaustin1100@
jaustinantiques.com
www.jaustinantiques.com

JMW Gallery
144 Lincoln Street
Boston, MA 02111
Tel: (617) 338-9097
Email: mail@jmwgallery.com
www.jmwgallery.com

John Alexander Ltd.
10–12 West Gravers Lane
Philadelphia, PA 19118
Phone: (215) 242-0741
Email: info@johnalexanderltd.com
www.johnalexanderltd.com

John Toomey Gallery
818 North Boulevard
Oak Park, IL 60301
Tel: (708) 383-5234
Fax: (708) 383-4828
Email: toomey@interaccess.com

Just Glass Auctions
Tel: (718) 456-9093
www.justglass.com

JW Art Glass
8466 N. Lockwood Ridge Road #252
Sarasota, FL 34243
Tel: (941) 351-6759
www.jwartglass.com

Kimberley Jane Gray Antiques
1205 Slocum Street
Dallas, TX 75207
Tel: (214) 752-8855

Lillian Nassau Ltd.
220 East 57th Street
New York, NY 10022
Tel: (212) 759-6062
Fax: (212) 832-9493
www.lilliannassau.com

Mission Era Ltd.
106 Orchard Street
Belmont, MA 02178
Tel: (617) 484-4800
Fax: (617) 864-3862

The Mission Oak Shop
109 Main Street
Putnam, CT 06260
Tel: (203) 928-6662

Nohjunc Antiques
Port Townsend Antique Mall
Space 62, 802 Washington Street
Port Townsend, WA 98368
Tel: (360) 379-0875

Old City Mission
162 N. Third Street
Philadelphia, PA 19106
Tel: (215) 413-3040

Our Mission Antiques
525 Hidden Pines Trail
Holly, MI 48442
Tel: (810) 634-7612
Fax: (810) 634-7500

Pearce Fox Decorative Arts
162 North Third Street
Philadelphia, PA 19106
Tel: (610) 688-3678
Email: ei216@aol.com

Peter-Roberts Antiques, Inc.
39 Bond Street
New York, NY 10012
Tel: (212) 477-9690
Fax: (212) 477-9692
Email: pra.nyc@verizon.net

Pete's Pots
P.O. Box 2724
Norcross, GA 30091
Tel: (770) 446-1419

Phil Taylor Antiques
224 Fox-Sauk Road
Ottumwa, IA 52501
Tel: (641) 682-7492

Preston Jordan
P.O. Box 55
Madison, NJ 07940
Tel: (201) 593-4866
Fax: (201) 822-0505

Quaint Antiques
2025 Secor Road
Lambertville, MI 48144
Tel/Fax: (313) 856-7272

Rockridge Antiques
5601 College Avenue
Oakland, CA 94618
Tel: (510) 652-7115

Seiz Pottery
401 W. Chestnut Street
Chatham, IL 62629
Email: john@seizpottery.com
www.seizpottery.com

Skinner Auctions Inc.
63 Park Plaza
Boston, MA 02116
Tel: (617) 350-5400
www.skinnerinc.com

Split Personality
P.O. Box 419
Leona, NJ 07605
Tel: (201) 947-2291

Strictly Mission
Cambridge Antique Market
201 McGrath-O'Brien Highway
Cambridge, MA 02141
Tel: (617) 868-9655

Stuart F. Solomon Antiques
9 3/4 Market Street, 2nd Floor
Northampton, MA 01060
Tel: (413) 586-7776
Email: antiques@ssolomon.com
www.ssolomon.com

Tim Gleason Gallery
194 Elizabeth Street #2
New York, NY 10012
Tel: (212) 966-5777
Fax: (212) 966-5063

Voorhees Craftsman
1415 North Lake Avenue
Pasadena, CA 91104
Tel: (888) 982-6377
Email: Steve@
VoorheesCraftsman.com
www.voorheescraftsman.com

William Doyle Galleries
175 East 87th Street
New York, NY 10128
Tel: (212) 427-2730
Fax: (212) 369-0892
Email: info@DoyleNewYork.com
www.doylenewyork.com

Woodsbridge Antiques
P.O. Box 239
Yonkers, NY 10705
Tel: (914) 963-7671

UNITED KINGDOM

Antiques on the Square
2 Sandford Court
Church Stretton
Shropshire SY6 6BH
Tel: 011 44 1694 724111

Art Furniture
158 Camden Street
London NW1 9PA
Tel: 011 44 20 7267 4324
Fax: 011 44 20 7267 5199
Email: arts-and-crafts@
artfurniture.co.uk
www.artfurniture.co.uk

Arts and Crafts Antiques
Manchester
Tel: 011 44 161 945 7775
Fax: 011 44 161 945 5318
Email: David@
artsandcraftsantiques.com
www.artsandcraftsantiques.com

**The Arts and Crafts
Furniture Co.**
49 Sheen Lane
East Sheen
London SW14 8AB
Tel/Fax: 011 44 20 8876 6544
www.artsandcraftsfurnitureco.co.uk

A.S. Antique Galleries
26 Broad Street
Pendleton
Salford
Manchester M6 5BY
Tel: 011 44 161 737 5938

Bernard Quaritch Ltd.
5–8 Lower John Street
Golden Square
London W1F 9AU
Tel: 011 44 20 7734 2983
Fax: 011 44 20 7347 0967
Email: rarebooks@quaritch.com
www.quaritch.com

Bonhams
101 New Bond Street
London, W1S 1SR
Tel: 011 44 20 7629 6602
Fax: 011 44 20 7629 8876
www.bonhams.com

Christie's South Kensington
85 Old Brompton Road
London SW7 3LD
Tel: 011 44 20 7724 2229
Fax: 011 44 20 7321 3321
www.christies.com

Christopher Wood
18 Georgian House
10 Bury Street
London SW1Y 6AA
Tel/Fax: 011 44 20 7839 3963
Email: cwood@
christopherwoodgallery.com
www.christopherwoodgallery.com

**Hill House Antiques &
Decorative Arts**
P.O. Box 17320
18 Chelsea Manor Street
London SW3 2WR
Tel: 011 44 7973 842 777
www.hillhouse-antiques.co.uk

JAG Decorative Arts
58–60 Kensington Church Street
London W8 4DB
Tel/Fax: 011 44 20 7938 4404
Email: jag@jagdecorativearts.com
www.jagdecorativearts.com

The Millinery Works Gallery
85–87 Southgate Road
London N1 3JS
Tel/Fax: 011 44 20 7359 2019
Email: antiquetrader@
millineryworks.co.uk
www.millineryworks.co.uk

Paul Reeves
32b Kensington Church Street
London W8 4HA
Tel: 011 44 20 7937 1594
Email: paul@
paulreeveslondon.com
www.paulreeveslondon.com

Retrospect
539 Woodborough Road
Mapperley, Nottingham NG3 5FR
Tel: 011 44 115 956 1182

Sandy Stanley Antiques
Vicarage House
58–60 Kensington Church Street
London W8 4DB
Tel: 011 44 7973 147 072
Email: info@sandystanley
antiques.com

Stamford Antiques Centre
The Exchange Hall
Broad Street
Stamford, Lincs PE9 1PX
Tel: 011 44 1780 62605

Strachan Antiques
40 Darnley Street, Pollokshields
Glasgow G41 2SE, Scotland
Tel: 011 44 141 429 4411
Email: alex.strachan@
btconnect.com

Sunburst Decorative Arts
2 Cavendish Arcade
The Crescent, Buxton
Derbyshire SK17 6BQ
Tel: 011 44 1298 23050

Sylvia Powell Decorative Arts
Suite 400, Ceramic House
571 Finchley Road
London NW3 7BM
Tel: 011 44 20 8458 4543
Email: dpowell909@aol.com
www.sylviapowell.com

Troy
4 Cleveland Terrace
London Road
Bath BA1 5DF
Tel: 011 44 1225 445 678
Email: cmlilium@aol.com
www.troy.uk.net

AUSTRALIA

Andrew Shapiro
162 Queen Street
Woollahra NSW 2025
Tel: 011 61 2 9326 1588
Fax: 011 61 2 9326 1305
Email: info@shapiro
auctioneers.com.au
www.shapiroauctioneers.com.au

Bathurst Street Antiques
Robin Cooper
128 Bathurst Street
Hobart TAS 7000
Tel: 011 61 3 6236 9422
Fax: 011 61 3 6236 9329
Email: bathurstantiques@
iprimus.com.au
www.antique-art.com.au/gallery/
dealers/bathurst/dealer.htm

Becky's Old Wares
Mark Chippendale
2 Burgan Place
Rivett ACT 2611
Tel: 011 61 6 288 0589
Fax: 011 61 6 288 5440

E. A. Joyce & Son
Steven Joyce
15 Castray Esplanade
Hobart
TAS 7000
Tel: 011 61 3 6223 8266
Fax: 011 61 3 6223 6496

Ritzy Bits
Irina & Rex McKillop
13 Sherlock Street
Kaleen ACT 2617
Tel: 011 61 418 623 007
Fax: 011 61 262 538 429
Email: RITZYBITS@bigpond.com.au

AUSTRIA

Bel Etage
Wolfgang Bauer
Mahlerstrasse 15
A-1010 Vienna
Tel: 011 43 1 512 23 79
Fax: 011 43 1 512 23 79 99
Email: office@beletage.com
www.beletage.com

Galerie bei der Albertina – Zetter
Lobkowitzplatz 1
A-1010 Vienna
Tel: 011 43 1 513 14 16
Fax: 011 43 1 513 76 74
Email: zetter@galerie-albertina.at
www.galerie-albertina.at

Elisabeth Michitsch Kunsthandel
Spiegelgasse 15
A-1010 Vienna
Tel: 011 43 1 512 83 13
Email: office@
elisabeth-michitsch.at
www.elisabeth-michitsch.at

Patrick Kovacs Kunsthandel
Rechte Wienzeile 31
A-1010 Vienna
Tel: 011 43 1 587 94 74
Email: office@patrick-kovacs.at
www.patrick-kovacs.at

BELGIUM

Export Furniture
Boulevard Eisenhower 109
Tournai 7500
Email: info@exportfurniture.com
www.exportfurniture.com

Tiny Esveld
Oostmalsesteenweg 295
Rijkevorsel 2310
Tel/Fax: 011 32 3 312 5190
Email: gallery@tinyesveld.com
www.tinyesveld.com

FRANCE

Chenel, Alain
Villa Printemps
12 Montée Desambrois
06000 Nice
Tel: 011 33 4 93 13 48 72
Fax: 011 33 4 93 85 85 33

Galerie Yves Gastou
12 rue Bonaparte
75006 Paris
Tel: 011 33 1 53 73 00 10
www.galerievesgastou.com

Louvre des Antiquaires
2 Place du Palais Royal
75001 Paris
Tel: 011 33 1 42 97 27 27
www.louvre-antiquaires.com

GERMANY

Art 1900
Kurfürstendamm 53
10707 Berlin
Tel/Fax: 011 49 30 881 5627
www.art1900.de

Dénes Szy
Königsallee 27–31
40212 Dusseldorf
Tel/Fax: 011 49 211 323 98 26

NETHERLANDS

Cherob
Elandsgracht 109–111
Amsterdam 1016 TT
Tel: 011 31 252 415215
Email: john@cherob.com
www.cherob.com

SPAIN

Belle Epoque
Antonio Lopez 2
Cádiz
Tel: 011 34 956 226 810

MUSEUMS

UNITED STATES AND CANADA

The Arts & Crafts Society
1194 Bandera Drive
Ann Arbor, MI 48103
www.craftsmanperspective.com

The Art Institute of Chicago
111 South Michigan Avenue
Chicago, IL 60603
Tel: (312) 443-3600
www.artic.edu

Charles Hosmer Morse Museum of American Art
445 North Park Avenue,
Winter Park, FL 32789
Tel: (407) 645-5311
www.morsemuseum.org

Delaware Art Museum
800 South Madison Street
Wilmington, DE 19801
Tel: (302) 571-9590
Fax: (302) 571-0220
www.delart.org

Elbert Hubbard Roycroft Museum
P.O. Box 472
363 Oakwood Avenue
East Aurora, NY 14052
Tel: (716) 652-4735
www.roycrofter.com/museum.htm

Gardiner Museum of Ceramic Art
60 McCaul Street
Toronto, ON M5T 1V9
Tel: (416) 586-8080
Fax: (416) 586-8085
Email: mail@gardinermuseum.on.ca
Gardinermuseum.on.ca

Los Angeles County Museum of Art (LACMA)
5905 Wilshire Boulevard
Los Angeles, CA 90036
Tel: (323) 857-6000
www.lacma.org

The Metropolitan Museum of Art
1000 Fifth Avenue
at 82nd Street
New York, NY 10028-0198
Tel: (212) 535-7710
www.metmuseum.org

Museum of Arts & Design
40 West 53rd Street
New York, NY 10019
Tel: (212) 956-3535
www.americancraftmuseum.org

Neue Galerie New York
1048 Fifth Avenue
New York, NY 10028
Tel: (212) 628-6200
Fax: (212) 628-8824
Email: museum@neuegalerie.org
www.neuegalerie.org

**The Stickley Museum
at Craftsman Farms,
Parsippany**
2352 Rt. 10-West, # 5
Morris Plains, NJ 07950
Tel: (973) 540-1165
Fax: (973) 540-1167
Email: CraftsmanFarms@att.net
www.stickleymuseum.org

Textile Museum of Canada
55 Centre Avenue
Toronto, ON M5G 2H5
Tel: (416) 599-5321
Fax: (416) 599-2911
Email: info@textilemuseum.ca
www.museumfortextiles.on.ca

**Virginia Museum
of Fine Arts**
2800 Grove Avenue
at the Boulevard
Richmond, VA 23221-2466
Tel: (804) 340-1400
www.vmfa.state.va.us

**The Wolfsonian Museum of
Modern Art and Design**
1001 Washington Avenue
Miami Beach, FL 33139
Email: webmaster@
thewolf.fiu.edu
www.wolfsonian.org

UNITED KINGDOM

**Birmingham Museum
& Art Gallery**
Chamberlain Square
Birmingham B3 3DH
Tel: 011 44 121 303 2834
www.bmag.org.uk

**Brighton Museum
& Art Gallery**
Royal Pavilion Gardens
Brighton BN1 1EE
Tel: 011 44 1273 290 900
www.brighton.virtualmuseum.info

**Cheltenham Art Gallery &
Museum**
Clarence Street
Cheltenham GL50 3JT
Tel: 011 44 1242 237 431
Email: ArtGallery@
cheltenham.gov.uk
www.cheltenhammuseum.org.uk

Dorman Museum
Linthorpe Road
Middlesbrough TS5 6LA
Tel: 011 44 1642 813 781
Fax: 011 44 1642 358 100
Email: dormanmuseum@
middlesbrough.gov.uk
www.dormanmuseum.co.uk

Glasgow School of Art
167 Renfrew Street
Glasgow G3 6RQ, Scotland
Tel: 011 44 141 353 4500
www.gsa.ac.uk

Godalming Museum
109a High Street
Godalming, Surrey GU7 1AQ
Tel: 011 44 1483 426 510
Fax: 011 44 1483 523 495
www.godalming-museum.org.uk

**Hunterian Museum and Art
Gallery and Mackintosh
House Gallery**
82 Hillhead Street
University of Glasgow
Glasgow G12 8QQ
Tel: 011 44 141 330 5431
Fax: 011 44 141 330 3618
www.hunterian.gla.ac.uk

Macclesfield Silk Museum
Roe Street
Macclesfield, Cheshire SK11 6UT
Tel: 011 44 1625 613 210
Fax: 011 44 1625 617 880
Email: silkmuseum@tiscali.co.uk
www.silk-macclesfield.org

Manchester Art Gallery
Mosley Street
Manchester M2 3JL
Tel: 011 44 161 235 8888
Fax: 011 44 161 235 8899
www.manchestergalleries.org

**Museum of Domestic
Design and Architecture**
Middlesex University
Cat Hill, Barnet
Herts EN4 8HT
Tel: 011 44 20 8411 5244
Fax: 011 44 20 8411 6639
Email: moda@mdx.ac.uk
www.moda.mdx.ac.uk

The Stained Glass Museum
The South Triforium
Ely Cathedral
Ely, Cambridgeshire CB7 4DL
Tel: 011 44 1353 660 347
Fax: 011 44 1353 665 025
www.sgm.abelgratis.com

Victoria and Albert Museum
Cromwell Road
London SW7 2RL
Tel: 011 44 20 7942 2000
www.vam.ac.uk

The Whitworth Art Gallery
The University of Manchester
Oxford Road
Manchester M15 6ER
Tel: 011 44 161 275 7450
Recorded Information:
011 44 161 275 7452
Education Line: 011 44161 275
7453
Email: Whitworth@man.ac.uk
www.whitworth.man.ac.uk

AUSTRIA

Museen der Stadt Wien
Karlsplatz
A-1040 Vienna
Tel: 011 43 1 505 87 47
Fax: 011 43 1 505 87 47
Email: mas@m10.magwien.gv.at
www.museum-vienna.at

BELGIUM

Musée Horta
Amerikaanse Straat/
Rue Américaine 23–25
1060 Brussels
Tel: 011 32 2 537 1692
www.hortamuseum.be

FRANCE

Musée des Beaux-Arts
3 place Stanislas
54000 Nancy
Tel: 011 33 3 83 85 30 72
Fax: 011 33 3 83 85 30 76

Musée de l'Ecole de Nancy
36–38 rue du Sergent Blandan
54000 Nancy
Tel: 011 33 3 83 40 14 86
Fax: 011 33 3 83 40 83 31
www.ecole-de-nancy.com

Musée d'Orsay
62 rue de Lille
75343 Paris
Tel: 011 33 1 40 49 48 14
www.musee-orsay.fr

GERMANY

**Museum für Kunst und
Gewerbe**
Steintorplatz 1
20099 Hamburg
Germany
Tel: 011 49 40 2486 2732
Fax: 011 49 40 2854 2834
www.mkg-hamburg.de

Index <small>(Page numbers in *italics* refer to captions)</small>

Acknowledgments

PUBLISHER'S ACKNOWLEDGMENTS

Dorling Kindersley would like to thank Neale Chamberlain for digital image coordination.

The Price Guide Company would like to thank the following people for their substantial contributions to the production of this book:

Photographer Graham Rae for his patience, humor, and wonderful photography, as well as John McKenzie, Byron Slater, and Adam Gault for additional photography.

All of the dealers, auction houses, and private collectors for kindly allowing us to photograph their collections, and for taking the time to provide a wealth of information about the pieces.

The team at Sands and at DK: Simon Murrell, David and Sylvia Tombesi-Walton, Paula Regan, and Mandy Earey for all their skill and dedication to the project.

Also special thanks to Cathy Marriott, Dan Dunlavey, Jessica Bishop, Karen Morden, and Sandra Lange at the Price Guide Company (UK) for their editorial contribution and help with sourcing information.

Thanks also to digital-image coordinator Ellen Sinclair, European consultants Martine Franke and Nicolas Tricaud de Montonnière, and consultants John Wainwright, Keith Baker, John Mackie, David Rago, and Suzanne Perrault.

PACKAGER'S ACKNOWLEDGMENTS

Sands Publishing Solutions would like to thank Sarah Duncan for picture research, Pamela Ellis for compiling the index, and Sam Spence for her design assistance and grasp of Photoshop. Thanks also to the teams at Dorling Kindersley and The Price Guide Company.

PICTURE CREDITS

DK Picture Librarians: Richard Dabb, Neale Chamberlain

The publisher would like to thank the following for their kind permission to reproduce their photographs:
(Abbreviations key: t=top, b=bottom, r=right, l=left, c=center)

15: Mary Evans Picture Library (t); 20: Getty Images/Hulton Archive (r); 26: www.bridgeman.co.uk (tr), V&A Images (bc, br); 30: akg-images (br); 31: www.bridgeman.co.uk (tl, tr), V&A Images/Given by Mrs F. J. Bassett-Lowk (bc), V&A Images/Given by the Glasgow School of Art (c), V&A Images (bl); 66: Museum of New Zealand Te Papa Tongarewa (bl, bc); 71: www.bridgeman.co.uk (tl); 75: www.bridgeman.co.uk (br); 82: www.bridgeman.co.uk (br); 90: Corbis/E.O. Hoppé (br); 94: www.bridgeman.co.uk (cr), V&A Images (br); 104: Newcomb College Center for Research on Women (br); 112: Ohr-O'Keefe Museum of Art, Biloxi, Mississippi (br); 113: Ohr-O'Keefe Museum of Art, Biloxi, Mississippi (r); 120: © Christie's Images Ltd (bl); 153: Van den Bosch (tr); 159: Cheltenham Art Gallery & Museums (t); 160: Cheltenham Art Gallery & Museums (br); 164: Manx National Heritage (br); 165: Dover Publications, Inc. New York; 205: V&A Images (tl); 206: Getty Images/Hulton Archive (br); 218: © Christie's Images Ltd (l); 219: Corbis/Stapleton Collection (tl).

All other images © Dorling Kindersley and The Price Guide Company Ltd. For further information see: **www.dkimages.com**